World Power Assessment

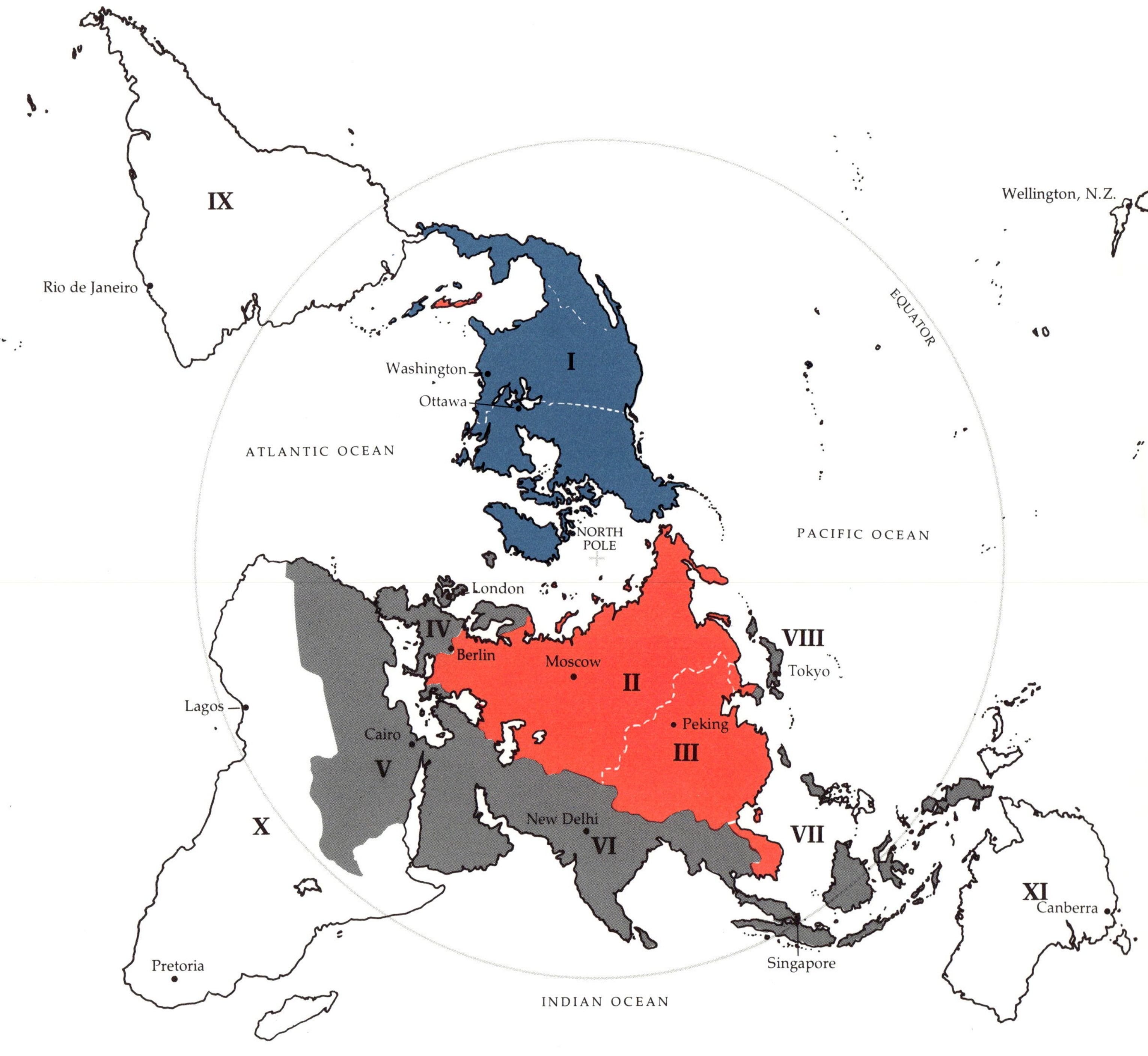

POLITECTONIC ZONES

I—North America, Central America
II—USSR, East Europe, Cuba
III—China (PRC), North Korea, Indochina
IV—West Europe
V—North Africa, Mideast
VI—South Asia
VII—Southeast Asia
VIII—Northeast Asia
IX—South America
X—Central and Southern Africa
XI—Australia, New Zealand

World Power Assessment

A CALCULUS OF STRATEGIC DRIFT

by RAY S. CLINE

WESTVIEW PRESS
Boulder, Colorado

Published in Cooperation with
THE CENTER FOR STRATEGIC AND INTERNATIONAL STUDIES
Georgetown University, Washington, D. C.

1975
ISBN 0-89158-011-5

Published in cooperation with the Center for Strategic and International Studies, Georgetown University.

Published 1975 in the United States of America in paperback by
The Center for Strategic and International Studies, Georgetown University.
1800 K Street, N.W.
Washington, D.C. 20006

Published 1975 in hardcover by
Westview Press, Inc.
1898 Flatiron Court
Boulder, Colorado 80301
Frederick A. Praeger, Publisher and Editorial Director

Library of Congress Cataloging in Publication Data

Cline, Ray S

World power assessment.

Includes index

1. International relations. 2. Alliances. 3. World politics—1945- I. Title
JX1395.C575 1975 327'.09'047 75-24129

ISBN 0-89158-011-5

Printed in the United States of America

Foreword

This book charts new ground in dealing with the old problem of international power politics. It explains why the balance of world power seems to be tipping toward the totalitarian states, the USSR and Communist China, and away from the United States. It describes the geographic distribution of economic, military, and political strength among nations as of 1975.

The author, Ray S. Cline, Executive Director of Studies at the Georgetown University Center for Strategic and International Studies (CSIS), outlines the strategic thinking of the USSR, the United States, and China. He assesses the present balance of power among groups of nations and the trend line indicating future conflict or stability in international relations. Finally, he suggests a specific new, alliance-oriented policy for the United States in the 1970s and 1980s.

Such an ambitious undertaking in so relatively few pages is bound to be, as the author is the first to acknowledge, a rough cut at what potentially can be accomplished with the novel methodology developed in this book. CSIS plans to bring out subsequent, updated issues of this study when and as more data and more refined research techniques make it possible.

The conceptual framework developed by Dr. Cline provides a unique contribution to systematic thinking about this complex policy problem confronting the Congress, the Executive Branch of the Government, and concerned citizens of all political persuasions. CSIS is fortunate to be able to present this comprehensive assessment of world power by a scholar and government official who has spent many years studying precisely these problems. Dr. Cline studied at Harvard and Oxford Universities prior to joining OSS (the Office of Strategic Services) in World War II. He worked in CIA for many years making strategic estimates of the world situation, rising to be CIA's Deputy Director for Intelligence, 1962-1966. He served overseas for a number of years, including several in the U.S. Embassy in Bonn, 1966-1969. His last public service post was as Director of Intelligence and Research, U.S. Department of State, 1969-1973. CSIS is pleased to present Dr. Cline's first published work as a private scholar since retiring from government at the end of 1973 and joining us at Georgetown.

DAVID M. ABSHIRE
Chairman, CSIS

Author's Preface

I am heavily indebted to all of my colleagues at the Georgetown Center, especially the Chairman, Dr. David Abshire, for support and assistance in this project. I also owe much to the many friends and associates in government service who mulled over these kinds of problems with me during the long years of my service in the Central Intelligence Agency and the Department of State. Deep appreciation is due my research assistant, Ms. Patricia Rader, my editorial assistants, Mrs. Sylvia Lowe and Mrs. Judith Berson, and my secretarial staff headed by Mrs. Ann Campagna. They have all been helpful in many ways far above and beyond the call of duty. Finally, as always, I must express my gratitude for all the wonderful support given by my best critics, my wife, Marjorie Wilson Cline, and my daughters, Judy and Sibyl, all three of whom are professional research analysts.

R.S.C.

Washington, D.C.
August 31, 1975

Table of Contents

I. INTRODUCTION

Chapter One: **"Politectonics"** ... 3

Chapter Two: **Measuring the Power of Nations** ... 7
Polarity ... 9
The Conceptual Framework ... 11

II. POWER MACROMETRICS

Chapter Three: **Critical Mass: Population and Territory** ... 15
Population ... 15
Territory ... 18
Comparisons by Politectonic Zones ... 22

Chapter Four: **Measuring Economic Capabilities** ... 35
Comparing the Gross National Economic Product of Nations ... 36
"Private Enterprise" versus "Command" Economies ... 37
Special Economic Strengths ... 40

Chapter Five: **Military Capability: The Strategic Force Balance** ... 53
Crucial Elements of Military Power ... 54
The Political Pressures Exerted by Nuclear Weapons ... 55
Trends in Nuclear Weapons Strength ... 56
Measuring Nuclear Capabilities ... 58
Numbers of Strategic Weapons ... 60
Defense Forces ... 61
Land-Based Missiles ... 62
Submarine-Launched Ballistic Missiles ... 67
Manned Long-Range Bombers ... 70
British, French, and Chinese Bombers ... 72
Conclusion: Perceived Nuclear Power Weights ... 73

Chapter Six: **Military Capability: Conventional Forces** 75
Control of the Seas and Global Reach 81
NATO versus Warsaw Pact Balance 83
Conclusion 85

Chapter Seven: **Total Macrometric Power Pattern** 87
Politectonic Distribution of National Power 89

Chapter Eight: **National Strategy and National Will** 97
Soviet Strategy in a Global Perspective 99
Strategic Thinking in the United States 103
Evolution of U.S. Strategic Concepts in the "American Age" 104
The "Containment" Strategy 106
The "Free World" Alliance Strategy 108
U.S.-Soviet Diplomatic Atmospherics 111
The Age of Detente 1969-1975 112
The Nixon-Kissinger Strategy 114
The Strategic Concepts of Communist China (PRC) 116
The Rest of the World 122
Final Ratings of Major Nations 123

III. POLITECTONIC ASSESSMENT

Chapter Nine: **Final Assessment** 129
Clear and Present Danger 131
U.S. Policy: An Analogue from History 133
A New National Strategy 134
An Oceans Alliance 135

IV. APPENDICES

Appendix A: **A Closer Look at Recent Economic Trends** 143
Negative Growth for 1974 144
The OPEC Apex 152
The Rest of the Third World 152

Appendix B: **Special Trends in International Economics: Oil** 155
The Oil-Producing Countries 155
The United States 157
NATO 158
Japan 159
International Energy Agency 159
The Warsaw Pact 160
The People's Republic of China 162
Conclusion 162

Index: 167

MAPS, CHARTS, AND GRAPHS

Frontispiece: Map of Politectonic Zones ... ii

Chapter Three:
Population: 50 Largest Countries ... 17
Population: Remaining Countries ... 17
Territory: Major Countries ... 19
Critical Mass: Major Countries Weighted for Population and Territory ... 21
Critical Mass: Population + Territory ... 21
Politectonic Zones: Critical Mass of Larger Nations ... 23
Zonal Distribution of 152 Nations ... 28

Chapter Four:
1973 GNP: Leading 50 Countries ... 39
Energy Use 1970 ... Facing 40
Energy Supply and Demand ... Facing 40
Energy: Coal Equivalent ... 42
Non-Fuel Minerals ... 44
Non-Fuel Minerals: Bonus Weights ... 44
Crude Steel ... 45
Food Grains: Net Exporters ... 46
World Trade 1973 ... 48
Economic Strengths: Consolidated Ranklist with Bonus Values ... 49
Critical Mass and Economic Capability:
Larger Nations in Politectonic Zones ... 51

Chapter Five:
Land-Based ICBMs: Actual Strengths ... 57
Military Balance Sheet ... 57
U.S.-USSR Strategic Nuclear Weapons (Bombs and Warheads) ... 59
Strategic-Nuclear Offensive Weapons Arsenals in Mid-1975 ... 61
The Five Strategic Powers ... 63
U.S. and USSR ICBMs: Salient Features
and Numbers Deployed, 1975 ... 65
U.S. and USSR SLBM Forces: Salient Features and
Numbers in Inventory, Mid-1975 ... 69
U.S. and USSR Manned Bomber Forces ... 72
Perceived Strategic Weapons Strength, 1975 ... 73

Chapter Six:
U.S. Defense Spending as a Percent of GNP ... 77
U.S.-Soviet Defense Expenditure and Military Manpower ... 78
Military Strength: Force Levels ... 80
Naval Ship Construction 1962-1972 ... 83
Central NATO and Warsaw Pact Forces ... 84
Military Capability: Perceived Power ... 85

Chapter Seven:
Total Weights (C + E + M) 87
Politectonic Zones: Importance of Powerful Nations 90
Additional Nations of Importance 91
Major Nations 92

Chapter Eight:
U.S.-USSR Relations Since World War II 110
Strategy and Will: Perceived Power for Major Nations 124

Chapter Nine:
Perceived Power = (C + E + M) X (S + W) 130
An Oceans Alliance System: Core Group 136

Appendix A:
World Product: Selected Years 1950-1974 145
Growth Rates: Annual or Average Annual 146
World Population 147
GNP: Per Capita 148
GNP: 1974 149

Appendix B:
Oil Production 164
Oil Consumption 165
Proved Oil Reserves 166

I: Introduction

CHAPTER ONE

"Politectonics"

After three decades of extraordinary power in world affairs the United States finds itself in 1975 in a state of markedly diminished influence and strategic confusion. The country still has enormous economic and military power but this power is not focussed on the pursuit of a coherent national purpose or a strategy on which there is political consensus.

In the 1970s, alliances hitherto thought vital to U.S. security are drifting apart or simply drifting. In Vietnam the United States has suffered the first clearcut military defeat ever inflicted on it. As a result, the world has recently witnessed a humiliating U.S. withdrawal from the Indochina area and the collapse of a regime and a society in which successive U.S. Presidents had invested heavily in terms of lives, money, and prestige.

The buoyancy and vigor of earlier U.S. behavior have trailed off into national uncertainty, indecisiveness, and self-doubt. Public confidence in governmental policy-making is at its lowest point since before World War II. We all have to ask ourselves: what is happening in the international arena that has brought about this change, and just where does the United States really stand in the world balance of power? This book suggests some answers that emerge upon looking at the strength of nations in terms of global geography, economic interdependence, military capability, and shifting political alignments.

There is nothing very new in this approach to our problems. It is really a return to basics and the long perspectives of historical change. Shortly after the turn of the twentieth century, in 1904, the great British geographer, Sir Halford Mackinder, wrote an essay on "The Geographical Pivot of History." He emphasized the pivotal significance of the central Eurasian land mass on the international scene and this emphasis increased as his ideas evolved down into the period of World War II. In particular, Mackinder's dictum that the command of the Eurasian heartland (essentially Central Europe and Russia, from the Rhine to the Urals) would eventually lead to command of all of the world's resources and peoples, has formed the core of most informed discussion of strategic theory ever since. Mackinder looks more prescient every day as we search for insights into our present circumstances.

There is a striking analogy between present political and strategic trends, on the one hand, and new scholarly findings relating to the seabeds, as well as fundamental new geological concepts, on the other. It now seems that the earth's surface is made up of vast "tectonic plates"[1] containing entire continents and immense stretches of the surrounding seabeds. These continental plates form separate pieces of the earth's hard crust; they float on a more fluid inner core, and they have slowly drifted apart and then together over the millennia. Where they meet, mountain ranges are thrust up, volcanic and seismic pressures erupt, the great oceanic ridges and rifts are formed, and some underwater terrain slips beneath the edge of other tectonic plates and is slowly ground down back into the molten core of the earth.

A more graphic picture of what is taking place in a much quicker time frame in the gradual shifting of international power in this century could hardly be found. The strength of nations and of the clusters of nations allied to one another waxes and wanes in conformity with subterranean rhythms of growth and weakening of economic, military, and political currents.

No good word is in common use to describe the process of analyzing such changes. The old term, "geopolitics", which derived from Mackinder's model for world trends, fell into disrepute some time ago, largely as a result of distortions introduced in Germany in Haushofer's and Hitler's time. In its place we now most often hear theorists talk of a "balance of power" vaguely reminiscent of Metternichean nineteenth century Europe. This talk of "pentagonal" structures has proved to be largely irrelevant to what is actually taking place. The economics and ideology of the "concert of Europe" are not very relevant for the pluralistic U.S. open society and its relations with the Soviet or Chinese People's Republic autarchic dictatorships. We need a simpler, more realistic model for analyzing today's power balance.

Accordingly, this book undertakes to study the elements of power in international politics and the gradual shift in the balance of those elements among nations and groups of nations in terms of a new formula based on old truths. To suggest the geographical foundations of this method of strategic analysis, and yet emphasize that the kind of power we are talking about is essentially political and economic, as well as military, I use a new word, "politectonics". By this, I mean to denote the formation and breakup of power groupings, mainly regional in makeup, that determine the real balance of influence and force in today's international affairs.

In keeping with this approach, we center our analysis on the United States, the foremost single unit of continent-size power, and on the clusters of nations which associate themselves in one or more ways, some closely, some loosely, with the power of the United States. In addition, we analyze those clusters of nations which stand apart from the United States and, in some cases, directly or indirectly oppose U.S. power and influence.

By this method, we describe the world as made up of a number of discrete

[1] The word "tectonic" literally means pertaining to construction or building, or specifically to the structural deformation of the earth's crust, whereby continental plates are gradually shifting relative to one another. For a more detailed discussion, see Walter Sullivan, *Continents in Motion,* as summarized in *The New York Times Magazine,* January 12, 1975.

politectonic zones. The future international alignments of major nations within these are crucial. There are 11 such zones, as shown on the frontispiece map, of which the primary ones are: (I) North America, the heartland of which is the United States; (II) the USSR, the heartland of Eurasia; (III) China (PRC) and the Asian communist regimes in Korea and Indochina, which together occupy most of the mainland of East Asia.

On the periphery of Eurasia are five great peninsular or insular zones, the rimlands, which can be dominated from the center of the continental land mass but which are also at this time in history closely connected by transoceanic ties to other parts of the world. These five are: (IV) West Europe, the crucial, long-disputed area stretching from Greece to the United Kingdom, an extended Eurasian peninsula from the viewpoint of the Soviet heartland; (V) the Mideast, a long, disorganized belt of nations reaching from Iran across Asia Minor and the Arabian peninsula to the Arab littoral of the Mediterranean; (VI) South Asia, the subcontinent; (VII) Southeast Asia beyond Indochina, the vast ocean archipelago area containing Indonesia, the Philippines, Singapore, Malaysia, Thailand, and Burma; and (VIII) Northeast Asia, the Japan-South Korea-China/Taiwan triangle.

These zones, the rimlands of Eurasia, are surrounded by an outer circle of continents and peoples. This circle comprises mainly the lands of the Southern Hemisphere, which group themselves in three zones: (IX) South America, (X) Central and Southern Africa, and (XI) Australia and New Zealand.

The power of the individual nations in each zone and their links with one another as well as their relationships with nations in other zones are the stuff that world strategy and diplomacy deal with. The slow, sometimes nearly imperceptible shifting or drifting of the dominant elements in these zones, the dynamics of clusters of allied nations, are what we are looking for.

This gradual movement both within and back and forth among zones is indeed like the drift of continental plates on the earth's surface. The insights gained through this politectonic approach to international power largely coincide with the conventional wisdom of most Americans about international power and conflict in recent years. Attempts to measure the power of nations individually or in groups are exceedingly difficult and inexact, whatever approach is used. Judging the trend in power relationships among the earth's politectonic zones is even more difficult. Looking at the United States' place in the balance of power from such a viewpoint may, however, clarify an understanding of the dangers and opportunities in the world around us in an era of strategic drift and, in Washington at least, drifting strategy.

CHAPTER TWO

Measuring the Power of Nations

In the rhetorical atmosphere of the United Nations all of the 152 sovereign nations[1] of the world are equal, but everyone is aware that in the real world some nations are much "more equal" than others. Some have tremendous power, others very little. Before we can describe aggregates of strength among clusters of nations, it is necessary to analyze and measure national power. In modern times the nation state is the main aggregative unit of political force in international affairs.

A nation is a group of people, usually living in a specific territory, who share a common sense of history, customs, and—usually—language. A state is a sovereign body politic. Many modern states are homogeneous nations and many nations are sovereign states. On the other hand, there are many states which are multinational, as in the USSR, where the dominant Great Russian population is barely over half of a country which includes many still quite distinct cultural minorities that make up nations in their own right. The United States is a nation state with an astonishing mix of ethnic groups who deliberately came to North America to belong to a pluralistic body politic. Tribalism, especially in Africa, is rampant today within national boundaries. Religious minorities and linguistic factions battle in Ireland and Belgium and India. The melting pot does not meld, even in the United States, as fast as some have

[1] We have included for examination in this study 152 states not under foreign jurisdiction, including former Portuguese colonies, Mozambique, and the Cape Verde Islands, which became independent in June and July, 1975, respectively. Although other smaller Portuguese colonies have declared independence, and resource-rich Angola will become independent when and if the civil war in that colony is ended, at present they are not included.

An exceptional case is the British Colony of Southern Rhodesia which has also been included because it declared its independence from the United Kingdom in 1965 and has been pursuing an independent policy since that time, although it has never been officially recognized by other governments or by the UN. Of the 152 nations analyzed in this study, 136 were UN members as of July 31, 1975. Technically there are 138 UN members, but two of these are parts of the USSR, Byelorussia and the Ukraine, which were given votes to attract the USSR into the United Nations when it was formed.

Some of today's states are politically fragile; some fragmentation and some merging may occur. As of mid-1975, however, the 152 nations mentioned in this book represent the commonly perceived independent actors on the international stage.

supposed. Nevertheless, the world is now divided into sovereign states which have attained or are trying to take on the community consciousness of a nation. The nation state is the decisive political unit of action and responsibility in our era.

From the town meeting to the nation state, communities of all types and sizes dispense power insofar as they act as a group. All of them must work out systems for sharing privileges and burdens, as well as for settling disputes among their members. They must also set up some kind of sanctions to enforce compliance with those settlements, sanctions vested in some constituted authority whether it is an absolute monarch with his army, or a judiciary backed by civil police. Ultimately, power is the ability to coerce.

In a community embracing the whole world, at this period of history, there is no single legitimately constituted power for the effective settlement of disagreements about economic, military, and political conflicts. More important, there is no procedure in international relations which guarantees that sanctions will be applied to enforce compliance with such international settlements as can be agreed upon. The extent to which one country can pursue its international and domestic aims without regard to, or even against, the interests of others, is based in the final analysis on its own national power as compared with that of other nations. Power in the international arena can thus be defined simply as the ability of the government of one state to cause the government of another state to do something which the latter otherwise would not choose to do—whether by persuasion, coercion, or outright military force.

Power is a subjective factor; it need not actually be used to bring about the results desired by those who wield it. A nation's leaders make decisions affecting foreign policy on the basis of projections, either of what they perceive their own power to be or of what they estimate to be the power of others. Such projections may not always be accurate, but they nonetheless determine decisions.

International conflicts of interest, whether political, economic, or military, are played out like a game of chess. Perceived power is a decisive factor, even if it only prevents another's action, like a chessman which threatens every square on the board to which an opponent's piece might move. The threat may never be carried out and therefore superficially nothing may appear to have happened. As on a chessboard, however, the pattern of potential power and counter-power in the minds of the antagonists determines how the game proceeds from move to move and how it will end: whether one nation carries out its aims or the match is stalemated. Only in desperate cases does the struggle move into a true end game, when—in international affairs—other levels of political and economic conflict are transcended and nations at last resort to war.

A study of power, in the last analysis, is a study of the capacity to wage war, but it is also in the normal run of cases an appraisal of many other kinds of international competition, where differences are resolved within a political or an economic context. It is important to calculate carefully the capabilities and intentions of enemies or potential enemies. Thus, in thinking about an appropriate strategy for the United States and the strategic balance which we seek in the world, it is essential to return to some positive ideas about which nations of the world are sympathetic toward U.S. purposes and which of them are strong enough to be helpful to the United States.

A nation must not become mesmerized by the power potential of an adversary. An obsessive preoccupation with hostile governments can lead to error, either through exaggerated fear of the dangers they present or through anxiety to placate them. The *sine qua non* is to know what U.S. objectives are and whether or not they can be achieved. This will depend upon our own national power plus that power committed to our side by dependable alliances. Like good friends, good allies must be shown again and again the mutual benefits of free and voluntary association. As Walter Lippmann said, 30 years ago:

> *American commitments and interests and ideals must be covered by our armaments, our strategic frontiers, and our alliances.*[2]

These basics are what we must examine in the light of the real international environment of the 1970s. Circumstances change drastically but the basics persist. The U.S. problem is complicated by the fact that the whole era since World War II is in many ways unique, unprecedented. It has seen a vast explosion of populations, technologies, and a proliferation of economic goods and services. For the first time in history, two nations, greater in most respects than any of the rest, plainly possess the capability of using nuclear weapons and their delivery systems to destroy the cities and total industrial structure of any nation. This fact acts as a powerful restraint on the use of military force by all nations to pursue their national objectives at the expense of others. To a lesser extent it also acts to prevent conflicts at levels of intensity lower than total warfare.

Gradually, over the past quarter century, it has become apparent that the ultimate sanction of nuclear destruction is, if not quite "unthinkable", too awful—in the true sense of that much abused word—to contemplate except as a defensive last resort. Thus it is unlikely to be employed except in those improbable circumstances where such drastic punishment would fit the provocation. Lesser crimes of nation states tend to be dealt with by the conventional methods of diplomacy, economic suasion, and the implicit threat of non-nuclear military force. We must try to measure these more intangible forms of national power in order to see where the balance lies and which way it is shifting.

Polarity

A lot of fashionable nonsense has been written in recent years about the passage of world affairs from an era of bipolarity (U.S.-USSR conflict) to a condition of multipolarity. There is some truth in these assertions, but in many respects they are dangerously wrong. The world is still, to a remarkable extent, divided between a sphere of influence dominated by the USSR and populated by states aligned politically and economically as well as militarily with the USSR, and a much less clearly delimited sphere of influence dominated—less firmly—by the United States and populated by states aligned with the United States politically and economically as well as in some cases through military pacts and guarantees.

[2] Walter Lippmann, *U.S. Foreign Policy* (London: Hamish Hamilton, 1943), p. 4.

There are many nations outside or not clearly associated with either of these spheres of influence, but the United States and the USSR—and particularly conflicts on varying levels of intensity between them—profoundly affect every other part of the globe. In this sense, despite the proliferation of smaller nations and the increase in strength of some of the secondary powers, the modern world is still basically bipolar.

Perhaps a better way to put it is to say, in a strictly geographic sense, that the world is polar—because most of the continental land masses surround the North Pole. The great multicontinent Eurasia, containing 33 percent of the globe's land surface, lies within the Northern Hemisphere, and directly across the North Pole from it is the North American continent, comprising another 16 percent of the land surface of the earth.

The best way to examine the distribution of nations about the world is to look at a globe—not a flattened Mercator projection of it—and study it from a polar viewpoint, that is, literally by looking directly at the North Pole. The frontispiece map conveys the message. The United States and the USSR confront each other across the north polar wastes, the two of them together comprising the largest agglomeration of choice temperate zone territory and natural resources existing anywhere on earth.

Canada, in this strictly geographical sense, whether or not it likes the situation, becomes an important extension of the northern U.S. strategic border. Thus the geography of Canada impels its identification with North American security quite apart from the multiple economic and political ties between Canada and the United States. The Caribbean islands, Mexico, and Central America are strategically linked with the United States and continental defense perimeters, although these areas are also drawn culturally and politically toward South America and other regions (i.e., Britain and France).

Putting it crudely and literally, everything else is peripheral. Other nations cluster in zones abutting on Soviet territory around the edges of the vast Eurasian continent; many nations are linked by sea-lanes to one another and to North America; some nations, of course, are pulled in both directions at once, and a few nations try to escape their natural geographic linkages by forming political bonds outside the broad zones in which they are situated.

This has long been true, but the nuclear missile age for the first time added enormous significance to the polar factor because it leaves the two continental superpowers locked in position just 30 minutes away from each other's ability to destroy all the cities and most of the people in both countries. This power potential will probably never be used by either of the two scorpions in the bottle, but all other international relationships are profoundly altered by it. The bipolar relationship between the United States and the USSR, both of which tend to dominate the regions of the earth in which they lie, is crucial to all international developments. The strength of these nations and the strengths of Zone I and Zone II are central to the balance of power.

The Conceptual Framework

Obviously a calculus of national power must include an analysis of nuclear weaponry and its potential for the deterrence of war. Still, even if deterrence seems to have a high degree of credibility, other elements of strength become crucial factors in the calculus. Non-nuclear arms and forces, economic capacity, and economic resources materially affect the way national power is perceived and hence its effect. Coherence in formulating national purpose and the degree of consensus expressed as political will substantially alter the way military and economic power can be used.

Thus we can say national power, realistically described, is a mix of strategic, military, economic, and political strengths and weaknesses. It is determined in part by the military forces and the military establishment of a country but even more by the size and location of territory, the nature of frontiers, the populations, the raw-material resources, the economic structure, the technological development, the financial strength, the ethnic mix, the social cohesiveness, the stability of political processes and decision-making, and, finally, the intangible quantity usually described as national spirit.

To ease the task of describing elements of international power in their various combinations, I have evolved a formula relating these factors. It is not a magic measuring rod, for the variables are not truly quantifiable. It simply provides a shorthand notation or index system to replace words and judgments once these have been defined.

The formula is as follows:

$$Pp = (C + E + M) \times (S + W)$$

Its terms are defined thus:

Pp = Perceived Power
C = Critical Mass = Population + Territory
E = Economic Capability
M = Military Capability
S = Strategic Purpose
W = Will to Pursue National Strategy

All of these terms will become clearer as we manipulate our observations within this conceptual framework for measuring real power in the international arena.

It only takes a careful look at the size and state of the economic development of the nations of the world to realize that the majority of them have relatively little impact on international affairs or even on important developments in their own regions. In a serious strategic assessment only from 25 to 40 nations determine the pattern of the world balance of power at any one time. The rest either weigh so little in realistic power terms that they can be disregarded or perhaps could be viewed as iron filings that automatically arrange themselves around magnetic fields of force in the geographic zones or alliance systems to which they belong.

This is not to say the people of the less powerful countries are unimportant or that long-range strategic and humanitarian concerns can be ignored, especially since these also motivate citizens and governments. Yet by any consistent standards of gross measurement, the preponderance of power appears to be in the hands of a relatively few nations.

Actually some very simple quantifications appear to be adequate for the rough approximations of strength in world affairs on which most broad generalizations about the balance of power rest. We are dealing here in macrometrics, the technique of measuring in a broad context where precise detail is not very significant. The patterns and trends in international relationships are what we want to see, not the details; the forest, not the trees.

In the same vein, index numbers are used to weight values and quantify strengths in this book. They reflect subjective and, in a sense, arbitrary judgments based on broad perceptions. They are used to convey easily and manipulate arithmetically estimates of comparative strengths and weaknesses among nations and groups of nations. In fact, these macrometric values generally fit and also reflect the conventional perceptions of power.[3] More specific assessments and verbal qualifications can—and must—follow to give micromeasurements within this general framework, but they do not fundamentally change the macrometric patterns.

[3] It is crucial in using this calculus to understand that we are talking about perceptions of power by governments, which are often influenced by popular perceptions, and not necessarily about real power. Real power seldom changes rapidly, but perceptions are volatile, particularly in societies where public opinion is important and ideas circulate freely. Many of the judgments in this book may need to be changed substantially if situations change and particularly if the perceptions of these situations change.

II: Power Macrometrics

$$P_p = (C + E + M) \times (S + W)$$

Critical Mass: Population and Territory

$Pp = (C + E + M) \times (S + W)$

The first factor in the formula for measuring perceived power in international affairs is what I call critical mass (C), a judgment on the size or mass of a nation. This perception is often blurred or diffuse, but it is fundamentally based on the amount of territory under a state's control and the number of people supported economically by that territory. While it is hard to quantify, there does seem to be a kind of critical mass—a reflection of population and area—that a nation must ordinarily possess to make itself felt in world affairs. Human beings are generally more important than land in most cases, since they are mobile and vocal and can bring their energies to bear on other human beings. Nevertheless the sheer size and space of a nation has its effect on the psychology of its inhabitants and more particularly on the thinking of its nearby neighbors.

In view of these age-old facts, we begin our measurement effort with this crude over-simplification: $Pp = C$. Obviously additional factors and coefficients are needed to make a more accurate formula for perceived power. It is revealing, nevertheless, to make a first approximation of the strength of nations in the international balance in this traditional way.

Population[1]

The first factor to look at in considering the importance of states is people. It is the sense of community among human beings that identifies the nation state and infuses it with life. The Table of Countries arranged in order of their population size (page 17) shows that about 90 percent of the roughly four billion people in the world live in countries which have a population of 12 million or more. There are just 50 countries of this size. It is true that a few countries with very small populations—Israel and Saudi Arabia, for example—have a disproportionate influence in international affairs because of some special circumstance that can be identified under some other term in our equation. But it is hard to think of most of the nations with a population of less than 12 million as having great power in their own right, independent of the interests or actions of other larger nations.

[1] All figures on population and territory in this chapter are taken from the *National Basic Intelligence Factbook*, January 1975, DOCEX, Library of Congress, Washington, D.C.

If an even more selective process singles out those countries with a population of more than 50 million, the total is only 15 nations. They are, in order:

China (PRC)
India
USSR
United States
Indonesia
Japan
Brazil
Bangladesh
Pakistan
West Germany (FRG)
Nigeria
Mexico
United Kingdom
Italy
France

With a few anomalies, mainly from populous Asia, most of these countries have been viewed as "great powers" for hundreds of years. In some cases, especially China, India, and above all, Bangladesh, a large population may be a mixed blessing; it is nonetheless true that the sheer mass of 50 million people or more constitutes a force to be reckoned with. The People's Republic of China, India, the Soviet Union, the United States, Japan, the Federal Republic of Germany, the United Kingdom, Italy, and France—these are the countries to whose policies and fortunes the world pays heed. Adding 19 more countries to this list makes it include the 34 most populous nations, those with 20 million or more inhabitants. There are 42 nations with more than 15 million people each, and altogether the 50 most heavily populated states have within their borders approximately three and one-half billion of the world's inhabitants. These 50 nations are certainly "more equal" than all the rest.

From the viewpoint of assessing what I have called the critical mass of countries, it is useful to arrange these countries into ranklists weighted according to population and area. For this purpose an arbitrary scale of 10 permits the nations to be rated in size groups, with equal importance (maximum of 5 points) being attached to predominance in numbers of people or in extent of territory.

The first step is to make a list including the 50 most populous nations in order of descending size, with weights attached from 5 down to 1 according to groups selected with arbitrary breakpoints in size of population purely for convenience (see page 17.) Nations with populations under 12 million are awarded no value.

Population: 50 Largest Countries

	Country	Population (Millions)	Perceived Power Weight
1	China (PRC)	930	
2	India	590	
3	USSR	250	
4	United States	212	5
5	Indonesia	129	
6	Japan	110	
7	Brazil	107	
8	Bangladesh	80	
9	Pakistan	70	
10	West Germany (FRG)	62	
11	Nigeria	62	4
12	Mexico	58	
13	United Kingdom	56	
14	Italy	56	
15	France	52	
16	Philippines	42	
17	Thailand	40	
18	Turkey	40	
19	Egypt	37	
20	Spain	35	
21	Poland	34	
22	South Korea	34	
23	Iran	33	
24	Burma	30	
25	Ethiopia	27.6	3
26	Colombia	25.1	
27	Argentina	24.8	
28	South Africa	24.7	
29	Zaire	24.5	
30	North Vietnam	24.1	
31	Canada	22.6	
32	Yugoslavia	21.2	
33	Rumania	21.1	
34	South Vietnam	20.5	
35	Afghanistan	18.9	
36	Sudan	17.5	
37	Morocco	17.0	
38	East Germany (DRG)	16.8	2
39	Sri Lanka	16.6	
40	Algeria	16.5	
41	North Korea	16.2	
42	China/Taiwan	15.8	
43	Tanzania	14.9	
44	Czechoslovakia	14.7	
45	Peru	14.6	
46	Netherlands	13.5	1
47	Australia	13.5	
48	Kenya	13.1	
49	Nepal	12.4	
50	Venezuela	12.0	

Population: Remaining Countries

Under 12 Million
Malaysia
Uganda
Iraq
Hungary

Under 10 Million
Chile
Belgium
Ghana
Cuba
Greece

Under 9 Million
Mozambique
Bulgaria
Portugal
Sweden

Under 8 Million
Austria
Cambodia
Syria
Ecuador
Malagasy Republic

Under 7 Million
Switzerland
Yemen (Sana)
Cameroon
Southern Rhodesia
Saudi Arabia

Under 6 Million
Upper Volta
Guatemala
Tunisia
Mali
Bolivia
Denmark
Haiti

Under 5 Million
Malawi
Ivory Coast
Zambia
Finland
Dominican Republic
Niger
Guinea
Senegal
Rwanda
El Salvador

Under 4 Million
Norway
Chad
Burundi
Israel
Laos
Somalia
New Zealand
Dahomey
Ireland
Uruguay

Under 3 Million
Honduras
Sierra Leone
Jordan
Paraguay
Albania
Lebanon
Libya
Singapore
Togo
Nicaragua
Jamaica

Under 2 Million
Costa Rica
Central African Republic
Liberia
Panama
Yemen (Aden)
Mongolia
Congo (Brazzaville)
Mauritania
Bhutan
Lesotho
Trinidad and Tobago

Under 1 Million
Kuwait
Mauritius
Guyana
Cyprus
Botswana
Fiji
Gabon
Gambia

Under 500 Thousand
Guinea-Bissau
Oman
Swaziland
Luxembourg
Malta
Equatorial Guinea
Cape Verde Islands
Barbados
Bahrain
Iceland
Bahamas
United Arab Emirates
Qatar
Western Samoa
Maldives

Under 100 Thousand
Tonga
Liechtenstein
Monaco
Andorra
San Marino
Nauru

Under 1 Thousand
Vatican City

Territory[2]

Land area is also basic to our weighting system of critical mass. The distribution of territory among nations is as inequitable as the distribution of population. There are approximately 58 million square miles of land surface in the world (versus about 140 million square miles of ocean surface). If the "big boys" with 1,000,000 square miles or more each are selected out, they have nearly one-half of the total land mass.

They are:

	Country	*Thousands of Square Miles*
1	**USSR**	8,600
2	**Canada**	3,850
3	**China (PRC)**	3,700
4	**United States**	3,620
5	**Brazil**	3,290
6	**Australia**	2,970
7	**India**	1,210
8	**Argentina**	1,070

It is true that the three biggest countries have enormous areas that are waste, desert, or are otherwise ill-suited for any kind of cultivation. Only about 26 percent of the Soviet Union's territory is arable or cultivated and much of the rest is permafrost. Canada has even less arable or cultivated land (6 percent) and China little more (11 percent). This factor scales these giants down in size considerably so that they roughly match the United States, which has nearly half (46 percent) of its territory in arable land or cultivated pasture. Thus the big four are on a level by themselves. Not far behind, on another level of size, Australia, India, and Argentina have almost half or more of their land cultivated or arable; Brazil has the smallest amount, at 17 percent.

These eight are enormous countries by any standard, and they are so perceived by friends and by enemies. Their size allows them agricultural resources and the possibility of defense in depth against military attack or occupation.

Some other nations, not so large, control particularly important land or sea corridors or valuable natural resources. Still others have achieved considerable impact by developing special economic skills or commodities which are in demand in international trade. Nevertheless, large area, if accompanied by a large population, almost automatically confers the status of power and will be so interpreted by strategists both at home and abroad. All eight of the geographically largest nations have populations of over 12 million although Australia, with 13½ million people, is a marginal member of this group.

If one extends the list of countries with substantial territory to include nations with one-half million square miles of area or more, the list extends only to 17, with additions as follows:

[2] Raw material endowment is not included in the discussion of critical mass because it is reflected in the measurement of current economic power in Chapter IV.

	Country	*Thousands of Square Miles*
9	**Sudan**	970
10	**Algeria**	950
11	**Zaire**	900
12	**Mexico**	760
13	**Indonesia**	740
14	**Libya**	680
15	**Iran**	640
16	**Saudi Arabia**	620
17	**Mongolia**	600

A number of these have enormous desert areas within their boundaries, but all except Saudia Arabia, Libya, and Mongolia are in the list of the 50 most populous nations in the world. If our list is extended further to include the United Kingdom, which is surely a nation of consequence, 69 countries in all are included and nearly 80 percent of the land surface of the globe. These 69 nations are those each of which control territory of 94 thousand square miles or more. Of these 69, many (31) have a population of less than 12 million, and some of them much less. Since quite a few of the larger territories are desert or waste, a small population may mean the country cannot be developed into a modern, powerful nation, or that the prospect is still a long way off.

The second step in assessing critical mass is to make a ranklist of the countries with very large territory and weight them as we did for population, in groups from 5 down to 1. Such a list follows:

Territory: Major Countries

	Country	*Sq. Mi.*	*Perceived Power Weight*
1	**USSR**	8.6 m.	
2	**Canada**	3.9 m.	5
3	**China (PRC)**	3.7 m.	
4	**United States**	3.6 m.	
5	**Brazil**	3.3 m.	
6	**Australia**	3.0 m.	4
7	**India**	1.2 m.	
8	**Argentina**	1.1 m.	
9	**Sudan**	970 th.	
10	**Algeria**	950 th.	
11	**Zaire**	900 th.	
12	**Mexico**	760 th.	
13	**Indonesia**	740 th.	3
14	**Libya**	680 th.	
15	**Iran**	640 th.	
16	**Saudi Arabia**	620 th.	
17	**Mongolia**	600 th.	

	Country	*Sq. Mi.*	*Perceived Power Weight*
18	**Chad**	496 th.	
19	**Peru**	496 th.	
20	**Niger**	490 th.	
21	**South Africa**	470 th.	
22	**Mali**	470 th.	
23	**Ethiopia**	460 th.	
24	**Colombia**	440 th.	
25	**Bolivia**	420 th.	
26	**Mauritania**	420 th.	
27	**Egypt**	390 th.	2
28	**Tanzania**	360 th.	
29	**Nigeria**	350 th.	
30	**Venezuela**	350 th.	
31	**Pakistan**	310 th.	
32	**Mozambique**	300 th.	
33	**Turkey**	300 th.	
34	**Chile**	290 th.	
35	**Zambia**	290 th.	
36	**Burma**	260 th.	
37	**Afghanistan**	250 th.	

Country	Sq. Mi.	Perceived Power Weight
38 **Somalia**	240 th.	
39 **Central African Republic**	240 th.	
40 **Malagasy Republic**	230 th.	
41 **Kenya**	220 th.	
42 **Botswana**	220 th.	
43 **France**	210 th.	
44 **Thailand**	200 th.	**1**
45 **Spain**	200 th.	
46 **Cameroon**	180 th.	
47 **Sweden**	170 th.	
48 **Iraq**	170 th.	
49 **Morocco**	160 th.	
50 **Paraguay**	160 th.	
51 **Southern Rhodesia**	150 th.	
52 **Japan**	140 th.	
53 **Congo (Brazzaville)**	130 th.	

Country	Sq. Mi.	Perceived Power Weight
54 **Finland**	130 th.	
55 **Malaysia**	130 th.	
56 **Norway**	120 th.	
57 **Ivory Coast**	120 th	
58 **Poland**	120 th.	
59 **Italy**	120 th.	
60 **Philippines**	120 th.	
61 **Yemen (Aden)**	110 th.	**1**
62 **Ecuador**	110 th.	
63 **Upper Volta**	110 th.	
64 **New Zealand**	100 th.	
65 **Gabon**	100 th.	
66 **Yugoslavia**	100 th.	
67 **West Germany (FRG)**	100 th.	
68 **Guinea**	100 th.	
69 **United Kingdom**	94 th.	

If we add the appropriate weights for the largest territorial holdings to the 50 nations with the largest populations, we have a ranklist providing weights for the term "C" in the perceived power formula. Countries weighted as being in the lowest two groups in extent of area, that is, with less than 500,000 square miles, are not added to our consolidated list at all unless their population size (over 12,000,000) already qualified them for it. There are many refinements in the power equation to be made for each country on the basis of economic, military, and political factors, and some nations may be designated as powerful in a special sense because of those other factors. If countries with small populations and large territories later come into consideration because of other strengths, their total power rating will also be increased on the basis of the weight values given them for territorial extent, even though the territorial factor alone does not qualify for the consolidated list of "critical mass".

The ranklist compiled on this basis contains only three additional countries included purely because of the size of their territories. Since all three happen to be nations with enormous deserts and relatively small populations, they do not alter the character of the ranklist very much. (See page 21.)

The final step in this technique of analyzing critical mass is to rearrange the ranklist by putting countries in descending order of consolidated value for critical mass, i.e., population and territory, as they have been weighted. Countries which have both less than 500,000 square miles of territory and less than 12,000,000 population are not included in this consolidated ranklist. The procedure we have followed generally gives a little more importance to people than to territory, since populous countries of an adequate size can exploit economic resources, mobilize armies, and act to influence other people.

The consideration of population and territory by themselves as basic factors constituting critical mass in the international arena ends up with countries at the

Critical Mass: Major Countries Weighted for Population and Territory

	Country	Perceived Power Weight: Population	Perceived Power Weight: Territory
1	China (PRC)	5	5
2	India	5	4
3	USSR	5	5
4	United States	5	5
5	Indonesia	5	3
6	Japan	5	1
7	Brazil	5	4
8	Bangladesh	4	0
9	Pakistan	4	2
10	West Germany (FRG)	4	1
11	Nigeria	4	2
12	Mexico	4	3
13	United Kingdom	4	1
14	Italy	4	1
15	France	4	1
16	Philippines	3	1
17	Thailand	3	1
18	Turkey	3	2
19	Egypt	3	2
20	Spain	3	1
21	Poland	3	1
22	South Korea	3	0
23	Iran	3	3
24	Burma	3	2
25	Ethiopia	3	2
26	Colombia	3	2
27	Argentina	3	4
28	South Africa	3	2
29	Zaire	3	3
30	North Vietnam (Indochina)	3	0
31	Canada	3	5
32	Yugoslavia	3	1
33	Rumania	3	0
34	South Vietnam	3	0
35	Afghanistan	2	2
36	Sudan	2	3
37	Morocco	2	1
38	East Germany (DRG)	2	0
39	Sri Lanka	2	0
40	Algeria	2	3
41	North Korea	2	0
42	China/Taiwan	2	0
43	Tanzania	1	2
44	Czechoslovakia	1	0
45	Peru	1	2
46	Netherlands	1	0
47	Australia	1	4
48	Kenya	1	1
49	Nepal	1	0
50	Venezuela	1	2
51	Libya	0	3
52	Saudi Arabia	0	3
53	Mongolia	0	3

Critical Mass: Population + Territory

	Country	Weight
1	China (PRC)	10
2	USSR	10
3	United States	10
4	India	9
5	Brazil	9
6	Indonesia	8
7	Canada	8
8	Mexico	7
9	Argentina	7
10	Japan	6
11	Pakistan	6
12	Nigeria	6
13	Iran	6
14	Zaire	6
15	West Germany (FRG)	5
16	United Kingdom	5
17	Italy	5
18	France	5
19	Turkey	5
20	Egypt	5
21	Burma	5
22	Ethiopia	5
23	South Africa	5
24	Sudan	5
25	Algeria	5
26	Australia	5
27	Colombia	5
28	Bangladesh	4
29	Philippines	4
30	Thailand	4
31	Spain	4
32	Poland	4
33	Yugoslavia	4
34	Afghanistan	4
35	South Korea	3
36	North Vietnam (Indochina)	3
37	Rumania	3
38	South Vietnam	3
39	Morocco	3
40	Tanzania	3
41	Peru	3
42	Venezuela	3
43	Libya	3
44	Saudi Arabia	3
45	Mongolia	3
46	East Germany (DRG)	2
47	Sri Lanka	2
48	North Korea	2
49	China/Taiwan	2
50	Kenya	2
51	Czechoslovakia	1
52	Netherlands	1
53	Nepal	1

top of the list which are *prima facie* of consequence or certainly of so much potential consequence that any assessment of the international balance of power must pay special attention to them.

This means that the major countries in the world as calculated purely on the basis of people and land are the ones which almost any observer of international events would call to mind. It is still a crude list but one that we can work with and modify with confidence that we are talking about real power. The big five are China, the USSR, the United States, India, and Brazil. If we focus our consideration on those nations with weight values above 4 in the lowest consolidated weight groupings, we have a good rough approximation of the countries, 27 in all, that count in an international sense and tend to influence the actions of other nations. This list needs much refinement but even at this stage it conforms to most subjective judgments of the way things are in the real world today.

Comparisons by Politectonic Zones

It may be useful to note how these major nations are distributed among the politectonic zones of the globe. The top 25 to 35 countries will be the center, though not the exclusive subject, of our ongoing assessment. The weights that we have assigned constitute units of perceived power, a kind of abstract measure of international importance. The power of the leading nations in each zone, based on the simple criteria of size and population, accumulates in terms of units of perceived power. (See page 23)

The story told by these three tables would not be complete if we did not indicate the relative size and population of each of the eleven politectonic zones illustrated by the frontispiece map in Chapter I.

The North American Zone (I), which includes Central America and the Caribbean, except for Cuba, has a total land area of about 9.3 million square miles, which is 16 percent of the world total, and a population of about 325 million. It is a rich and productive region dominated by the United States because of that country's central location, its control of most of the temperate zone of the continent, and its large, productive population. Command of the Atlantic-Pacific sea passage via the Panama Canal adds an extra element of strategic importance to this zone in addition to its polar juxtaposition to Eurasia.

In comparison, Zone II is a little over 9.6 million square miles of which the greatest part (8.6 million) lies within the USSR. Mongolia accounts for most of the remainder, while the six East European Communist states plus Cuba add up to less than one-half million square miles. The total population of these states, including Cuba, is about 365 million. It is also rich and productive, especially in the temperate zone of the Soviet Union and in the Central European heartland. Strategically the central land mass, which touches on all the peninsular and insular regions of Eurasia, is in a dominant position, its greatest weakness being geographic and climatic limitations on access to the oceans. Because of the size of the USSR and its authoritarian method of government, the 130 million or so Great Russians in the USSR exercise greater influence over the peoples and resources of this whole zone (II) than do the 211 million people in the United States in Zone I.

Politectonic Zones:

Critical Mass of Larger Nations

	Country	Critical Mass	Total of Perceived Weights
I	United States	10	25
	Canada	8	
	Mexico	7	
II	USSR	10	10
III	China (PRC)	10	10
IV	West Germany (FRG)	5	20
	United Kingdom	5	
	Italy	5	
	France	5	
V	Iran	6	26
	Turkey	5	
	Egypt	5	
	Sudan	5	
	Algeria	5	
VI	India	9	15
	Pakistan	6	
VII	Indonesia	8	13
	Burma	5	
VIII	Japan	6	6
IX	Brazil	9	21
	Argentina	7	
	Colombia	5	
X	Nigeria	6	22
	Zaire	6	
	Ethiopia	5	
	South Africa	5	
XI	Australia	5	5
		Total	173

The Asian Communist Zone (III) is still another continental-sized region dominated strategically by a single country, the People's Republic of China. While North Korea and North Vietnam maintain some independence of action by keeping their political lines to Moscow open, the cultural backgrounds of their populations and their geographical proximity make this entire region primarily a Chinese preserve. North Vietnam, while apprehensive about being drawn into a Peking-dominated hegemony, has its hands full organizing the recently conquered territory of old Indochina (Cambodia, Laos, and South Vietnam) politically and economically. It will be obliged to cooperate with China for some time to come, using Moscow to counterbalance its obligations to Peking. The whole zone bulks very large in East Asia. It covers about four million square miles of territory and sustains a population of about one billion people, most of them in China, constituting one-fourth of the total population in the world.

The friction at the edges of politectonic zones is nowhere better illustrated than in the case of communist Asia. The dispute between China (PRC) and the USSR over the 4,500 mile border between the two countries and over Mongolia, now thoroughly incorporated in the Soviet political and economic system, is a perennial source of conflict, and actual fighting breaks out periodically along the Amur River and in Sinkiang.

Furthermore, China and North Vietnam are supporting revolutionary movements and guerrilla forces in the bordering Southeast Asian states: Burma, Thailand, and Malaysia. Similarly, where Peking-controlled Tibet meets India's client states across the Himalayas, border disputes and bitter political conflict have been going on for 15 or 20 years despite Indian Prime Minister Nehru's determined effort to establish a friendly relationship with China during Prime Minister Chou En-lai's "peaceful coexistence" policy phase in the mid-1950s. This cordiality broke down abruptly when the Chinese attacked Indian armies on the frontier in 1962 and administered a quick, thorough defeat to Indian defense forces. Politectonic drift and peripheral clashes appear inexorable when adjoining zones are dominated by powers with different cultures, different social and political systems, and markedly different world views.

Proceeding counterclockwise around the periphery of Eurasia, the first peninsular region is West Europe. At times high hopes have been held for a political evolution that would unite many of these nations into a single community organized for security, economic interchange, and political legislation. Today this concept is still far from becoming a reality, and the states of West Europe take on a common identity mainly by their economic free trade system (EEC) and by sheltering within the North Atlantic Pact defense system. Zone IV, then, is made up of those states not incorporated in the autocratic Soviet system that embraces East Germany and East Europe. It is a small region, but its population is substantial and has produced technology and living standards as high as or higher than any in the world today.

As we define the region, 27 states are included, ranging from the Vatican City (population 1,000 on one and one-half square miles), Andorra, Liechtenstein, and Malta, on the smaller side, to France, Germany, the United Kingdom, Italy, and Spain, on the larger. Zone IV has a total area of about one and one-half million square miles with a population of a little over 365 million.

Because of a common ethnic background and cultural affinities, West Europe lines up with North America without drastic friction in most matters, thus constituting the bi-zonal association usually called the Atlantic Community. The political symbolism of this concept and the practical defense arrangements of the North Atlantic Treaty are important features in present-day international affairs.

On the other hand, West Europe borders on Zone II along an entirely artificial line through Central Europe where Soviet armies and Soviet policy stopped at the end of the 1940s—Churchill's "Iron Curtain". This has been a conflict-prone border ever since, with a focal point of tension in West Berlin and periodic trouble in a divided Germany. The people of both Czechoslovakia and Hungary have been suppressed by Soviet armies to prevent those countries from being drawn into the West European cluster of states, with which East Europe has many ties.

There are two states along this Central European border which have doggedly resisted inclusion in the Soviet sphere of influence, while remaining under domestic Communist Party dictatorships and holding aloof from West Europe. They are Yugoslavia, which escaped Soviet controls in the Stalin era to become subsequently steadfastly "neutral", and Albania, which leans on Peking to preserve its independence from the West, from Yugoslavia, and from the Soviet Union. For purely geographic reasons, and because of their determination to stay out of Soviet clutches, these states are included as marginally part of West Europe.

The North African states and those of the Mideast constitute a politectonic zone (V) separated by the Mediterranean and Black Seas, on one side, and the Sahara Desert, on the other, from bordering regions. Its diversity is greater than its unity, but religion (Islam) and a sense of Pan-Arabism tie it together. One of the larger states, Iran, is in fact not Arab at all. The state which creates most of the tension in the area by its very existence is Israel. It is small but dynamic and its Hebraic heritage sets its inhabitants off sharply from the other Semitic peoples of the area.

The tribalism and complex history of Zone V is reflected in the number of separate states which comprise it, many of them very small. This zone lies at the crossroads of Asia, Europe, and Africa, and contains the strategic Suez link between the Mediterranean and the Indian Ocean. It has probably been the most fought-over region of the world since the days of ancient Egypt and the Roman Empire. Now, of course, its enormous oil reserves inevitably make the Mideast a ripe plum for contesting influences from neighboring politectonic zones.

The area between the Sahara and the Mediterranean, basically Arab in background, contains eight states with a population of about 100 million and territory, which is not very hospitable or productive for the most part, amounting to about four million square miles. In the Arabian Peninsula itself there are 12 states (counting the United Arab Emirates as one), with a population of about 40 million and territory amounting to a little less than two million square miles, one-third of which belongs to the six million people of Saudi Arabia.

Turkey, Israel, and Iran are culturally distinct although geographically situated in the Mideast. Their populations of 39.5 million, 3.3 million and 32.7 million, respectively, live within territorial boundaries comprising about 300 thousand square miles, 8 thousand square miles, and 636 thousand square miles. In total, Zone V supports a population of about 215 million on a little less than 7 million square miles of land, much of it desert.

The subcontinent of South Asia is a politectonic zone (VI) in the most literal sense. Geologically it drifted from a more southerly location millions of years ago and collided with Asia, uplifting the Himalayas which still separate it from Central Asia. It comprises only eight states, including the new mini-states, the Maldives. The Zone VI population reaches the staggering total of about 790 million, mostly situated in India, on a total territory of about 2 million square miles.

What is left of Southeast Asia, Zone VII, once Indochina has been treated in accord with its political coloration as part of communist Asia, is largely an island territory of nearly one and one-half million square miles supporting a population of about 250 million. Indonesia has approximately one-half of the people and land in Zone VII.

Here the fault line separating the mainland states from Zone III to the north is unstable, and this has been the most turbulent zone of recent years because of the conflict which ended only in 1975 with the severing of South Vietnam, Cambodia, and Laos from this grouping of states and the effective establishment of North Vietnamese control over these 30-odd millions of people and 225 thousand square miles of fertile subtropical territory.

The remaining peripheral region of Eurasia, Zone VIII, is a small but politically and geographically disparate cluster of three states: Japan, South Korea, and China/Taiwan. Its total population is about 160 million and its territory only about 195 thousand square miles. It constitutes a pivotal strategic triangle, each point of which interlocks with the others, and the whole sits in the center of a larger triangle where mainland Chinese, Soviet Far Eastern, and U.S. Pacific interests meet. It is stable in the sense that a major change of structural strategic position in any part of Northeast Asia would tend to destabilize the relationship of the larger powers, none of which at present appears anxious for this to happen.

On the other hand, Zone VIII is under tremendous pressure from all sides, and an unanticipated or unavoidable change in any of these three countries could cause the region to disintegrate as a strategic unit. China/Taiwan is a politically cohesive nation of nearly 16 million people, but its territory is claimed by the Communist regime in Peking which ousted the Government of the Republic of China (China/Taiwan) in 1949. While Peking probably does not want to incur the risks and costs of taking the island now, it has made "Recover Taiwan" one of its most constantly reiterated slogans. The Chinese people living in Taiwan have a standard of economic well-being three times as high as that on the mainland and a considerably less autocratic form of government. They have no intention of succumbing to communist rule if they can help it.

South Korea is also part of a divided country, in this case a more equitably divided one. North Korea, with Soviet and Chinese Communist support, tried to unify the peninsula by military force in 1950 and still threatens to do so. South Korea is strong enough and politically coherent enough to fight against any attack from the North, so long as it can count on military assistance from the

United States. Since the Korean peninsula as a whole has long been perceived as a dagger pointing at the heart of Japan, Japan has every interest in maintaining the present status quo.

Japan, also, appears to be able to sustain the enormous pressures on this region so long as it remains part of the U.S. Pacific security system. It has little military strength, but its level of economic development carries great influence throughout East Asia, and the size of its population makes it the northern equivalent of Indonesia in the long chain of islands that flank the continent along an arc nearly 3,000 miles in length.

On the outer crescent of the globe are three politectonic zones whose strategic fate is ultimately tied up with the evolution of power in the Eurasian and North American zones. At this point in history they are only beginning to exert leverage in the international arena and the power position of the leading nations in these outer zones is therefore relatively limited. Their potential importance is enormous, however, and the way they evolve in this decade will unquestionably foreshadow the ultimate role they play in strategic global conflicts.

These three zones are rather arbitrarily designated as Latin America south of Panama, Central and Southern Africa below the Sahara, and the South Pacific island region of Australia and New Zealand, which includes Fiji, Nauru, Tonga, and Western Samoa. The significance of geography, political coherence, and economic development is nowhere so dramatically illustrated as in the comparatively restricted role played in world affairs by Zones IX, X, and XI, which collectively include nations with about 500 million people in them and a total land area of over 16 million square miles.

To recapitulate, the 27 nations whose comparative importance in terms of people and territory we have tried to measure are the most prominent elements in the eleven politectonic zones throughout which roughly four billion people are scattered. The total population of each zone and the way approximately 52 million square miles of territory are distributed (omitting Antarctica) is shown in the following table:

Zone	Population *(Millions Rounded)*	Territory *(Millions of Square Miles)*
I	325	9.3
II	365	9.6
III	1,000	4.0
IV	365	1.5
V	215	7.0
VI	790	2.0
VII	250	1.5
VIII	160	0.2
IX	210	6.8
X	280	6.6
XI	17	3.0

Zonal Distribution of 152 Nations

Zone I.

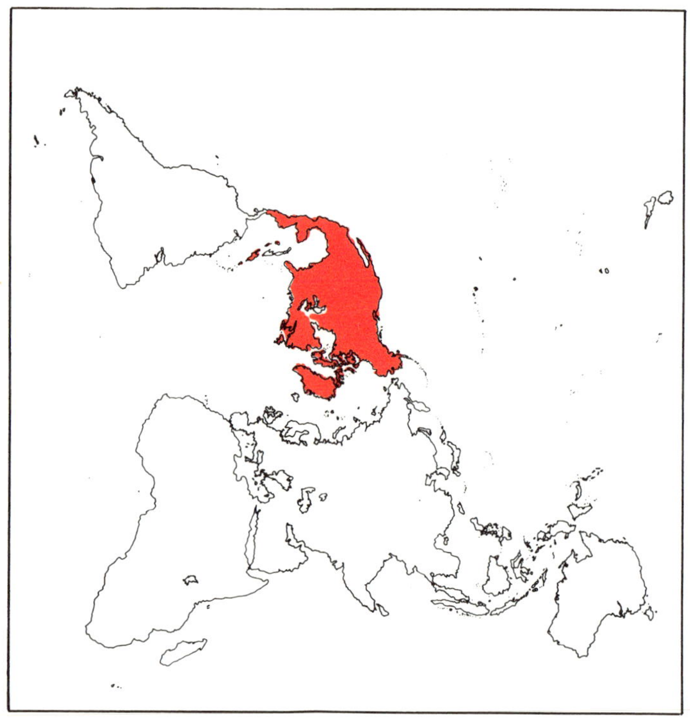

Bahamas
Barbados
Canada
Costa Rica
Dominican Republic
El Salvador
Guatemala
Haiti
Honduras
Jamaica
Mexico
Nicaragua
Panama
Trinidad and Tobago
United States

Zone II.

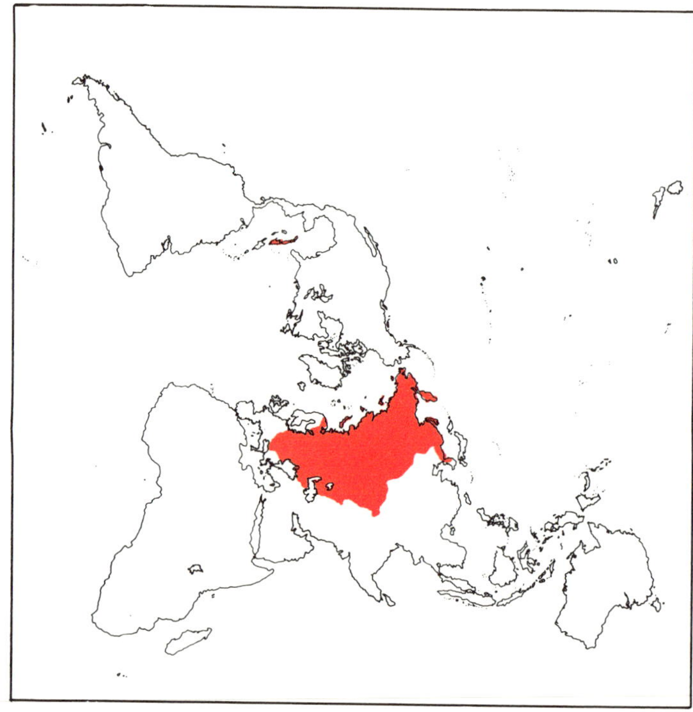

Bulgaria
Cuba
Czechoslovakia
Germany (GDR)
Hungary
Mongolia
Poland
Rumania
USSR

Zone III.

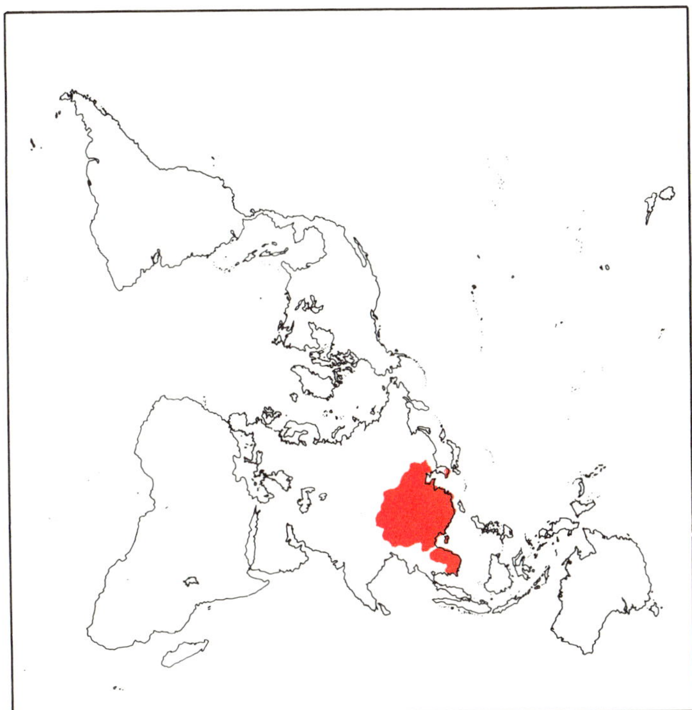

Cambodia
China (PRC)
Korea, North
Laos
Vietnam, North
Vietnam, South

Zone IV.

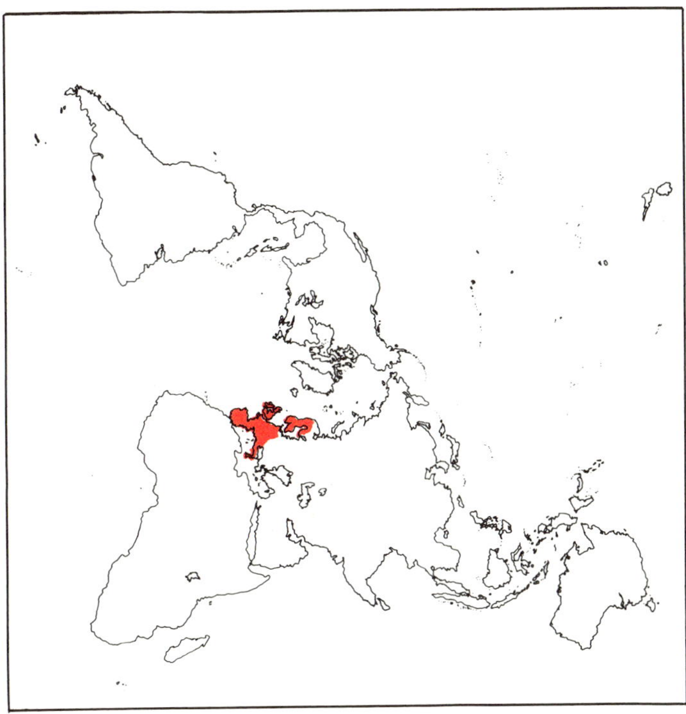

Albania
Andorra
Austria
Belgium
Cyprus
Denmark
Finland
France
Germany (FRG)
Greece
Iceland
Ireland
Italy
Liechtenstein
Luxembourg
Malta
Monaco
Netherlands
Norway
Portugal
San Marino
Spain
Sweden
Switzerland
United Kingdom
Vatican
Yugoslavia

Zone V.

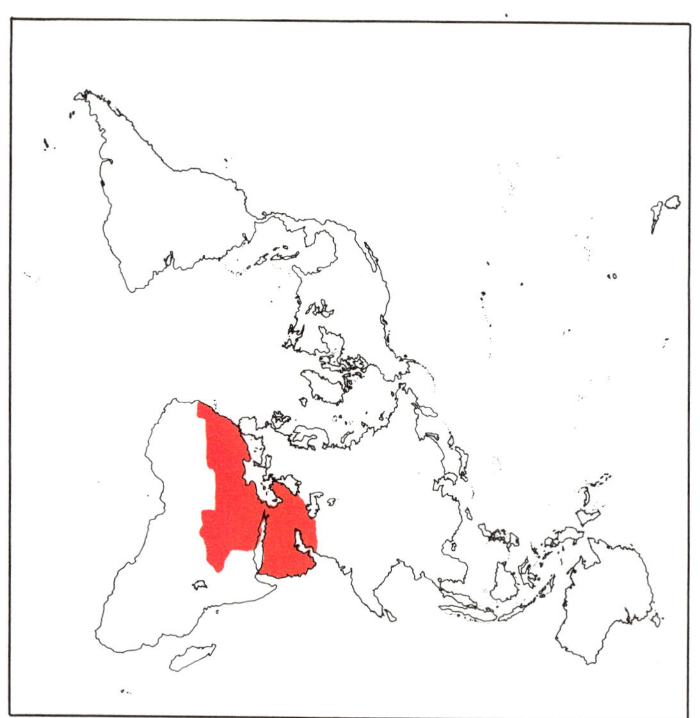

Algeria
Bahrain
Egypt
Iran
Iraq
Israel
Jordan
Kuwait
Lebanon
Libya
Mali
Mauritania
Morocco
Oman
Qatar
Saudi Arabia
Sudan
Syria
Tunisia
Turkey
United Arab Emirates
Yemen (Aden)
Yemen (Sana)

Zone VI.

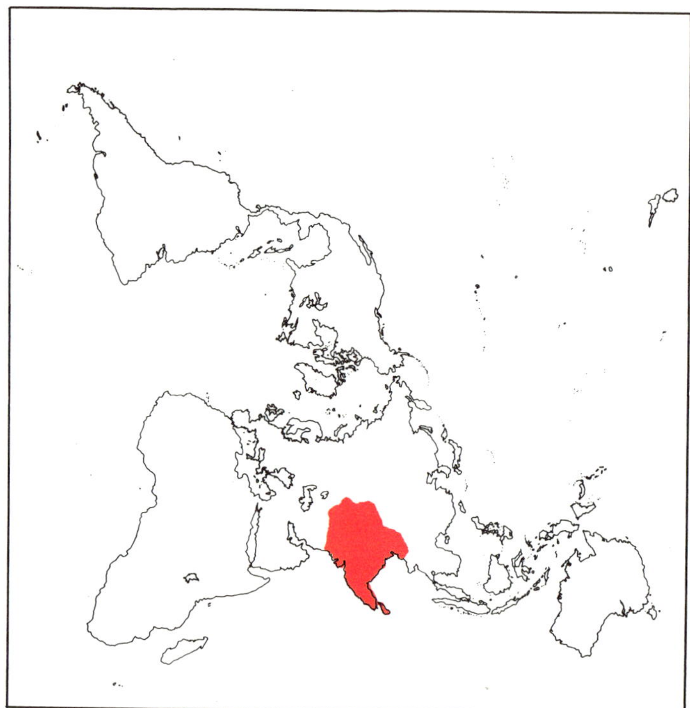

Afghanistan
Bangladesh
Bhutan
India
Maldives
Nepal
Pakistan
Sri Lanka

Zone VII.

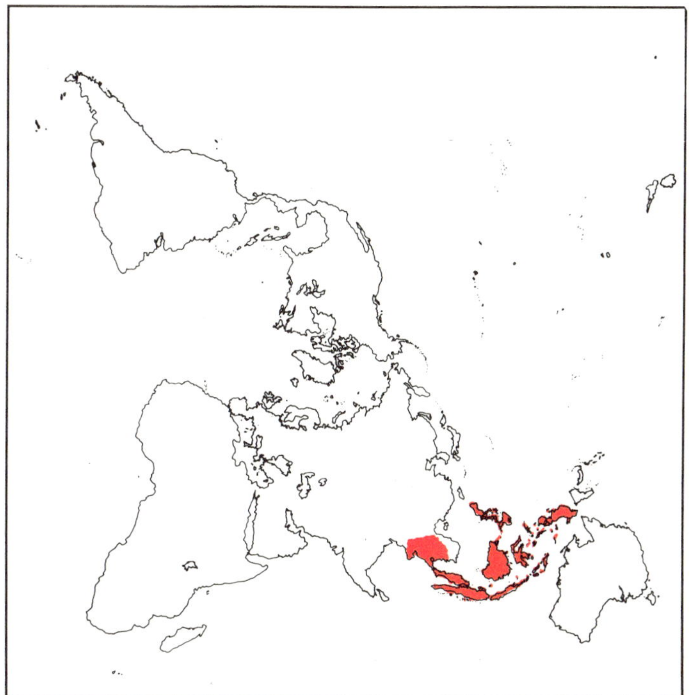

Burma
Indonesia
Malaysia
Philippines
Singapore
Thailand

Zone VIII.

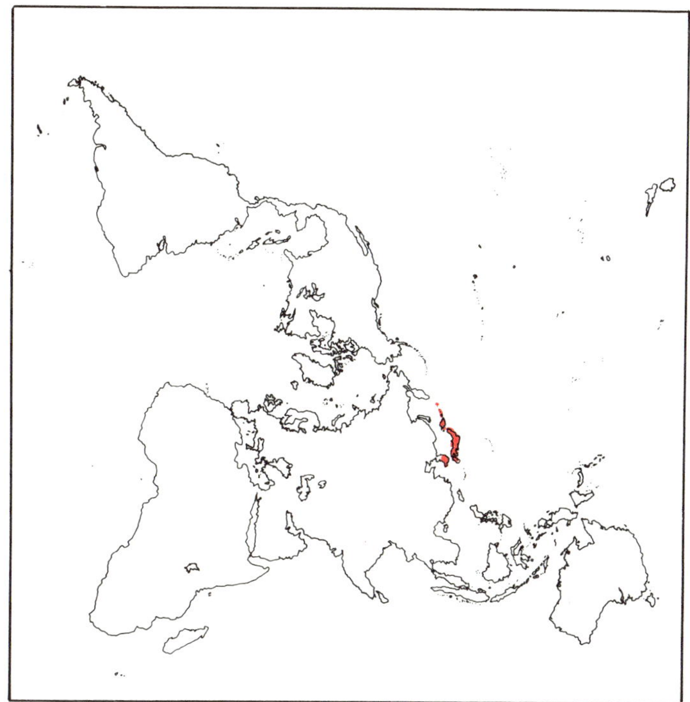

China/Taiwan
Japan
Korea, South

Zone IX.

Argentina
Bolivia
Brazil
Chile
Colombia
Ecuador
Guyana
Paraguay
Peru
Surinam
Uruguay
Venezuela

Zone X.

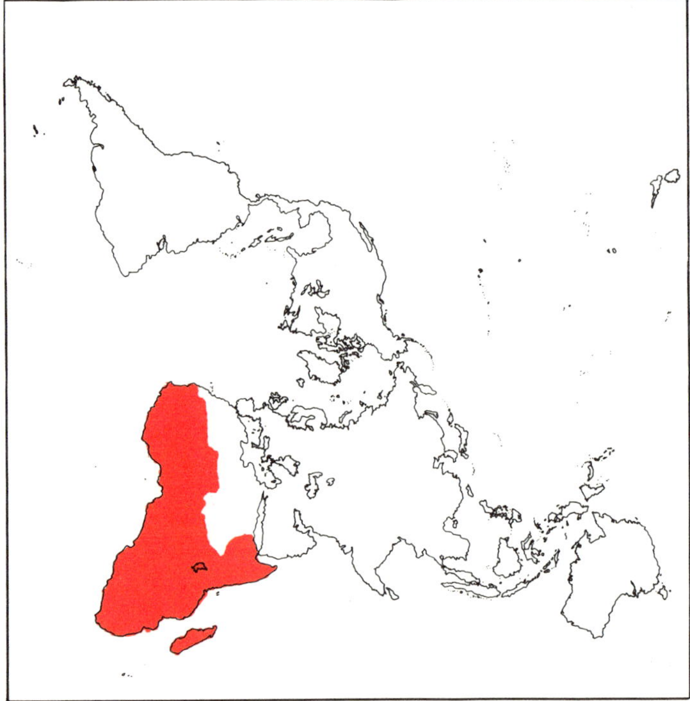

Botswana
Burundi
Cameroon
Central African Republic
Chad
Congo (Brazzaville)
Dahomey
Equatorial Guinea
Ethiopia
Gabon
Gambia
Ghana
Guinea
Guinea-Bissau
Ivory Coast
Kenya
Lesotho
Liberia
Madagascar
Malawi
Mauritius
Mozambique
Niger
Nigeria
Rwanda
Senegal
Sierra Leone
Somalia
South Africa
Southern Rhodesia
Swaziland
Tanzania
Togo
Uganda
Upper Volta
Zaire
Zambia

Zone XI.

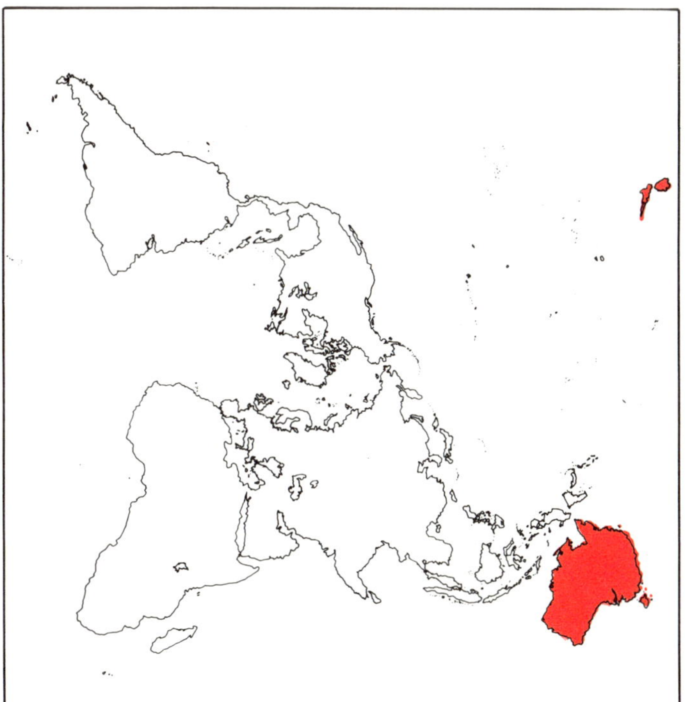

Australia
Fiji
Nauru
New Zealand
Tonga
Western Samoa

Measuring Economic Capabilities

$Pp = (C + E + M) \times (S + W)$

In developing a formula for measuring and comparing national power it is clear that calculations based solely on acreage and people would be misleading unless adjusted to show particular economic strengths. In other words, the formula Pp = C is too crude a measure; the equation is more useful—though still incomplete—if it reads Pp = C + E. What the people of a country have actually accomplished with the available land and natural resources is a critical factor in their own and others' perceptions of their power. Economic strength is equally important as the basis on which a nation is able to build organized military capabilities, manufacture arms, and provide the logistic and technical support needed by modern armies, navies, and air forces. The next task in our assessment of world power is therefore to look at countries from the economic viewpoint, since economic achievement is generally the measuring rod in international affairs that can most tangibly be put to use. While here, as elsewhere, we are dealing with macrometrics designed to support general conclusions, some precision of quantification is possible.

The broadest way of calculating the extent of a country's mobilized economic strength is to assess the total of economic goods and services produced annually or within another specified period, that is, the value of the gross national product (GNP) or a related concept. If qualified with appropriate caveats about other aspects of a nation's economic structure, particularly its natural resources, its technological skills, and its international trade, comparisons among nations which are based on GNP are extremely revealing, while admittedly imperfect. Furthermore, GNP is a standard of concrete measurement made familiar by repeated worldwide use in the information media.

Working with GNP statistics can be a treacherous undertaking, since reliable data usually become available at least a year late, since reporting systems vary, since constant dollars must be used for comparisons in time and fluctuating currency conversion values must be used for comparisons between countries. Skilled economists can disagree on a multitude of details, but the gross orders of magnitude are nonetheless significant. As we go on we will add weights to account for such special economic strengths as sources of energy, but our first rough approximation is based on GNP. Weights for the initial economic analysis are assigned on the basis of a systematic compilation of GNP data issued by the U.S. Government in January 1975. While most of the statistics reflect the calendar year 1973, this compilation is an internally consistent up-to-date source for the wide variety of data needed to calculate economic capability as a factor in the international power context. It is certainly among the best worldwide comparisons of GNP values.[1]

Comparing the Gross National Economic Product of Nations

What quickly emerges from an examination of these data is that most of the world's activity resulting in economic goods and services takes place in a relatively small number of countries. Among these the United States is in a class by itself. The 1975 GNP of the United States will probably be about $1,500 billion—or a trillion and a half 1975 dollars. In current 1974 dollars the 1974 GNP was about 1,400 billion and in 1973, when reliable data for most other countries are available, GNP in current dollars was about 1,300 billion. The difference between these numbers is mostly due to inflation, since there has been an overall decline rather than new growth in GNP in the United States since 1973.

The total value of economic goods and services in the whole world in 1973 was about 5,000 billion or five trillion 1973 dollars, so the United States alone produced and disposed of about one-fourth (26 percent) of the world product in 1973. The total and the percentage will not greatly differ for 1975 since the growth of the world economy has been drastically slowed down by the 1974-1975 recession and is not likely to start growing appreciably again until the latter part of 1975. In the United States, for example, real output (discounting inflation) dropped about 2 percent in 1974 and will probably drop more in 1975. This is what economists call negative growth—the first experience of it in many years for the United States. In any case, the basic pattern of economic relationships presented in final 1973 statistics persisted in mid-1975.[2]

The Soviet economy for a number of years has been operating at a level just less than one-half of the GNP of the United States. In 1973 the Soviet GNP was about $625 billion.[3] The two superpowers together thus account for nearly 40 percent of the world's economic output, and, with Japan and the Federal Republic of Germany, for over one-half of the global GNP. Another five nations, France, the United Kingdom, the People's Republic of China, Italy, and Canada, in 1973 produced goods and services of over U.S. $100 billion; these, plus the preceding four, account for 70 percent of the world's output. The 20 nations having GNPs in 1973 over U.S. $50 billion make up 80 percent of the whole and the top 50 nations account for 90 percent of the economic goods and services of the entire globe.

[1] *National Basic Intelligence Factbook,* January 1975, DOCEX, Library of Congress, Washington, D.C.

[2] Herbert Block, *Political Arithmetic of the World Economies,* (Washington, D.C.: The Center for Strategic and International Studies ((CSIS)), Georgetown University, 1974). For comparative purposes, recent economic trends in the historical context of the past 25 years have been examined in a special research report by Herbert Block. The results are presented in Appendix A, which contains a series of tables on GNP in terms of 1974 U.S. dollars. Not all nations have provided sufficient data to permit using this 1974 material in this chapter, but the trends in major countries and groups of countries are comparable to those set forth in *Political Arithmetic.*

[3] Block, *op. cit.,* p. 80.

"Private Enterprise" versus "Command" Economies

The economic systems in the USSR and China differ fundamentally from the systems of the other economic giants. The United States, Japan, West Germany (FRG), France, the United Kingdom, Italy, and Canada basically have private-enterprise economies. The centrally planned or authoritarian socialist economy typified by the Soviet Union is essentially a command economy which produces on order from the top rather than in response to consumer demand anticipated by private entrepreneurs. In practice, no pure economic system exists, since each of these two fundamental types has found it practical to incorporate some small admixture of the processes characteristic of the other. Nevertheless, the United States, Japan, and West Germany are in most important respects oriented around the private-enterprise, free-exchange market, while the USSR leans toward a centrally planned and controlled economy.

In a free-enterprise economy, the means of production are mostly privately owned, and this production is carried out at the initiative of private owners or managers. Legislation and administrative regulation condition the market factors which entrepreneurs must take into account, but in general the question of what commodities and how much of each are to be produced is decided on the basis of price and cost calculations by individual firms. Distribution is determined by the market mechanism as the production process adjusts itself to changes that occur in response to buyer demand. The complicated process of interrelating thousands of production systems is accomplished without central direction, mainly by the profit motive, at every level of economic activity.

In these economies the government takes care of communal wants, sees to it that the market processes remain orderly, and tries to make sure that the aggregate demand is sufficient to avoid involuntary unemployment on a socially or politically untenable scale. Although competition results in some waste, this system rewards innovation and flexible response to situation changes. Because the individual decision-makers are motivated mainly by profit, the attainment of high levels of productivity is of major concern, and finer tuning of economic judgments takes place than is possible in a centrally controlled system. To enhance their profits, private producers often look to markets outside their national boundaries. They also are likely, if political conditions permit, to export capital and manufacture abroad where raw materials or labor may be less expensive.

Most of the countries in the world, except the Soviet-East Europe economic bloc and communist Asia, are to a considerable degree free-enterprise economies. They are all involved to some extent in the worldwide trading system which spans the Atlantic, Pacific, and Indian Oceans. The USSR and China have so far deliberately insulated themselves from this market except in specific cases. Fundamentally, the two great Communist states are autarkic in economic structure and process. However, the USSR and China began to extend foreign economic and military aid in the mid-1950s, and more recently they have modestly increased their foreign trade. Moscow in particular tends to tie other Communist nations to special economic arrangements which keep them out of the mainstream of world trade.

Among the less developed nations, an economic philosophy has been voiced in favor of solving problems of poverty by redistribution of the world's wealth to benefit the Third World at the expense of the rich nations, rather than through growth beneficial to all. The demands of the UNCTAD (United Nations Conference for Trade and Development) countries are increasingly shrill. They strike responsive notes in industrial nations which have intermittent humanitarian impulses to aid various countries in this Third World or at least to buy them off.

These countries dedicated to a redistributive world economy are encouraged in their demands by Communist China. Peking sternly requires productivity and rapid growth in its own society but tries to identify with the poor, weak, and colored peoples of the earth in demanding equalizing measures from the larger, more developed economic powers. The proponents of the redistributive school of economic thought are trying to gain leverage through cartelizing important economic raw materials.

In the centrally planned or command economy, the material means of production are the property of the state or at least thoroughly state controlled. What and how much is to be produced is worked out according to government plan, which is meant to allocate the available resources and technical know-how to integrate and balance the interdependent production processes. High priority for military weapons and armament-supporting industry can be maintained even if consumers are unhappy about the quantity and quality of consumer goods. This may be wasteful and does not necessarily encourage the greatest effort on the part of workers. Lack of incentive is a constant problem in the USSR, particularly in agriculture. It is also extremely difficult for any government to control and manage in an efficient balance all the parts of an economy.

A positive aspect of the command economy is that it can control the use of available resources and thus push the development of growth in any chosen sector. By this method the USSR and Communist China have tried to industrialize quickly. China is still, as its leaders say, an underdeveloped country, but has its own atomic weapons and missiles. The Soviet Union has been able to build its military weapons technology and production to a level of rough parity with the United States despite a much weaker economic infrastructure.

The competition and industrial diversity on which the private-enterprise system is built allows for more efficient managerial decisions based on price/cost relations and offers a better chance that innovations will be made than in a command economy. In the case of the United States, the achievement of higher and higher levels of technology, and the development of advanced managerial expertise, are its greatest strengths in the international market. The U.S. domination of the world computer industry and the extensive use of computers in U.S. industry are indicative of this technological lead. These aspects of economic strength deserve more detailed treatment than the data available and the scope of this book have allowed.

In looking at economic capabilities of the major nations that carry weight in foreign affairs, whether of the free-enterprise or command type, a ranking of the top 50 countries in order of their total economic output, i.e., GNP, indicates substantial disparities of strength.

The vast superiority of the United States in consumer goods and services along with its great capacity for industrial and military production requires us to assign the United States a weight of 10 in units of perceived international power. It is without question economically the richest and strongest nation in the world and is generally perceived as such. We weight the USSR at 8 versus the United States' 10, rather than 5 versus 10 as straight arithmetic of comparative GNP would suggest. Command economies can allocate more easily than consumer-oriented economies their more limited resources to military and industrial products which loom high in international perceptions of power. The multiple choices of carbonated beverages, cosmetics, and convenience-packaged foods in the United States are the envy of the world but they do not add to perceptions of national strength as steel mills, hydroelectric dams, nuclear missiles, and tanks do. Tilting our weights to reflect the Soviet predilection for visible economic might is justifiable, indeed essential, in the interests of realism.

Using 1973 data for precision and comparability, a list can be compiled which groups the nations of lesser GNP than the United States and the USSR according to economic output. Japan and Germany are in the same class as the two superpowers. Below them we have grouped nations with GNPs less than $300 billion but more than $100 billion, less than $100 billion but more than $40 billion, and so on, with breakpoints at $20 billion and $7 billion. Only 50 nations are in this ranking of over 7 billion 1973 dollars. The fact that 1975 figures in constant 1975 dollars will differ somewhat when they become available—not very much in view of the worldwide recession—does not alter the basic relationships underlying our estimates. This ranklist follows:

1973 GNP:

Leading 50 Countries

(US Billion 1973 Dollars[4])

	Country	*GNP**	*Perceived Power Weight*
1	**United States**	$1289	**10**
2	**USSR[5]**	624	**8**
3	**Japan**	412	**6**
4	**West Germany (FRG)**	348	**5**
5	**France**	239	
6	**United Kingdom**	175	
7	**China (PRC)**	172	**4**
8	**Italy**	138	
9	**Canada**	111	
10	**India**	70	
11	**Poland**	60	
12	**Brazil**	60	
13	**Netherlands**	55	
14	**Spain**	54	
15	**Australia**	54	**3**
16	**Sweden**	50	
17	**Mexico**	49	
18	**East Germany (DRG)**	48	
19	**Belgium**	42	
20	**Iran**	40	

(continued)

Country	GNP*	Perceived Power Weight
21 Czechoslovakia	39	
22 Switzerland	38	
23 Rumania	34	
24 Argentina	33	2
25 Austria	28	
26 South Africa	26	
27 Yugoslavia	24	
28 Turkey	24	
29 Denmark	21	
30 Hungary	19.2	
31 Norway	18.8	
32 Finland	16.8	
33 Bulgaria	15.7	
34 Indonesia	14.3	
35 Venezuela	14.0	
36 Greece	13.8	
37 South Korea	11.2	
38 Nigeria	10.6	
39 Thailand	10.5	
40 Philippines	10.5	1
41 Portugal	10.1	
42 New Zealand	9.2	
43 Colombia	8.8	
44 Saudi Arabia	8.8	
45 Egypt[6]	8.8	
46 Israel	8.7	
47 China/Taiwan	8.6	
48 Peru	8.0	
49 Pakistan	7.8	
50 Chile	7.8	

[4] *National Basic Intelligence Factbook,* January 1975, DOCEX, Library of Congress, Washington, D.C.
[5] Block, *op. cit.,* p. 80.
[6] *World Military Expenditures and Arms Trade,* U.S. Arms Control and Disarmament Agency, Washington, D.C. (1973), p. 31.
* For the purpose of this chart Gross Domestic Product (GDP) has been used for those countries for which GNP data were not available.

Special Economic Strengths

A number of specific economic characteristics with international implications are reflected within the gross activity of the whole economy as measured by GNP levels. These economic strengths tend to have special impact on the perceived image of national power in the international arena, either at home or abroad. People and governments are impressed with actual production of commodities particularly when they figure significantly in international economic exchange. For this reason it is corrective in terms of our analysis to weight further the ranklists of the larger countries so far compiled by providing "bonus" economic weights as appropriate for special strengths. These specific economic factors are assign the United States a weight of 10 in units of perceived international power. It is without question economically the richest and strongest nation in the world and is generally perceived as such. We weight the USSR at 8 versus the United States' 10, rather than 5 versus 10 as straight arithmetic of comparative GNP would suggest. Command economies can allocate more easily than consumer-oriented economies their more limited resources to military and industrial products which loom high in international perceptions of power. The multiple choices of carbonated beverages, cosmetics, and convenience-packaged foods in the United States are the envy of the world but they do not add to perceptions of national strength as steel mills, hydroelectric dams, nuclear missiles, and tanks do. Tilting our weights to reflect the Soviet predilection for visible economic might is justifiable, indeed essential, in the interests of realism.

Using 1973 data for precision and comparability, a list can be compiled which groups the nations of lesser GNP than the United States and the USSR according to economic output. Japan and Germany are in the same class as the two superpowers. Below them we have grouped nations with GNPs less than $300 billion but more than $100 billion, less than $100 billion but more than $40 billion, and so on, with breakpoints at $20 billion and $7 billion. Only 50 nations are in this ranking of over 7 billion 1973 dollars. The fact that 1975 figures in constant 1975 dollars will differ somewhat when they become available—not very much in view of the worldwide recession—does not alter the basic relationships underlying our estimates. This ranklist follows:

1973 GNP:

Leading 50 Countries

(US Billion 1973 Dollars[4])

	Country	*GNP**	*Perceived Power Weight*
1	United States	$1289	10
2	USSR[5]	624	8
3	Japan	412	6
4	West Germany (FRG)	348	5
5	France	239	
6	United Kingdom	175	
7	China (PRC)	172	4
8	Italy	138	
9	Canada	111	
10	India	70	
11	Poland	60	
12	Brazil	60	
13	Netherlands	55	
14	Spain	54	
15	Australia	54	3
16	Sweden	50	
17	Mexico	49	
18	East Germany (DRG)	48	
19	Belgium	42	
20	Iran	40	

(continued)

not sufficient in themselves to raise a nation with small population and low GNP to high rank, but the countries possessing them project an image of power which provides useful leverage in international relations. These specific economic strengths therefore magnify perceptions of the capabilities of countries, including those already at the top of the list of powerful nations.

An endless number of economic factors might be taken into account, but in this first attempt to assess perceived power in this way we have selected five for which reasonably good data are available. To these five we have assigned equal value, with the total possible weights equal to the highest GNP value weight. The inclusion of these factors is intended to augment the standards for comparison of economic strengths. They are: energy, crucial non-fuel minerals, steel manufacture, food, and foreign trade. Others would be useful additives, but these five are recognized and highly visible elements of national economic capability. The judgments leading to such weighting are very general and to some extent arbitrary, but they reflect the common perceptions of international power.

One of the most valuable economic resources in the world of the twentieth century, particularly for nations of advanced industrial technologies, is the supply of energy sources, consisting mainly of coal, oil, and gas—the fossil fuels. The relationship between production and consumption of energy is a decisive modifier of economic capability since a surplus or shortage of energy materially affects industrial capacity, trade, and balance of payments. In advanced industrial states the amount of energy that must be imported is a crucial constraint on national strategy.

The United States and the USSR are prodigious producers and consumers of coal, oil, and gas. The nuclear power age is at hand but for the next few years nuclear power does not bulk large statistically in energy supply anywhere, not even in the United States, the country farthest advanced in nuclear reactor technology.

The U.S. model of energy use is a special case. The United States uses over 35 percent of the world's total energy, but U.S. losses from inefficient conversion of fuel into energy, particularly in the massive and wasteful U.S. transportation system, amount to more than the total availability of energy in most nations. The sharply rising demand curve indicates that, for ten years at least, energy will have to be imported in quantity to meet consumer requirements unless these are legislatively restricted.

Consumption is, and will remain for some time, greater than domestic production, but the scale of economic activity is so high that an option for self-sufficiency exists if policies should be adopted at the national level to encourage energy conservation measures and heavy investment in increased domestic production.

Japan and the Western European countries are predominately consumer nations and are in a much less flexible position in international energy negotiations. Many of the oil-exporting states, on the other hand, consume little of the energy they produce. This situation results in an accumulation of petrodollars which creates financial vulnerability as well as commercial strength for the exporting countries. Unless investment in growth industries at home and abroad can siphon off these funds to help build balanced economies, petrodollars may be a financial resource that benefits the oil producers very little.

The 50 largest energy producers in the world can be compared with one another by a conversion of all forms of their energy production to the equivalent of metric tons of coal. By putting data on energy consumption in parentheses immediately following the figures for energy production, vulnerabilities as well as strengths are indicated in the same chart. Where the shortfall in domestic supply to meet consumer needs is large, the benefits of being a big producer of energy are negated. Allowing 2 as the maximum weight and adding these bonus weighting values only to the principal producers, the ranklist in descending order with breakpoints at 100 million and at 50 million metric tons of coal equivalent follows.[8]

Energy:

Coal Equivalent[9]
(Million Metric Tons)

	Country	*Annual Production*	*Annual Consumption*	*Perceived Power Weight*
1	**United States***	2,065	(2,424)	**2**
2	**USSR**	1,312	(1,179)	
3	**China (PRC)**	443	(444)	**1**
4	**Saudi Arabia****	379	(7)	
5	**Iran****	351	(29)	
6	**Canada**	257	(235)	
7	**Venezuela****	233	(27)	
8	**Kuwait****	203	(8)	
9	**West Germany (FRG)*****	171	(332)	
10	**Poland**	170	(150)	
11	**United Kingdom*****	159	(301)	
12	**Libya****	148	(9)	
13	**Nigeria****	118	(3)	
14	**Iraq****	93	(6)	
15	**India**	89	(104)	
16	**Australia**	89	(73)	
17	**Netherlands**	82	(76)	
18	**Czechoslovakia**	81	(99)	
19	**East Germany (DRG)**	78	(102)	
20	**United Arab Emirates****	77	(2)	
21	**Indonesia****	76	(16)	
22	**Algeria****	69	(8)	
23	**Rumania**	66	(65)	
24	**Mexico**	61	(69)	
25	**South Africa**	58	(71)	
26	**France*****	51	(214)	

[8] Current trends in the world oil situation are discussed at greater length in Appendix B. The details presented there illuminate, but in the broad context of all forms of energy production do not alter, the patterns presented in this table.

[9] *UN Statistical Yearbook, 1973* (1972 Statistics)

Country	Annual Production	Annual Consumption	Perceived Power Weight
27 Japan***	44	(344)	
28 Argentina	37	(41)	
29 Qatar**	32	(1)	
30 North Korea	30	(31)	
31 Italy***	27	(151)	
32 Yugoslavia	23	(33)	
33 Hungary	22	(34)	
34 Brazil	20	(52)	
35 Colombia	19	(13)	
36 Oman	18	(0)	
37 Spain	18	(60)	
38 Bulgaria	14	(35)	0
39 Egypt	14	(11)	
40 South Korea	12	(26)	
41 Trinidad & Tobago	11	(4)	
42 Turkey	11	(20)	
43 Norway	11	(18)	
44 Belgium	10	(65)	
45 Austria	9	(26)	
46 Chile	9	(15)	
47 Gabon**	8	(0)	
48 Israel	8	(8)	
49 Syria	7	(3)	
50 Pakistan	7	(10)	

* The United States has such enormous production of energy that it has to be weighted evenly (weight of 2) with the USSR despite the fact that it has a shortfall in meeting demand (consumption) except through imports.
** Members of OPEC, these nations mostly have large supply surplus for export.
*** Note shortfall of these major U.S. allies in meeting demand.

Another significant index of economic strength among advanced nations is production of non-fuel minerals. Iron and steel are used in almost all heavy industry, in machinery production, in munitions, in transportation, and in plant construction. Hence, the availability of iron ore is critical for heavy industry. Other metals, like copper, bauxite, and uranium, are also vitally important, the latter for nuclear power plants as well as for weapons. Chemicals, electronics, and the other elements of modern industry are also essential, but iron and the three other scarce non-fuel minerals are central. Khrushchev used to denounce the "steel-eaters" in the Soviet government who took most of that essential commodity for military manufactures and heavy industry, irrespective of overall demand for such goods or efficiency of production.

There are a surprisingly small number of major producers of all four raw minerals. To give a bonus value in economic weights for these crucial inputs to industrial strength, we can list the principal producers and assign weights for large production of iron ore, copper, bauxite, and uranium.

Non-Fuel Minerals[10]

(Thousand Metric Tons)

Iron Ore

	Country	Production
1	USSR	113,467
2	United States	45,798
3	Australia	39,254
4	Brazil	28,628
5	China (PRC)	25,300
6	Canada	24,387
7	Liberia	22,543
8	India	22,126
9	Sweden	21,317
10	France	16,525
11	Venezuela	11,089

Copper

	Country	Production
1	United States	1,510
2	USSR	1,050
3	Chile	723
4	Zambia	717
5	Canada	709
6	Zaire	412
7	Peru	217
8	Philippines	213
9	Australia	171
10	South Africa	155
11	Japan	112
12	Yugoslavia	103
13	China (PRC)	100

Bauxite

	Country	Production
1	Australia	13,697
2	Jamaica	12,989
3	Surinam	6,777
4	USSR	4,700
5	Guyana	3,707
6	France	3,258
7	Guinea	2,650
8	Greece	2,435
9	Hungary	2,358
10	United States	2,235
11	Yugoslavia	2,197
12	India	1,692
13	Indonesia	1,278
14	Dominican Republic	1,087
15	Malaysia	1,076

Uranium

	Country	Production
1	United States	10,514
2	USSR*	n.a.
3	Canada	3,768
4	South Africa	3,077
5	France	1,213
6	Niger	215
7	Gabon	210

[10] *UN Statistical Yearbook, 1973* (1972 Statistics).

* Soviet production is estimated to be one-half to two-thirds that of the United States and may include production by Czechoslavakia, Hungary, Poland, Bulgaria, and Rumania though precise production figures are not available for these countries.

Non-Fuel Minerals:

Bonus Weights

	Country	Perceived Power Weight
1	United States	2
2	USSR	2
3	Canada	2
4	Australia	1
5	Brazil	1
6	France	1
7	South Africa	1

The production of steel is closely linked with an adequate supply of iron ore. A ranklist based on the production of crude steel indicates that most of the powerful nations have developed a substantial capacity for making this basic metal. For comparison purposes, the consumption statistics are given in parentheses for each country. Japan and West Germany produce steel for export in quantity. The United States, despite being one of the two largest steel producers, has been importing on a substantial scale. The weighted crude steel ranklist is as follows:

Crude Steel[11]

(Thousand Metric Tons)

	Country	*Annual Production*	*Annual Consumption*	*Perceived Power Weight*
1	**USSR**	125,589	(121,143)	
2	**United States**	120,875	(138,410)	2
3	**Japan**	96,901	(68,888)	
4	**West Germany (FRG)**	43,706	(39,972)	
5	**United Kingdom**	25,321	(22,651)	
6	**France**	24,054	(23,570)	1
7	**China (PRC)**	23,000	(26,092)	
8	**Italy**	19,815	(20,585)	
9	**Belgium**	14,477	(4,676)*	
10	**Poland**	13,474	(13,967)	
11	**Czechoslovakia**	12,727	(9,599)	
12	**Canada**	11,859	(12,851)	
13	**Spain**	9,530	(9,508)	
14	**Rumania**	7,401	(777)	
15	**India**	6,756	(9,227)	0
16	**Australia**	6,585	(6,214)	
17	**Brazil**	6,518	(7,642)	
18	**East Germany (DRG)**	5,670	(8,648)	
19	**Netherlands**	5,585	(4,927)	
20	**Luxembourg**	5,457	(4,676)**	
21	**South Africa**	5,343	(4,881)	
22	**Sweden**	5,248	(5,567)	

[11] *UN Statistical Yearbook, 1973* (1972 Statistics).
* Includes Luxembourg
** Includes Belgium

Equally important, and in some contexts more important than energy as a source of economic strength, is an adequate supply of food. One of the strongest bargaining chips which the United States has on the international table is its abundance of food grains, which are a key staple in international trade. Because of its size and its ideal location in the temperate zone, the United States has been able to apply capital-intensive techniques to agriculture and produce more food than Americans consume even at the high living standard that prevails in this country. The USSR has tried to emulate the U.S. model, as Khrushchev's great love affair with raising corn indicated, but despite its great size the USSR has less favorable growing conditions and much less efficient farm methods than the United States. In bad years the USSR has had to import substantial amounts of food grains, as it did in 1975.

China is only barely self-sufficient in good years. Some nations, like India, have chronic difficulties in maintaining essential food supplies. In the last few years a shift in the monsoon belt has created food-deficient areas in the Sahel in North Central Africa, and in South Asia. Only international relief shipments minimized the effects of widespread famine. Some scientists think a cooling trend of some duration may perpetuate these conditions. In any case, in the mid-1970s, an exportable surplus of food grains is an extremely valuable resource everywhere around the globe that commands respect and reciprocal exchange benefits for the exporters. Such major exporters are few. Canada and the United States control a larger percentage of the world's food supply than the Mideast oil exporters control of the world's petroleum. Our weighting values, with a maximum of 2, are easy to apply because so few countries have this exportable surplus. Short ranklists for key food grains are as follows:

Food Grains:

Net Exporters[12]

Wheat

Country	Thousand Metric Tons	Country	Perceived Power Weight
1 United States	22,609	1 United States	2
2 Canada	14,463	2 Canada	2
3 Australia	8,712	3 France	1
4 France	6,787	4 Argentina	1
5 Argentina	1,814	5 Australia	1
		6 South Africa	1

Rice

Country	Thousand Metric Tons
1 Thailand	2,076
2 United States	2,022
3 China (PRC)*	735
4 Burma	460
5 Egypt	456
6 Italy	338
7 Pakistan	300
8 Japan	199
9 Australia	178

Corn

Country	Thousand Metric Tons
1 United States	22,355
2 France	3,230
3 Argentina	3,038
4 South Africa	3,000

[12] *FAO Trade Yearbook, 1973* (1972 Statistics).

* Imports of corn and wheat have in recent years much more than offset exports of rice.

A final economic value must be added to the strength of major nations in order to compare them accurately. It is foreign trade. In international affairs, trade is often the instrument of foreign policy that settles issues short of war. It once was said that trade followed the flag; it now tends to follow from the perception of power, particularly economic power, and from the ability to maintain access to the marketplaces and lanes of commerce throughout the world.

The best way to measure trade as an instrument of foreign policy is to calculate a country's share of the world total. The conventional means of measurement used by economists for a nation's total trade is the averaging of the money value of total exports plus total imports. To some extent the volume of trade also suggests how vulnerable an economy is to fluctuations in prices or supply, but this is offset by other factors, particularly what percentage of its GNP a nation derives from foreign trade. The volume of U.S. trade is by far the greatest in the world. This means that its markets and its commodities are important in the eyes of most trading nations. On the other hand, trade represents only about 6 percent of the U.S. GNP and interruption of supplies by cartels or by military action is consequently less crippling than it would be to many other countries. By way of comparison, British trade is about 20 percent of its GNP and the Federal Republic of Germany's, about 18 percent.

The major autarkic command economies, the Soviet Union and China, are also protected from outside leverage. Their foreign trade is about 3 percent of their respective GNPs; by design, they participate relatively little in world commodity exchange. Their trade is often motivated by an interest in acquiring advanced foreign technology and sometimes by an attempt to exert political leverage. Most other large nations are part of a world trading community that normally depends on market mechanisms to regulate price and volume of exchange.

As is true for most other factors, the bulk of the world's commerce is also conducted by a few large nations, primarily the North Pacific-North Atlantic trading partners of West Europe, North America, and Japan. The USSR makes its way into the top ten primarily on the strength of its planned exchanges with the Eastern European communist nations which it dominates politically as well as economically. The top nine countries, all formally allied with the United States for common military defense purposes, conduct 60 percent of total world trade. If we add all of the nations whose total trade (i.e., one-half of exports plus imports) in 1973 was more than $4 billion, the ranklist would include 19 more nations and account for an additional 24 percent of world trade. This indicates a total for the top 28 nations of over 80 percent of international commerce. The weighted ranklist of major nations in order of value of world trade is as follows, with columns included showing percentage of world trade and percentage of GNP for comparison purposes:

World Trade 1973[13]

World Trade $573 Billions

	Country	Exports + Imports / 2 — Value in Billion U.S. Dollars[14]	% Total World Trade	% Domestic GNP	Perceived Power Weight
1	United States	**72**	12.6	5.6	
2	West Germany (FRG)	**61**	10.6	17.5	
3	France	**37**	6.4	15.5	
4	United Kingdom	**35**	6.1	20.0	
5	Japan	**34**	5.9	8.2	2
6	Canada	**26**	4.5	23.4	
7	Italy	**25**	4.4	18.1	
8	Netherlands	**24**	4.2	43.6	
9	Belgium	**22**	3.8	52.4	
10	USSR	**21**	3.7	3.4	
11	Sweden	**11**	1.9	22.0	
12	Switzerland	**10**	1.7	26.3	
13	Australia	**9**	1.6	16.7	
14	East Germany (DRG)	**8**	1.4	16.7	
15	Spain	**7**	1.2	13.0	
16	Poland	**7**	1.2	11.7	
17	Denmark	**7**	1.2	33.3	
18	Brazil	**7**	1.2	11.7	
19	Czechoslovakia	**6**	1.0	17.9	1
20	Austria	**6**	1.0	21.4	
21	Norway	**5**	.9	26.6	
22	Iran	**5**	.9	12.5	
23	China (PRC)	**5**	.9	2.9	
24	South Africa	**4**	.7	15.4	
25	Hungary	**4**	.7	20.8	
26	Venezuela	**4**	.7	28.6	
27	China/Taiwan	**4**	.7	46.5	
28	Finland	**4**	.7	23.8	

[13] *Monthly Bulletin of Statistics,* United Nations, July 1975.
[14] *National Basic Intelligence Factbook,* January 1975.

To recapitulate our findings so far we can construct a consolidated ranklist additionally weighted for GNP and for these 5 bonus economic strengths. The order changes considerably. Several countries must be added to the 53 originally designated as having a significant critical mass.(See page 21.) They number 17, of which 14 are small with substantial economic activity (Sweden, Belgium, Switzerland, Austria, Denmark, Hungary, Norway, Finland, Bulgaria, Greece, Portugal, New Zealand, Israel, and Chile), and three are small states with large energy resources (Kuwait, Iraq, and the United Arab Emirates). The 70 countries thus ranked for critical mass, plus all economic capabilities, are as follows:

Economic Strengths:

Consolidated Ranklist with Bonus Values

(Perceived Power Weights)

	Country	*Critical Mass*	*GNP*	*Energy*	*Minerals*	*Food*	*Steel*	*Trade*	*Econ. Total*	*Total*
1	United States	10	10	2	2	2	2	2	20	30
2	USSR	10	8	2	2	—	2	2	16	26
3	Canada	8	4	1	2	2	—	2	11	19
4	China (PRC)	10	4	1	—	—	1	1	7	17
5	Japan	6	6	—	—	—	2	2	10	16
6	France	5	4	1	1	1	1	2	10	15
7	West Germany (FRG)	5	5	1	—	—	2	2	10	15
8	Brazil	9	3	—	1	—	—	1	5	14
9	India	9	3	1	—	—	—	—	4	13
10	United Kingdom	5	4	1	—	—	1	2	8	13
11	Australia	5	3	1	1	1	—	1	7	12
12	Italy	5	4	—	—	—	1	2	7	12
13	Iran	6	3	1	—	—	—	1	5	11
14	Mexico	7	3	1	—	—	—	—	4	11
15	South Africa	5	2	1	1	1	—	1	6	11
16	Indonesia	8	1	1	—	—	—	—	2	10
17	Argentina	7	2	—	—	1	—	—	3	10
18	Poland	4	3	1	—	—	—	1	5	9
19	Nigeria	6	1	1	—	—	—	—	2	8
20	Spain	4	3	—	—	—	—	1	4	8
21	Pakistan	6	1	—	—	—	—	—	1	7
22	Turkey	5	2	—	—	—	—	—	2	7
23	Netherlands	1	3	1	—	—	—	2	6	7
24	East Germany (DRG)	2	3	1	—	—	—	1	5	7
25	Zaire	6	—	—	—	—	—	—	0	6
26	Egypt	5	1	—	—	—	—	—	1	6
27	Yugoslavia	4	2	—	—	—	—	—	2	6
28	Algeria	5	—	1	—	—	—	—	1	6
29	Rumania	3	2	1	—	—	—	—	3	6
30	Venezuela	3	1	1	—	—	—	1	3	6
31	Colombia	5	1	—	—	—	—	—	1	6
32	Burma	5	—	—	—	—	—	—	—	5
33	Ethiopia	5	—	—	—	—	—	—	—	5
34	Sudan	5	—	—	—	—	—	—	—	5
35	Philippines	4	1	—	—	—	—	—	1	5
36	Thailand	4	1	—	—	—	—	—	1	5
37	Saudi Arabia	3	1	1	—	—	—	—	2	5
38	Czechoslovakia	1	2	1	—	—	—	1	4	5
39	Belgium	—	3	—	—	—	—	2	5	5
40	Sweden	1	3	—	—	—	—	1	4	5
41	Bangladesh	4	—	—	—	—	—	—	—	4
42	Afghanistan	4	—	—	—	—	—	—	—	4
43	South Korea	3	1	—	—	—	—	—	1	4
44	Peru	3	1	—	—	—	—	—	1	4
45	Libya	3	—	1	—	—	—	—	1	4
46	China/Taiwan	2	1	—	—	—	—	1	2	4
47	North Vietnam	3	—	—	—	—	—	—	—	3
48	South Vietnam	3	—	—	—	—	—	—	—	3
49	Morocco	3	—	—	—	—	—	—	—	3
50	Tanzania	3	—	—	—	—	—	—	—	3
51	Mongolia	3	—	—	—	—	—	—	—	3
52	Switzerland	—	2	—	—	—	—	1	3	3

Country	Critical Mass	GNP	Energy	Minerals	Food	Steel	Trade	Econ. Total	Total
53 Austria	—	2	—	—	—	—	1	3	3
54 Denmark	—	2	—	—	—	—	1	3	3
55 Finland	1	1	—	—	—	—	1	2	3
56 Chile	2	1	—	—	—	—	—	1	3
57 Norway	1	1	—	—	—	—	1	2	3
58 Hungary	—	1	—	—	—	—	1	2	2
59 Sri Lanka	2	—	—	—	—	—	—	—	2
60 North Korea	2	—	—	—	—	—	—	—	2
61 Kenya	2	—	—	—	—	—	—	—	2
62 New Zealand	1	1	—	—	—	—	—	1	2
63 Iraq	1	—	1	—	—	—	—	1	2
64 Nepal	1	—	—	—	—	—	—	—	1
65 Bulgaria	—	1	—	—	—	—	—	1	1
66 Greece	—	1	—	—	—	—	—	1	1
67 Portugal	—	1	—	—	—	—	—	1	1
68 Israel	—	1	—	—	—	—	—	1	1
69 Kuwait	—	—	1	—	—	—	—	1	1
70 United Arab Emirates	—	—	1	—	—	—	—	1	1

Finally, we ought to readjust the table which shows the comparative importance of the larger nations in the several politectonic zones. It is necessary to add weights for those nations whose international power we can perceive to have been substantially enhanced by taking GNP and other economic strengths into account.

Focussing on the top of the adjusted list we now have a meaningful breakpoint at 31 nations (perceived power weights of 6 and over), geographically dispersed, which are by every indication so far the leading elements of international power. Even at this early stage of analyzing world balance of power, it is easy to see that (a) the United States is stronger than the USSR and towers over the others, (b) North America is naturally a dominant zone because of the strengths of the three large nations in it, (c) West Europe is an extremely valuable piece of real estate potentially stronger than the whole of North America but (as we shall see later) handicapped in the effective use of power because it lacks political unity, and (d) the Soviet-East Europe Bloc—with or without the borderline Communist renegade, Yugoslavia—constitutes a formidable power center closely rivalling North America.

N.B. The ideas in this chapter are dependent in part on the helpful comments and suggestions of Dr. Penelope Hartland-Thunberg, CSIS Director of Economic Research.

Critical Mass and Economic Capability:

Larger Nations in Politectonic Zones

	Country	*Perceived Power Weight*	*Total Weights*
I	United States	30	60
	Canada	19	
	Mexico	11	
II	USSR	26	48
	Poland	9	
	East Germany (DRG)	7	
	Rumania	6	
III	China (PRC)	17	17
IV	France	15	76
	West Germany (FRG)	15	
	United Kingdom	13	
	Italy	12	
	Spain	8	
	Netherlands	7	
	Yugoslavia	6	
V	Iran	11	30
	Turkey	7	
	Egypt	6	
	Algeria	6	
VI	India	13	20
	Pakistan	7	
VII	Indonesia	10	10
VIII	Japan	16	16
IX	Brazil	14	36
	Argentina	10	
	Venezuela	6	
	Colombia	6	
X	South Africa	11	25
	Nigeria	8	
	Zaire	6	
XI	Australia	12	12

Military Capability: The Strategic Force Balance

$Pp = (C + E + M) \times (S + W)$

The ultimate recourse in disputes between nations is to military force. The threat of war, if credible, precipitates national action as nothing else can do. Fear that survival is at stake is a prime motivating factor. As Clausewitz said long ago, "War is a mere continuation of policy by other means", and hence "is an act of violence intended to compel our opponent to fulfill our will" by application of the "utmost use of force".[1]

Conflicts among nations usually start with political arguments and diplomatic pressures and proceed through increasingly important offerings or withholdings of economic benefits. If either side considers the conflict absolutely vital, it can threaten to go to war and in the end call upon its military units and weapons in a final violent act of persuasion. At the point of threatening to use armed force, mobilized military capabilities become all-important, whether the readiness of the superior force settles the issue without actual fighting or war breaks out and final arbitration takes place on the battlefield. In any calculation of perceived power it is essential, then, to expand our formula for calculating national power to include military capability, that is, to read: $Pp = C + E + M$.

The most powerful weapons in the long history of war are universally considered to be nuclear missiles even though, except for Hiroshima and Nagasaki, atomic weapons remain untested under battle conditions. The overwhelming preponderance of Soviet and U.S. strategic nuclear strength is the dominant fact of international life. These two powers can literally extinguish the life of any other nation in a few moments, devastating it beyond recovery. Other nuclear powers pale into insignificance in comparison, but there is a certain aura of belonging to the "nuclear club" that sets off the United Kingdom, France, China (PRC), and now possibly India, from the rest. Even those nations like Japan, Sweden, Argentina, Israel, and China/Taiwan, which are widely perceived to have the technological capability of manufacturing nuclear weapons, enjoy with their neighbors a certain marginal advantage of respect or fear.

Nuclear weapons are so destructive that their capacity to deter other nations from using them is their greatest military benefit. Except in an extremity hard to

[1] Carl von Clausewitz, *On War*, (London and Boston: Routledge & Kegan Paul, 1968), Vol. I, p. 2 and p. 23.

imagine or the passage of command authority to a madman, the United States and the USSR presently deter each other from nuclear war and seem likely to do so for at least another five or ten years. Obviously, either of these giant nuclear powers can easily deter the secondary nuclear powers from using their much more limited arsenals.

It is the implicitly threatened use of nuclear bombs or missiles—either as nuclear "blackmail" or nuclear "shield"—that brings enormous pressure to bear on international conflict situations. In a sense, the less responsible a nation's leadership, the greater the nuclear threat, for its use becomes more credible. Insofar as political leadership is moderate, and especially to the extent that it is accountable to public opinion, it can exploit nuclear capability only as a deterrent rather than as a realistic threat. Yet without this ultimate strategic weapon, no nation today can pretend to be completely free to pursue an independent line in international affairs to the bitter end. Non-nuclear powers win contests of will only on the sufferance of the USSR and the United States. In a true national life-or-death issue they would have to give way unless they could secure U.S. and Soviet forbearance.

Fortunately, international conflicts are seldom pursued to the point of national survival or destruction. Such military action as has taken place since World War II has involved only conventional weapons. The era has not been a peaceful one by any measure, but no conflict has yet involved the actual employment of nuclear arms. The closest escape came probably during the Cuban missile crisis of October 1962, when Soviet inferiority in strategic weapons-delivery systems and U.S. superiority in conventional weapons systems in the Caribbean forced the USSR into a humiliating withdrawal of its missiles.

It is clear that in circumstances like these, conventional military strength is the key to safe confrontations of the short-of-war variety. It also assures nations under attack from more aggressive neighbors that they can put up some defense until the nuclear powers can contain the conflict and adjudicate or arbitrate it. Up to a certain point, a nation with effective conventional military forces can even defy the restraining influence of the nuclear powers and triumph over less well-armed states. North Vietnam's takeover of Cambodia, South Vietnam, and Laos, in the face of the efforts of the United States to prevent it, is an eloquent demonstration of this point. The crucial difference, of course, probably was in varying levels of national will, but Cambodia's and South Vietnam's armies were finally beaten on the battlefield with conventional weapons while the United States stood by.

Crucial Elements of Military Power

Perceptions of military power are highly subjective, but it is clear that a weighting system for military capability has to take into account two crucial elements. First, it must give primary importance to nuclear deterrence, either total, as in the case of the USSR and the United States, or limited, as in the case of the United Kingdom, France, and China. The perceived power of a nation is enhanced immeasurably if a nation's nuclear-weapons strength is sufficient to face conventional challenges right down to the last step into nuclear war without fear that its actual war-fighting capabilities in a nuclear exchange would prove so greatly inferior that the nation could not afford the risk of continuing the struggle. Only the USSR and the United States can pass this test at present.

Since most conflicts will probably be fought with conventional non-nuclear forces, a second crucial element is the maintenance of respectable armies, navies, and air forces for general-purpose combat. While they are probably of use only in less than national life-or-death confrontations, this is the way all conflicts begin.

Conventional capability is doubly important because its use or the threat of its use guards the lower rungs of the ladder of escalation to nuclear warfare. A nation that can defend itself on even terms against a conventional thrust does not have to contemplate taking the awesome step to nuclear weapons. In this chapter we will analyze only strategic nuclear forces, reserving the equally important assessment of conventional military forces to the next chapter.

The Political Pressures Exerted by Nuclear Weapons

When national leaders are compelled to consider the strength of the strategic forces at their disposal, in a crisis severe enough to present the risk of nuclear conflict, the question uppermost in their minds must be the damage that their societies could suffer in the event of war. Moreover, even when the possibility of actual conflict remains remote, as it will unless a nation's most vital interests are at stake, perceptions of each other's ultimate capabilities will limit the demands that national leaders feel free to make. It is impossible to forecast with confidence the interplay of move and counter-move, but awareness of the risk of war, and a sense, however vague, of the ultimate balance of military strengths will act on men's minds and set tacit limits on their actions.

The limits on adversary actions set by direct nuclear deterrence are obvious enough. For example, it is quite clear that the leaders of the Soviet Union could not at present order an all-out attack on North American cities without facing the unacceptable prospect that Soviet cities would in turn be destroyed. If this, indeed, were the only practical implication of the strategic balance, as some pundits assert, we scarcely need bother to calculate the relative military capabilities of the United States and the Soviet Union, or, in fact, of any of the nuclear powers. No rational adversary would be likely to run the risk of provoking a nuclear attack on itself.

Deterrence depends upon the total balance of forces, not on the atmospherics of diplomatic exchanges. The current detente is often justified as preventing nuclear holocaust, but it is in fact a political relationship made possible by the rough parity of deterrent nuclear power of the U.S. and Soviet military forces. Holding a population hostage in the face of a nuclear threat may confer very great political leverage, but only if the imminence of destruction is credible. Such leverage is automatically negated when the population of the aggressor is equally vulnerable, as in the case of the USSR and the United States.

Military planning must nevertheless proceed on the basis of a possible surprise attack, however remote its likelihood. If strike-back forces are adequate in that setting, they will serve to deter all-out attacks in any conceivable circumstances. Policy, on the other hand, cannot be formulated exclusively in terms of all-out attacks and all-out responses. It is the danger that economic and political conflicts will escalate to the point where threats of nuclear war are implicit, that U.S. and Soviet policymakers must think about and be prepared to deal with. The political-psychological pressure exerted by the mere existence of nuclear weapons is the significant element in international power calculations.

Recently the nuclear balance between the USSR and the United States has changed from a marked U.S. superiority over the USSR in strategic weapons to some rough equivalent of parity. Looking ahead, The United States will undoubtedly continue to maintain a reliable deterrent against direct nuclear attack, for at least five to ten years, but the Soviet Union will add some additional new capabilities, including "counterforce" attack options aimed at destroying the fixed land-based missiles of the United States, the People's Republic of China, and France. Well before this point is reached, the growing nuclear forces of the Soviet Union could acquire a margin of perceived superiority in the eyes of political leaders all over the world. This image of superior strength would enhance Soviet influence and prestige at the expense of the United States. Inevitably, the effect would be to induce third parties to try to conciliate Soviet demands at the expense of U.S. interests. In the sense of giving the USSR a kind of tacit veto over the policies of other states, particularly nearby ones, this situation is often described as "Finlandization"; the classical term for neutralization. Military capability, if it is visible and overwhelming, can force former adversaries into an impotent neutrality.

Political judgments are based on gross and unsophisticated perceptions. It is not the opinion of technical experts that matters but rather the sometimes "unscientific" views of political leaders at home and abroad. Much of what follows deals with the factual aspects of the measurement of strategic power, but it should never be forgotten that in the world of international diplomacy, military strategy is politics, not a branch of engineering.

Trends in Nuclear Weapons Strength

The perceptions that shape political evaluations and strategic plans are not fixed in the present; they are dynamic. A growing and innovative arsenal will be perceived as more powerful than one which is static—even if the latter still retains an advantage in purely technical terms. This is perfectly appropriate because political practitioners must always attempt to anticipate future power trends and not base their policies on a short-term view. The lead-time for development and production of modern advanced weapons is from five to ten years. Hence it is prudent to note the trend line and rate of change along with absolute numbers as of the present.[2]

A time graph showing numbers of the most visible and highly advertised strategic weapon, the intercontinental land-based missile, reveals a rather startling reversal of comparative U.S. and Soviet numerical strengths over a 15-year period.

[2] Data for this chapter are taken primarily from Annual Reports by Secretaries of Defense or Chairmen of the Joint Chiefs of Staff. The overall analysis and some details are based on a special unpublished research report prepared for use in this book by Edward Luttwak. It also draws upon two books by Edward Luttwak, *The Strategic Balance 1972* (Washington, D.C.: CSIS, 1972), and *US-USSR Nuclear Weapons Balance* (Washington, D.C.: CSIS, 1974).

Land-Based ICBMs: Actual Strengths

Year	*USSR*	*U.S.*
1960	35	18
1961	50	63
1962	75	294
1963	100	424
1964	200	635
1965	270	854
1966	300	904
1967	460	1,054
1968	800	1,054
1969	1,050	1,054
1970	1,300	1,054
1971	1,510	1,054
1972	1,550	1,054
1973	1,575	1,054
1974	1,590	1,054
1975/77	1,618 (*SALT I Limits*)	1,054

It is impossible to state precisely how the political leaders of the lesser powers measure strategic strength; certainly not by means of detailed numerical studies. More likely men's views of the military balance are impressionistic, based on images mainly qualitative in nature. Thus bombers may be thought of as "old-fashioned" regardless of how effective they may be in the calculations of professional analysts, while weapons publicly and repeatedly described as "giant ICBMs" and "super-missiles" make a deep impression which far transcends their actual military usefulness.

The clear-cut difference in the numbers of the missiles allowed to each side in the 1972 SALT I Interim Agreement and Protocol had a considerable psychological impact, while the countervailing technical military factors such as accuracy of guidance systems, whose importance is so obvious to the professional experts, went almost unnoticed. After the signature of the accords, even casual readers of the daily press learned, from constant repetition, that the United States was allowed to deploy only 1,054 ICBMs as against 1,618 for the Soviet Union and that the maximum limits on SLBMs were 710 for the United States and 950 for the Soviet Union. It was a far smaller number of observers who were aware of the substantial U.S. advantage in numbers and combat capability of bombers, or in the number of separately deliverable nuclear warheads. Actual strengths in major strategic weapons as of 1975 are as follows:

Military Balance Sheet

U.S.		USSR
1,054	**Intercontinental Missiles**	1,590
656	**Submarine-Launched Missiles**	700
498	**Strategic Bombers**	160

Many non-expert observers concluded that the United States had conceded a certain position of strategic superiority to the Soviet Union, and that the SALT I accords were therefore a clear signal of a decline in U.S. strategic power across the board. While Soviet superiorities in SALT I were seen as finite and contractual, the technological and qualitative advantages of the United States were usually perceived as a wasting asset, to be discounted in estimates of future power relationships, just as future money repayment is discounted by bankers.

In view of all these factors, to measure roughly the broad, quasi-psychological effects of power we are studying, we have adopted a weighting system for military capability that allows a maximum of 20 perceived power weights, roughly equivalent to economic capability. A maximum of 15 weights is allotted for effective nuclear deterrence based on nuclear war-fighting capability, and another maximum of five for conventional military strength. Most of the nations of the world will qualify only in the latter category. Obviously, these weighted elements of perceived power can be calculated only in gross, macrometric terms. We present specific statistics in detail only to anchor our assessment of military capability as an instrument of national policy in reality. In the nuclear field this is mainly a U.S.-Soviet matter. The weighting of all the individual nations' strength is presented in the next chapter, which examines conventional military forces and expenditures.

Measuring Nuclear Capabilities

The standard way of measuring the destructive effect of nuclear weapons is to calculate the equivalent force in conventional explosive material (TNT). This gives each weapon a yield of kilotons (thousands of tons of TNT) or megatons (millions of tons of TNT). In World War II the total of conventional bombs dropped by the U.S. Air Force amounted to only two megatons, the yield of one or two ordinary nuclear bombs today.

In trying to think about the unthinkable, military planners have devised more sophisticated methods of measuring actual weapons capabilities. One is to rate every weapon on the "one-megaton equivalent" scale, which measures the destructive power nuclear weapons would have if actually delivered on target. Like ordinary chemical explosions, nuclear detonations produce destructive effects which spread outward in all directions, with diminishing impact as distance increases. Targets are unavoidably over-destroyed at the core of the explosion, so that much of the energy yield of explosive weapons is wasted. The more powerful the device—other things being equal—the smaller the proportion of the energy yield which is actually effective on target. A simple formula can be used to convert the gross nominal yield of nuclear weapons in megatons or kilotons into one-megaton equivalents (o.m.e.), as a rough measure of real destructive power against surface targets, such as cities.

In a "city-busting" scenario, which lies at the heart of most early theory of strategic deterrence and certainly figures centrally in the popular imagination of nuclear war, the actual number of bombs or warheads that can be aimed at targets is very important. The United States has more aircraft and smaller missiles with multiple warheads. Hence it far outclasses the USSR at present in numbers of strategic weapons and megaton equivalence. The o.m.e. method is a measuring technique better suited to war-gaming and close-precision analysis of nuclear exchanges than to macrometric perceptions of military power. Numbers of weapons or what the U.S. Defense Department calls "force-loadings" make more sense to most observers.

U.S.-USSR Strategic Nuclear Weapons (Bombs and Warheads)

("Force Loadings")

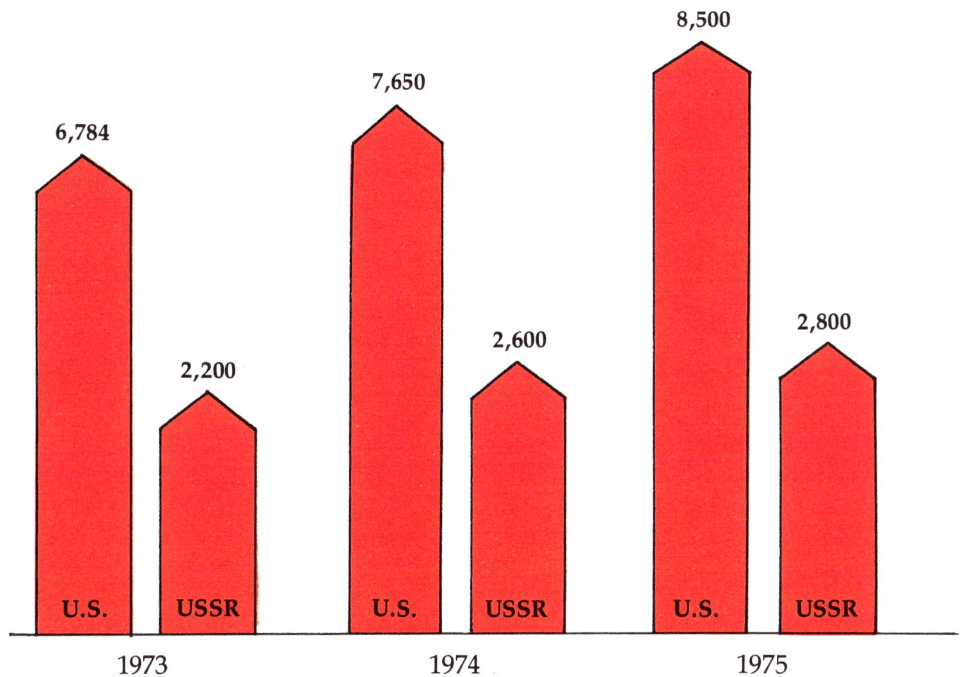

There is another useful measurement, the calculation of throw-weight—or missile payload. Throw-weight figures tell us something useful, i.e., what a missile can carry to target. The delivery capacity of missiles, like the payload of bombers (at stated ranges), defines the ultimate potential capabilities of strategic forces.

Even without major new discoveries, the energy yield extracted from every pound of payload has been steadily augmented over the years as the technology of nuclear weapons has become increasingly refined. Similarly, accuracies have been improving as more refined guidance equipment is produced. Given these technological changes, in the long run the measure of strategic capability will be set by the capacity of the vehicles available to deliver payloads. This factor becomes especially important if numbers of missiles are limited by agreement (as in SALT I and II) but numbers of warheads are not.

As the USSR introduces the three heavy new missiles it has been testing in the past year into operational use, it will be working toward the ceilings prescribed in SALT II. At those high ceilings the USSR would double its present throw-weight of about 6 million pounds, to about 12 million pounds, in land-based ICBM forces alone. The throw-weight of the U.S. ICBM force is now about

2 million pounds.[3] These ceilings will not be reached for several years, however, so the throw-weight advantage is a future or potential capability that does not alter the present balance.

Overall missile throw-weights would only measure actual capabilities, even in the future, if the missile and nuclear technologies of all sides were equally advanced, and if the strategic arsenals were oriented to the same goals. At the moment the United States appears to enjoy a significant, though diminishing, advantage in numbers of warheads, warhead yield/weight ratios, missile accuracies, booster efficiency, and electronic counter measures (ECM) for bombers. In throw-weight, the United States is markedly inferior to the USSR, whose missiles and silos are much larger.

Since the early 1960s, the United States has deployed forces optimized for attacks on cities and other dispersed targets, as indicated by the very small warheads of the *Poseidon* submarine-launched missiles (40 kiloton) and the modest-sized (170 kiloton) warheads of newer ICBMs, the *Minuteman-3s*. As against this, the Soviet Union has deployed very large warheads (20-25 megaton nominal yield) on most of its "heavy" land-based missiles.

Numbers of Strategic Weapons

A simple numerical summary of the array of U.S. and Soviet weapons systems and strategic-nuclear forces is presented below. The characteristics of the new Soviet missile types just now beginning to be deployed are described on page 65, but these weapons are not included on page 61. Probably about 50 *SS-19s,* 10 *SS-18s,* and 10 *SS-17s* have been deployed in the USSR as of mid-1975. The United States, of course, has no new missiles to deploy.

The United States and the Soviet Union also have other means of long-range delivery that are often regarded as non-strategic because they are qualitatively inferior or at least their performance is in some way limited. These include Soviet medium bombers which can reach U.S. territory on one-way missions only; U.S. tactical strike aircraft deployed in Europe and capable of reaching the USSR, and Soviet long-range cruise missiles on board nuclear and non-nuclear submarines. The United States has 7,000 nuclear weapons deployed in Europe and many more deployed at sea and at other military bases overseas in addition to its 8,500 nuclear weapons designated as strategic—a total of about 22,000. For its part, the Soviet Union deploys a large (about 600) but rather antiquated force of "intermediate" (IRBM) and "medium" (MRBM) range ballistic missiles targeted on West Europe and China.

Among the lesser nuclear powers, only France deploys a full "triad" of offensive forces; that is, intercontinental land-based missiles (ICBM), submarine-launched ballistic missiles (SLBM), and long-range bomber forces. The United Kingdom still retains a somewhat larger force of medium-range "*V*" bombers which could deliver nuclear weapons on the Soviet Union, but its only official strategic force consists of four ballistic-missile submarines. The People's Republic of China has not yet deployed a submarine element in its

[3]*Annual Report, Defense Department, FY 1975,* p. 46.

Strategic-Nuclear Offensive Weapons Arsenals in Mid-1975

ICBMs-Intercontinental Ballistic Missiles

	U.S.	USSR
Total ICBMs:	1,054	1,590
"heavy"*	0	288
"old"	54	209
"light"	1,000	1,093
Fitted with multiple warheads (MRV)	0	some
Fitted with multiple, independently targetable warheads (MIRV)	550	some

SLBMs-Submarine-Borne Ballistic Missiles

	U.S.	USSR
Total SLBMs (incl. under conversion):	656	760
SLBMs on "modern nuclear submarines"*	656	676
SLBMs on "older nuclear submarines"*	0	24
SLBMs on diesel-electric submarines	0	60
Fitted with MRV	176	some
Fitted with MIRV, operational	352	0
SLBMs counted as "strategic" under SALT I and Vladivostok tentative agreement rules	656	700

Manned Long-Range Bombers

	U.S.	USSR
Total, gross inventories	498	210+
Operational, heavy	330	160
Modern medium bombers	66	50+
Bombers counted as "strategic" under SALT I and Vladivostok tentative agreement rules	498	160
Total offensive delivery vehicles defined as "strategic" under Vladivostok tentative agreement rules	2,208	2,450

*SALT I definitions

strategic arsenal but has a fairly large force of medium bombers and is slowly building a land-based missile force targeted on the Soviet Union. In addition, Chinese fighter-bombers capable of delivering nuclear weapons could reach Soviet and Indian targets. For the time being, India has only the capability of producing a handful of plutonium bombs which could no doubt be delivered on Chinese and Pakistani targets by aircraft. There is as yet no evidence of any Indian missile-development effort.

Defense Forces

There is an obvious imbalance between these vast offensive forces and the rather weak strategic defenses deployed on all sides, an imbalance that is historically unprecedented. In particular, there are no substantial missile defenses, probably because the USSR and the United States both calculated the costs were too massive and such defenses would only spur both sides to deploy ever more numbers of expensive and unneeded offensive missiles. Under the terms of the 1972 Anti-Ballistic Missile (ABM) Treaty, as amended in 1974, the Soviet Union and the United States may each deploy only a single missile-defense complex, with no more than 100 interceptor missiles. No such treaty restriction applies to the other countries that are potential targets of ballistic-missile attack, but in their case there are intrinsic limitations, since the cost of ABM defenses is extraordinarily high and the relevant technologies are very complex.

As against this abnegation of missile defenses, large air-defense forces, consisting of ground-based radar networks, manned fighters, anti-aircraft missiles, and anti-aircraft (AA) guns remain in service in the Soviet Union and China, while smaller air-defense forces, consisting primarily of manned interceptors, are deployed in the United States, the United Kingdom, and France, as in many other countries. These defensive forces have little effect on the strategic nuclear equation, particularly as far as the USSR and the United States are concerned.

A final element in strategic defenses, though one not usually designated as such, are the extensive antisubmarine-warfare (ASW) forces deployed by the major powers. There is no technical distinction between tactical (i.e., shipping protection) and strategic ASW, although operationally the use of the forces would be quite different. The United Kingdom, the Soviet Union, and the United States all deploy nuclear-powered attack submarines, the most effective single ASW weapon, though by its very nature any ASW campaign would have to be a coordinated effort involving land-based search aircraft, surface warships, and seabed acoustic sensor grids, as well as attack submarines. For the time being, the peculiar properties of sea water continue to limit the range and reliability of the most important detection equipment, sonar, in all its various forms. Ballistic-missile launching submarines, while by no means immune to attack, are relatively secure.

Land-Based Missiles

There has been a striking divergence between the land-based missile policies of the superpowers. Long before the signature of the SALT I accords, the United States made the momentous decision to abandon the development of intermediate-range missiles (IRBMs), to scrap existing forward-based ballistic missiles, and unilaterally to limit its deployment of intercontinental ballistic missiles (ICBMs) to 1,054 units.

Since that time, the United States has concentrated on qualitative improvements with the deployment of separately targetable multiple-warhead (MIRV) systems, improved accuracies, and, presumably, reliabilities, in a single type of ICBM, the *Minuteman-3,* first deployed in 1970.

As a result of this policy, and the rapidity with which older weapons were withdrawn, the United States retains in service fewer than half of the land-based ballistic missiles it has built over the years, even though many of those scrapped were at least comparable to weapons which remain in the Soviet arsenal. In contrast, the Soviet Union has retained in service all but a very few of the strategic missiles it has deployed; the purely numerical superiority of the Soviet ICBM force, which apparently counted for so much in the SALT negotiations,

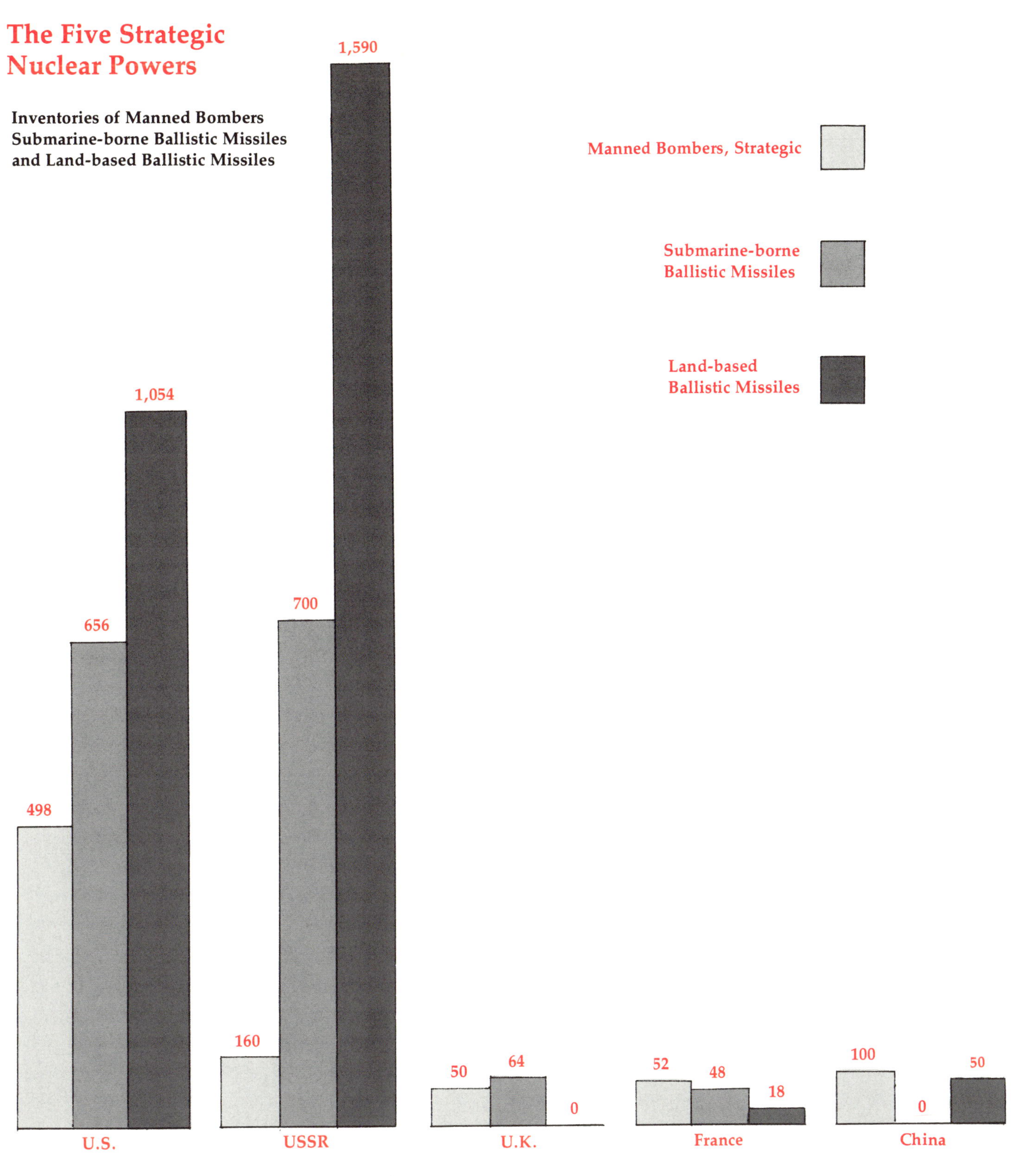
The Five Strategic
Nuclear Powers
Inventories of Manned Bombers
Submarine-borne Ballistic Missiles
and Land-based Ballistic Missiles
Manned Bombers, Strategic
Submarine-borne
Ballistic Missiles
Land-based
Ballistic Missiles
1,590
1,054
700
656
498
160
50
64
0
52
48
18
100
0
50
U.S.
USSR
U.K.
France
China

was largely a result of this policy. Shrewdly, the Soviet Union accorded a much higher priority to political visibility than to purely technical considerations.

If a weapon can reach deep into enemy territory to strike at homeland population centers, it is in a sense "strategic". If such a weapon is armed with a nuclear device, it becomes "strategic-nuclear", whether or not it has full intercontinental range. The Soviet medium- and intermediate-range ballistic missiles targeted on Europe and China fall within this class, even if they cannot reach U.S. targets, for without their deployment the Soviet Union would have to allocate ICBMs for this purpose.

There is a second feature of the Soviet ICBM deployment policy that is also in clear contrast to U.S. policy. Instead of concentrating the full range of Soviet technical advance in a single weapon type, at least three distinct classes of ICBMs have been produced: a small solid-fuel class, a medium-sized liquid-fuel class, and a heavy class. Even the medium-sized class has larger throw-weights than the U.S. *Minuteman-3,* and this, together with the numerical superiority of the Soviet ICBM force, has resulted in an altogether greater throw-weight capacity of the order of at least 6 million pounds for the Soviet Union versus 2 million for the United States, as mentioned previously. When the present Soviet launchers are replaced with planned newer models, the throw-weight of the Soviet force will be at least 10 and probably 12 million pounds, approximately a 5:1 or 6:1 advantage over the existing U.S. land-based ICBM force. That ratio will only be attained in the 1980s. There is still time for the United States, if it so chooses, to alter the trend.

The Soviet warhead development efforts which seek to translate the potential throw-weight advantage into actual strike capabilities have lagged behind, although the gap is being narrowed. Soviet MIRV systems reached the advanced testing stage only in 1974, and their first operational deployments took place only in mid-1975. Details on U.S. and Soviet land-based ICBMs on page 65.

Mobile ICBMs are not strategically significant at present but they are potentially less vulnerable to counterforce attacks than are present fixed-site ICBMs housed in protected silos. This class of weapons, which is growing in importance, was not covered by the SALT I Interim Agreements, nor was any prohibition on weapons of this class included in the tentative SALT II agreement, although it seems certain that restrictions will have to be imposed on their mode of deployment, in order to permit verification, if their numbers increase.

Many configurations for mobile ICBMs have been suggested: air-launched missiles deployed on aircraft held on ground alert, land-mobile deployments on road or rail networks, and closed-circuit land-mobile deployments, where ICBMs would rotate from shelter to shelter on rail or truck-like platforms inside secure areas. In the United States there are still some very large military reservations which could be used for the purpose, and, of course, both the Soviet Union and China would have no difficulty in finding vast and secure deployment areas.

There are both added costs and technical complications in mobile ICBM design. Nevertheless, should improvement in ICBM accuracies render fixed-site, land-based missiles very vulnerable to counterforce attacks, air- or land-mobile ICBMs may well be adopted in order to avoid exclusive dependence on

U.S. AND USSR ICBMs: Salient Features and Numbers Deployed, 1975

		Year First Deployed	Number Operational	Warhead Systems: Number of	Warhead Systems: Yield Mt./Kt.	Throw-Weight 1,000 Lbs.
U.S.						
Minuteman-2		1966	450	1	1–2 Mt.	1
Minuteman-3		1970	550	3	170 Kt.	2
Titan-2		1962	54	1	9 Mt.	8
USSR						
"old"						
	SS-7	1962	190	1	5 Mt.	3
	SS-8	1963	19	1	5 Mt.	3
"light"						
	SS-13	1969	60	1	1 Mt.	1
	SS-16	1975	Some	1	1 Mt.+	1
"medium"						
	SS-11 Mod. 1	1966	967	1	1–2 Mt.	1.5
	SS-11 Mod. 3	1973	66	3 MRV	300 Kt.	1.5
	SS-17	1975	10	4 MRV	1 Mt.	4.5
	SS-19	1975	50	6 MIRV	300 Kt.	6
"heavy"						
	SS-9 Mod. 2	1967	250	1	20 Mt.	12
	SS-9 Mod. 4	1971	Some	3 MRV	5 Mt.	12
	SS-18 Mod. 1	1974	10	1	20 Mt.	15
	SS-18 Mod. 2	1976	---	6-8	2 Mt.	15
MRBMs	SS-4	1959	500+	1	1 Mt.	
IRBMs	SS-5	1961	100+	1	1 Mt.	

submarine and manned bomber systems. Verification of arms limitations, however, would become exceptionally difficult in that circumstance.

Aside from the considerable technical uncertainties inherent in our estimates of comparative U.S. and Soviet ICBM forces, U.S. policy confronts a deeper and politically more significant ambiguity as to the whole direction of the Soviet ICBM program. While the United States publishes its program years in advance, the Soviet Union makes nothing public, except for some general claims of superiority. Furthermore, even after several years of supposedly intimate negotiations, very little, if anything, has been learned about the goals and modalities of Soviet strategic policy. Thus, for example, it is not known what role the counterforce mission plays in Soviet policy—beyond what may be inferred from the evidence of past missile deployments, which suggest that this role is important. In fact, we have almost no information at all on Soviet strategic policy, only on actual capabilities.

There is no such uncertainty with respect to the Soviet *SS-18,* the most powerful ICBM ever built. This very large launcher has a throw-weight at least seven times that of the *Minuteman-3.* It reflects a major military investment. Unless its development reflects bureaucratic irrationality of monumental proportions, it must have a purpose other than that of the common run of Soviet ICBMs. This purpose can only be to deliver a heavy-weight MIRV payload of several large individual warheads. It has been tested with seven MIRVs. The military role of such warheads is apparently to attack U.S. ICBM silos and command centers. The Soviet development of this counterforce-oriented missile must be viewed with concern in the West since it is inconsistent with the prevailing notion of strategic stability, which requires that something like present levels of retaliation—strikeback or second-strike capability—be predictable and assured for both sides so that deterrence for the prevention of war will be mutually reliable.

Owing to the more advanced state of U.S. warhead technology which results in a more efficient use of launcher throw-weight, it is sometimes suggested that the latest U.S. land-based missile, *Minuteman-3,* is potentially a counterforce weapon and thus comparable to the giant Soviet *SS-18.* It is true that with very high accuracies a small warhead such as that of the *Minuteman-3* could be effective against Soviet ICBM silos. Indeed with the accuracies now commonly achieved by short-range precision-guided missiles, it would be possible to destroy heavily protected ICBM silos with warheads much smaller than those of the *Minuteman-3.* But it is one thing to guide an anti-tank rocket precisely to a target a few thousand yards away and quite another to launch ballistic warheads over ranges of thousands of miles. It is not difficult to imagine ways of dramatically improving present accuracies, given time and abundant resources, but so far no real attempt has been made in the United States to achieve any such results. The variety of research and development efforts to improve strategic ballistic missile accuracies has had the more modest goal of achieving refinements in existing guidance systems rather than to produce entirely new ones. Radical improvement would require warheads that have maneuverability and a good terminal guidance system.

The provisions of the SALT I Interim Agreement limit U.S. and Soviet ICBM forces to 1,054 and 1,618 units respectively. In addition, there is a sub-limit of 313 units on "heavy" missiles for the Soviet Union; the United States is allowed none. At the time the sub-limit on "heavy" missiles seemed highly important, and indeed agreement on this provision was a central goal of the U.S. negotiating team. If the sub-limit on "heavy" ICBMs was obtained in exchange for the Soviet concession of the very high overall ICBM ceiling, on the assumption that only the "heavy" missiles had a counterforce potential, then the benefits have been rather illusory. The counterforce potential of the "medium" missiles, particularly the new MIRV *SS-19,* is not greatly inferior. Thus it is not clear that a sub-limit on "heavy" ICBMs will be retained, in the proposed ten-year treaty whose outlines were agreed on at Vladivostok, at an overall ceiling of 2,400 long-range bombers and missiles with a sub-limit of 1,320 on SLBMs and ICBMs fitted with MIRV systems.

Among the lesser nuclear powers, only China is proceeding with a full-scale land-based ballistic missile program. British efforts in this sector ceased more than a decade ago, and the French land-based missile force is limited to a planned total of 18 IRBMs. Although housed in protected silos, the French IRBMs are inevitably rather vulnerable. Since inaccuracy increases with range, Soviet weapons would have much higher kill probabilities against French IRBMs than against U.S. ICBM silos located further away. The French missile force, unlike the Soviet or the U.S. force, cannot offer assurance of retaliation.

The Chinese land-based missile program has advanced at a rather slower pace than was expected, especially with respect to full-range ICBM weapons. China remains a largely agrarian country, with only small islands of technical sophistication and modern industry. Moreover, there are indications that the Chinese are following a long-term development strategy rather than searching for quick-fix solutions. Large-scale facilities for producing nuclear materials are being built, and substantial resources have been allocated to solid-fuel missile propulsion. In the meantime, China deploys perhaps 50 liquid-fuel MRBMs, which could reach cities in eastern Siberia, and a roughly similar number of liquid-fuel IRBMs. Both weapons are of poor overall quality and have slow reaction times. Longer-range weapons, limited ICBMs which may become operational quite soon, though as yet they are virtually untested, and a full-sized ICBM which probably will not be ready until the mid-1980s, are under development. If present national policies are followed on all sides, the Chinese will most probably choose to concentrate their short-term efforts on the deployment of a fully reliable deterrent against Soviet nuclear coercion, or even attack, since a strategic force targeted on the United States could serve only second-order political goals for many years to come.

The present Chinese land-based missile force thus consists of first-generation weapons mostly poorly protected against a disarming counterforce strike. Unlike the French IRBM force, however, the Chinese ballistic missile force is a growing concern. By the time a Chinese ICBM force is fully developed, it is possible that *all* fixed-site weapons will have become vulnerable. The Chinese may therefore proceed directly, in the mid-1980s, to deploy solid-fuel mobile ICBMs (and SLBMs).

Submarine-Launched Ballistic Missiles

The shift in the balance of strategic forces between the Soviet Union and the United States has been most marked with regard to the submarine element. Until 1969, the absolute qualitative superiority of the U.S. ballistic missile submarine force was so great that its numerical superiority, although also crushing, scarcely seemed to matter. From the beginning, the U.S. boats were equipped with solid-fuel *Polaris* missiles of great reliability, capable of underwater launch, and thus were able to target Moscow from vast areas of the North Atlantic as well as from the northern end of the Indian Ocean.

In contrast, the Soviet SLBM force was originally based on makeshift conversions of torpedo-firing attack submarines, vastly inferior to the *Polaris* type. With limited missile and launching capacities, Soviet submarines were also much less quiet in underwater cruise than U.S. boats. The diesel boats of course could not reach firing positions against U.S. territory without using their snorkel tubes, and were thus vulnerable to sonar and radar detection, and therefore attack. For these reasons the numerical advantage of the U.S. SLBM force, 656 versus approximately 130, understated the vast superiority of the forces. Even non-expert political observers could perceive the qualitative advantages of the U.S. submarine force.

Since 1969, the United States has been converting existing *Polaris* boats to accommodate a new type of missile, the *Poseidon,* which can be up to ten times as effective as the *Polaris-A2* against cities, industrial centers, airfields, and other large unprotected targets, since it can carry ten MIRVs. The United States has maintained a self-imposed 41-boat limit on its submarine force, which was first attained in the course of 1967. The only near-term change in the U.S. force will be the completion of this *Poseidon* conversion program. At present 23 boats have been converted; another seven will be in conversion during 1975, and the last of the 41 *Poseidon*-equipped boats is due to enter service in 1977. This force provides, for the present and foreseeable immediate future, a guaranteed retaliatory—strike-back—capability which insures deterrence independently of land-based ICBM and bomber forces.

U.S. restraint in improving rather than expanding its SLBM force, together with a very rapid deployment program on the part of the Soviet Union, has enabled the Soviet Union to reverse the numerical superiority of the U.S. SLBM force while at the same time considerably reducing its qualitative advantage. Since 1968, 34 of the new Soviet *Y*-class nuclear-powered submarines have been deployed, and beginning in 1973 some of them were fitted with a new type of missile, the *SS-N-8,* which has a range substantially greater than the *Poseidon* and is probably intended for MIRVing. In 1974, a modified boat, the *D-I,* came into use and in 1975, a new boat, the *D-II,* was observed under construction. The latter appears to be fitted to carry up to 20 tubes for the new submarine-launched missile *(SS-N-8).*

The pace and diversity of Soviet SLBM deployment efforts have not been hampered by the SALT I accords. The latter set a final limit of 950 allowable SLBM tubes on board nuclear-powered submarines for the USSR, as against 710 units for the United States. Even some of those observers who welcomed the SALT I accords and who saw the land-based missile imbalance as reasonable in the light of U.S. superiority in the bomber sector, were disturbed by the provisions covering the SLBM forces. Aside from the gross and highly visible inequality in the final ceilings, the provisions for substitution were highly favorable to the USSR.

The SALT I Protocol set the level of the Soviet SLBM force on board nuclear submarines at 740 tubes, which seemed high to most informed U.S. observers, and allowed the 950 tube ceiling to be reached by scrapping 210 older Soviet ICBMs or older SLBMs. The United States, on the other hand, could only add 54 tubes by scrapping the existing and more effective *Titan-2* force.

Under the terms of the Vladivostok agreement-in-principle, a total of 2,400 SLBMs, ICBMs, and long-range bombers may be deployed by each side includ-

U.S. and USSR SLBM Forces:

Salient Features and Numbers in Inventory, mid-1975

Submarines

	Propulsion	Year First Deployed	Number in Inventory	SLBM Tubes
U.S.				
George Washington/ Ethan Allen (Polaris)	nuclear	1960	11	16
Lafayette Class (Poseidon)	nuclear	1962	30	16
USSR				
G-class*	diesel	1960	20	3
H-class	nuclear	1963	8	3
Y-class	nuclear	1968	34	16
D-I class	nuclear	1973	11	12
D-II class	nuclear	1976	0	20

SLBMs

	Year First Deployed	Range N. Miles	Number in Inventory (Incl. under Conversion)	Warhead Systems Number of	Warhead Systems Yield Mt./Kt.
U.S.					
Polaris A-3	1964	2,500	176	3 MRV	200 Kt.
Poseidon C-3	1971	2,500	480	10 MIRV	40 Kt.
USSR					
SS-N-4	1960	300	24	1	1-2 Mt.
SS-N-5	1963	700	60**	1	1-2 Mt.
SS-N-6 Mod. 1	1968	1,300		1	1-2 Mt.
SS-N-6 Mod. 2	1974	1,600	544	1	1-2 Mt.
SS-N-6 Mod. 3	1974	1,600		3 MRV	200 Kt. *(estimated)*
SS-N-8	1973	4,200	132	1 (or MIRV)	2 Mt.+

* These boats are not defined as "strategic" under the SALT definitions.
** Of which 24 are housed in *H*-class boats and 36 in *G-II* class boats. (Only the former are counted in the official listing of strategic forces.)

ing up to 1,320 launchers fitted with MIRVs. It is unclear to what extent these limits will cause additional SLBMs to be deployed by each side. As far as the United States is concerned, the *Trident* submarine program calls for the deployment of ten boats, with a total of 240 tubes. If these were added to the force, SLBMs would account for 896 of the 2,400 total and 736 of the 1,320 MIRVed launcher sub-limit. By 1980, the first *Polaris* boats will be approaching their twentieth year of continuous operation. If the increasing threat to land-based ICBMs prompts a shift from *Minutemen* to SLBMs (and/or cruise missiles), this could mean that more *Tridents* would be deployed. A third and attractive alternative would be the deployment of a smaller, slower, and cheaper submarine than the fast 18,700 ton *Trident*.

The 950-unit SLBM force-level set by the SALT I agreement opened a wide range of deployment options to the USSR though the limit of 62 on the number of modern submarines would evidently become an operative constraint, just as the SALT I limit of 44 constrains the United States. No more *Y*-class boats are likely to be built beyond the 34 now operational, though their missiles will no doubt be upgraded. It is almost certain that the USSR will exercise its exchange option under Article III of the Interim Agreement, replacing older ICBMs with modern SLBMs, but it is not yet clear what the mixture of *D-Is* and *D-IIs* will be.

It seems probable that by 1977 or soon thereafter the last of the antiquated Soviet submarines, which are grossly uneconomical as missile platforms, will be withdrawn. The characteristics and numbers of SLBMs now in inventory in the Soviet and the U.S. Navies is the best guide to future developments.

Both the United Kingdom and France have followed the superpowers in deploying SLBMs on board nuclear-powered submarines, albeit in much smaller numbers. But while the former received complete missile launchers and other technical aid from the United States, the French program was based very largely on purely domestic technology. Owing to this fact, the French effort has resulted in the slower deployment of less capable forces, at considerably higher cost, than the British program. The British force of four boats, with a total of 64 tubes, is now in service. The French submarines also have 16 tubes each and under current plans a total of five (and perhaps six) boats are to be deployed. At present three boats are in service.

The People's Republic of China has had a single *G*-class boat for many years but without missiles. Official statements indicate that the Chinese are developing a nuclear-powered submarine but it is not known when SLBMs might become available for a submarine force. So far, Chinese strategic missiles have been based on liquid-fuel launchers, which are not suitable for deployment on board submarines. The Chinese are developing solid-fuel launcher technology, essential for effective SLBMs. It is possible of course that China may take a different approach to the problem of fixed-site missile vulnerability, and instead of going to sea in submarines, develop land-mobile ballistic missiles as mentioned above. Given the size of the Chinese mainland, a mobile system for IRBMs or ICBMs would be quite feasible (which is not the case for the United Kingdom or France). It obviously would be much cheaper to rotate IRBMs or even ICBMs on moving platforms than to keep them at sea, inside exceedingly expensive nuclear-powered submarines.

Manned Long-Range Bombers

Manned bombers belong to the only category of strategic weapons in which the United States still retains a net superiority, both qualitative and quantitative. This is true in spite of the fact that no new heavy bomber type has been deployed in the United States since the first *B-52s* became operational in 1955. The more modern medium bombers introduced later, the *B-58* and the *FB-111A*, have not proved entirely successful as strategic weapon carriers. Accordingly the *B-52s* have repeatedly been upgraded with improved electronics, structural reinforcement of airframes, and lately with some very effective air-to-ground weapons.

The key to bomber penetration against current air defenses is not mere speed but rather low-level flight to evade radar detection and electronic-warfare (EW) capabilities. It is for this reason that tankers are deployed alongside the bombers; even the *B-52s* need refueling for optimal low-altitude performance. In any case, the *B-52* has proved superior to more recently built supersonic aircraft.

Now, however, in the *B-1* program, the United States is developing an aircraft which is both a full-size intercontinental bomber with a theoretical payload almost twice that of the *B-52* and one which is supersonic. Ordinarily the *B-1s*, like the *B-52s*, would penetrate air defenses in low-altitude subsonic flight in order to underfly ground-based radar. The first *B-1s* will become operational at the end of the decade, assuming that there are neither technical problems nor policy changes.

There are in addition the carrier-based fighter-bombers and attack aircraft of the U.S. Navy deployed with the Sixth and Seventh Fleets. Theoretically these two could penetrate Soviet or Chinese airspace. They could bomb the cities of the Soviet Southwest and those adjacent to the Northwest Pacific with substantial payloads. U.S. aircraft carriers have nuclear weapons on board, and their primary tactical aircraft could serve as backup elements in strategic target attacks.

The Soviet Union's manned bomber forces have been assigned a much lower priority than the ICBM or SLBM forces in Soviet defense strategy. Two heavy bomber models, the *Tu-95* turboprop and the *Mya-4* jet were first deployed operationally in 1956 and both have been produced in small numbers since then.

In addition to these bombers, which have a full intercontinental range, the USSR also has large numbers of medium bombers *(Tu-16s)* which do not have a primary strategic role against the United States. Their primary targets are almost certainly in West Europe and China. The real deficiency of these bombers, shared by the heavy bombers, is neither the range/payload limitation nor their subsonic speed, but rather the inadequacy of their supporting ECM equipment and the lack of effective air-to-ground missiles.

Many observers assume that Soviet disinterest in the bomber sector of the strategic competition will continue and that this reflects a negative Soviet judgment on the effectiveness of the manned bomber in the missile age. More recently a new supersonic bomber with a variable-geometry wing design like that of the *FB-111* is being produced. It is called the *Backfire.* Although a variety of other missions are open to this aircraft, and its range appears limited at present, it must certainly be viewed as a potential intercontinental weapon.

Under the tentative provisions of the Vladivostok agreement-in-principle, a bomber counts as a single weapon within the overall weapon ceiling of 2,400 units. The sub-limit on MIRVed launchers does not apply. It seems, however, according to the vague public accounts of Vladivostok, that any missile carried on board aircraft with a range greater than 600 kilometers would count against the overall weapon ceiling, while bombers equipped with such longer-range missiles are counted as MIRVed weapons. This provision, if carried over into the actual ten-year treaty, would have a direct bearing on the U.S. cruise-missile program. Unlike ballistic missiles, cruise missiles fly within the atmosphere much as ordinary manned aircraft. Development programs are under way for long-range cruise missiles which would come under the 2,400 Vladivostok weapons ceiling and whose launcher aircraft would come under the 1,320 MIRVed vehicle ceiling.

Current U.S. plans call for the deployment of 499 of the 2,400 allowable weapon units to be taken up by bombers (255 *B-52s* and 244 *B-1s),* a reasonable figure since it would allow for the retention of the present 656-unit SLBM force, the addition of 240 *Trident* SLBM tubes, and maintenance of the deployed force of 1,000 *Minuteman* missiles.

The tentative Vladivostok rules define the U.S. *FB-111A* and the Soviet *Backfire* bombers as "nonstrategic", as well as the old Soviet *Tu-16.* For comparative purposes, however, they are listed on the following table showing Soviet and U.S. manned bombers.

U.S. and USSR Manned Bomber Forces

	Year First Deployed	*Number mid-1975 Operational*	*Unrefueled Max. Range Statute Miles*	*Theoretical Max. Payload Pounds*
U.S.				
B-52 G&H	1959	255	12,500	75,000
B-52 D	1956	75	11,500	60,000
FB-111A	1969	66	3,800	37,500
B-1	1980 (?)	—	—	150,000
USSR				
Tu-95	1956	75	7,800	40,000
Mya-4	1956	85	6,000	20,000
Tu-16	1955	500+	4,000	20,000
Backfire	1974	50+	4,500	40,000

British, French, and Chinese Bombers

During the 1950s, the United Kingdom undertook an ambitious bomber program based on the innovative "V" bombers. Now, however, all but 48 have been withdrawn from service or converted to other uses, and the remaining force has been reassigned to tactical missions. In theory, therefore, the British no longer have a strategic bomber force, but the United Kingdom retains a large stock of nuclear weapons, and all of its remaining fighter-bombers deployed in the Federal Republic of Germany could reach targets in the Soviet Union.

France's bomber force, the first element in the French mini-triad in point of time, deployed as of 1964, consists of 36 operational *Mirage-IVs.* These are small supersonic aircraft which require mid-air refueling to reach targets such as Moscow on two-way missions. Eleven U.S.-built tanker aircraft are available for this purpose. Owing to its small payload, the French bomber force lacks adequate ECM capabilities, while its fuel limitation prevents sustained low-level flight at high speed.

So far, the Chinese have not flight-tested a strategic bomber of local design, but have a force of 60 *Tu-16s* in service, which could reach Moscow on one-way missions from inland airfields in China. Chinese light bombers and locally produced fighter-bombers all have some degree of penetration capability against Soviet targets east of the Urals. Although numerically small and technically obsolescent by superpower standards, the Chinese bomber force remains important, since the only other strategic delivery vehicles of the Chinese, the land-based missiles, remain vulnerable to attack.

In the case of India and other potential third-level nuclear powers, manned aircraft are likely to prove the cheapest and most easily available means of nuclear delivery. A wide variety of aircraft, including ordinary fighter bombers with reasonable payloads, can attempt the nuclear delivery mission against targets territorially adjacent and not protected by sophisticated air defenses. Although this mission is not particularly exacting, an improvised force of aircraft can offer only a moderate possibility of success. A reliable delivery capability requires special training and much supporting equipment is essential. At the present time China has neither of these prerequisites and India is even less well provided.

Conclusion: Perceived Nuclear Power Weights

It is clear that the United States and the USSR now have unique strategic nuclear forces. They possess at present a near-absolute deterrent capability and a roughly equivalent capability for waging a nuclear war in the event that one —most irrationally—occurs. By comparison, China, the United Kingdom, and France have only minimal capabilities, sufficient perhaps to deter direct attacks by the major nuclear powers where the interests in dispute are marginal for the latter. In recent years the USSR has closed a wide strategic gap and has reached parity with the United States. At present the nuclear power of the two military giants is roughly equivalent. The crude weighting for our assessment is as follows:

Perceived Strategic Weapons Strength, 1975

Country	*Nuclear Deterrence and War Fighting*
USSR	**15**
United States	**15**
United Kingdom	**2**
France	**2**
China (PRC)	**2**

CHAPTER SIX

Military Capability: Conventional Forces

$$Pp=(C+E+M)\times(S+W)$$

As the last chapter indicates, the bipolar superpowers, the United States and the USSR, clearly dominate the strategic nuclear world, leaving by comparison only token nuclear strength to the People's Republic of China, the United Kingdom, and France. They also cast a strong deterrent shadow over conventionally armed states. Recent history, however, has found the USSR and the United States aligned on opposing sides in most conflicts between conventionally armed states. Hence these conflicts are usually settled, whether politically or in combat, without nuclear force coming into play. The fact that the arms and money which fuel such conventional conflicts frequently come from the USSR and the United States gives them special leverage with many states, but this relates more to a basic economic and political influence than to military capability.

In the last analysis, when one of the superpowers directly intervenes in a local conflict, as in the case of the United States in the Vietnam War, it is reduced to using only conventional arms and forces lest the onus of escalation cause political losses worldwide of a greater magnitude than the loss of a local war. Thus victory depends on conventional military strength rather than on nuclear capability.

North Vietnam fought on against conventional U.S. forces until these were finally withdrawn in 1973 and persevered against U.S. arms in the hands of a U.S. ally, South Vietnam, until final victory in 1975. A clearer proof of the power of conventional arms, when combined with a coherent strategy and an unshakable political will, could not be devised. It goes without saying that the cooling of the U.S. commitment to the war was what made Hanoi's victory possible. Plainly the United States possessed superior military power in both conventional and nuclear combat configurations, if it had chosen to apply that power without restraint to destroy North Vietnam. For many reasons this ultimate use of U.S. military power did not occur, but this does not mean that it does not exist. It simply points up the importance of the part of the formula for national power which we will treat in our final assessment of national purpose and the crystallization of national will in a conflict situation.

The fact that 500,000 U.S. forces fought a conventional war for several years against the North Vietnamese forces, which had no nuclear weapons, yet triumphed, shows that in this era we must attribute significant weights to traditional, non-nuclear military power. In this chapter we deal in macrometric fashion with key factors in the conventional military capability of the major nations plus a few other countries whose conventional forces, combined with strategic location, give them special significance in international conflicts.

Routine statistical inventories of military might can be largely ignored in the international power context. Most national regimes maintain armed forces primarily to keep their own populations under control; beyond that, the principal role of military forces-in-being is simply to protect national frontiers. What we are trying to measure here in a crude way is something else; it is the potential for exploiting conventional military capability to international advantage. Only exceptional nations are able to project their forces far enough beyond their own borders to be major actors on the international stage.

Conventional military strength can be assessed in the light of three specific attributes which can be exploited for national policy purposes. They are:

1. **Scale of Military Expenditures**
2. **Size of Armed Forces**
3. **Global Deployment and Sea Control Potential**

If we weight each of the first two factors at a maximum of 2, the top nations in each category can be assessed for different levels of military capability. Only the United States can claim a truly global deployment reach and a substantial potential for controlling the seas, but the USSR is approaching the level necessary to challenge this U.S. global reach. A weight of 1 is probably about right for the United States with regard to this unique, valuable, but wasting military asset. Control of the seas and the mobility required to project forces abroad is a vital factor in power equations. If it were unchallenged, U.S. capabilities of this kind would have to be weighted more heavily. As it is, the USSR, with its submarines, surface navy, and transport aircraft, is approaching a comparable capability. No other nation can play more than a regional role, so a small plus for the United States is appropriate.

The USSR and the United States both spend more than 5 percent of their GNP on military forces, equipment, and support services. They both have spent a substantially larger proportion of their wealth on military capability in previous years, but this level of military effort is still very high in 1975.

In the case of the United States, military expenditures are at the $90 billion level. The high personnel pay costs of an all-volunteer force and the effect of rapid inflation in recent years mean that this sum in terms of what it actually buys is substantially less than at any time since the Korean War.

The shrinkage of the relative share of U.S. GNP devoted to military programs is clearly shown on page 77[1].

[1] *Annual Defense Department Report, FY 1976,* p. I-24. All other statistics on military capability are from the *National Basic Intelligence Factbook,* or the U.S. Arms Control and Disarmament Agency 1975 report: *World Military Expenditures and Arms Trade 1963-1973.*

U.S. Defense Spending as a Percent of GNP

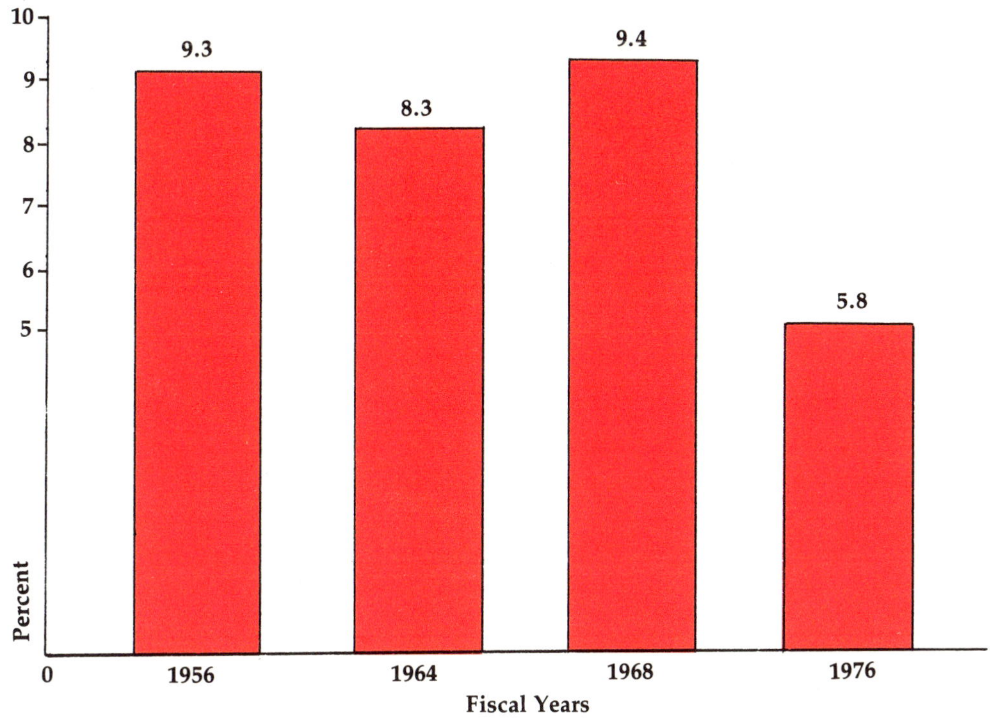

This level of military expenditure is probably close to the minimum that a major power can sustain and still be a force to reckon with independent of a strong ally or allies. In the 1930s, when the United States depended on neutrality and isolation for its security, outlays were on the order of 2 percent of GNP. By 1944, in a peak effort, they had reached 48 percent of GNP. Yet the United States emerged from World War II with a vibrant, expansive economy that made it almost inevitably the dominant world power for 20 years. The United States cut back its scale of effort immediately and in the entire postwar period has never exceeded the Korean War level of 12 percent. Plainly a nation with such demonstrable economic strength can fairly easily sustain a peacetime effort at its present level of about 6 percent of GNP.[2]

Comparisons between U.S. and Soviet efforts are tricky because of hidden cost factors in the Soviet budget and the complexities of the conversion of values from one national currency to another. Most estimates show the USSR on a rising level of expenditures on military programs over the past ten years in contrast to the up-and-down U.S. record. In constant dollars, the record is shown on page 78.[3]

[2] See Murray L. Weidenbaum, *Economics of Peacetime Defense,* (New York) Praeger, 1974, p. 25.
[3] *Annual Defense Department Report, FY 1976,* p. I-6.

U.S.-Soviet Defense Expenditures and Military Manpower

(Billion 1973 dollars, excludes military assistance and civil defense)

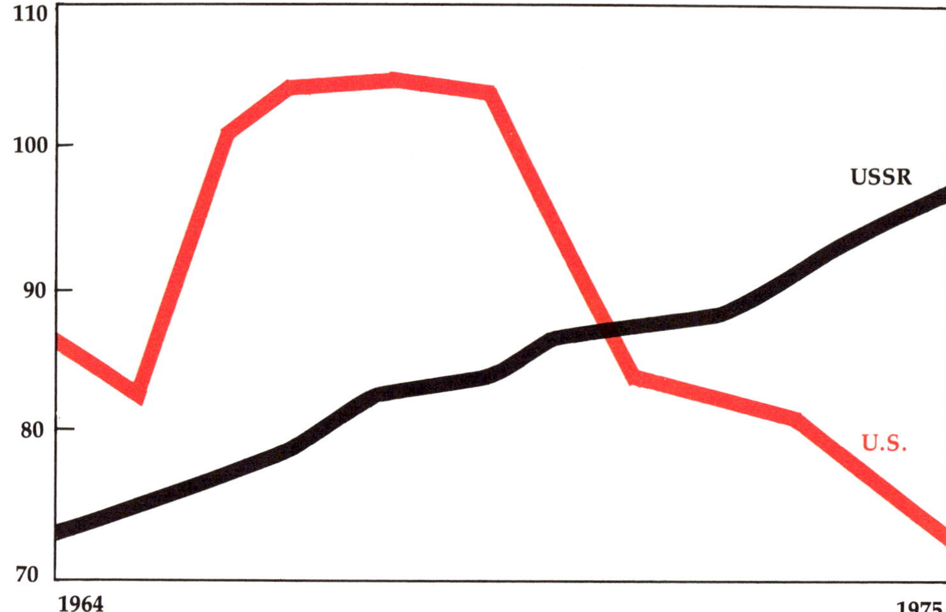

These are serious peacetime military efforts by the two superpowers, in support of major programs, as would be expected. Actually, the 6 percent level is just about the average for worldwide arms expenditures at present, the average having decreased a bit over the past decade. Conversion of worldwide military spending to a dollar basis gives the staggering annual total expenditure of over $250 billion, roughly 60 percent of which is U.S. and Soviet.[4]

Of the major countries which possess substantial elements of other kinds of power, only eight spend more than 5 percent of their GNP on military programs. Besides the USSR and the United States, they are:

Egypt	15%
Iran	11%
China (PRC)	8%
East Germany (DRG)	6%
Nigeria	5%
United Kingdom	5%

In addition to these countries, several other nations maintain a very high level of military expenditures.[5] They are located in conflict areas of intersecting great power interests, some of them quite recently actual battle zones.

The outstanding example is Israel, which is on a war footing and spends 45 percent of its GNP for military purposes. This would not be possible over a long period without the substantial aid Israel receives from the United States. The reasons for its high military readiness are apparent, however, when it is noted that all of the Arab states ringing Israel and a number of others have unusually high rates of military expenditure. Egypt is noted above at 15 percent; Syria spends 12 percent of its GNP, Jordan 16 percent, Saudi Arabia 14 percent, and

[4] *World Military Expenditures and Arms Trade 1963-73,* Table I, p. 14.
[5] *Ibid.*

Iraq 12 percent. Yemen (Aden), the United Arab Emirates, and Qatar all spend more than 9 percent of GNP on military programs. Both U.S. and Soviet assistance have contributed to making these high expenditures feasible and, in fact, most of the arms come from the two superpowers.

The Republic of China/Taiwan, an island state with a giant hostile neighbor that would like to annex it, is the Israel of the Far East. Like Israel, it has a modern economy, a relatively advanced technology, an energetic population, efficient government, and a strong defense force. Its level of military expenditures runs at about 9 percent of a GNP that has been rapidly expanding for a number of years.

North Korea also spends 9 percent of its GNP on military strength, in this case to maintain pressure on its non-communist neighbor, South Korea. North Vietnam has just conquered its neighbor, South Vietnam, and has come to dominate Cambodia and Laos. Thus, in the context of military strategy, North Vietnam is now synonymous with the old territory called Indochina. North Vietnam has been spending about 25 percent of its GNP on the war. This level, which will drop as fighting in Indochina comes to an end, was possible because of extensive aid from both the USSR and Communist China.

Albania, protecting itself from all its neighbors and from the USSR, with aid from Communist China, spends at the rate of 9 percent of GNP for military programs.

Cuba and Somalia, both beneficiaries of extensive Soviet aid, are in the over 5 percent of GNP category, as are the Sudan, Burma, Pakistan, and Portugal. For purposes of our formula, all of the nations with expenditures above the 5 percent level are assigned 2 units of weight for their military effort.

Most of the North Atlantic Treaty countries maintain military programs costing 2-4 percent of GNP—this includes the Federal Republic of Germany, France, Italy, Greece, and Canada—as do Spain, Yugoslavia, India, Indonesia, Australia, South Korea, Brazil, Zaire, and South Africa. Among the major allies of the United States, only Japan is in the 1 percent category.

In view of their geographical contiguity and active, organized defense interrelationship, the NATO powers which spend between 2 percent and 5 percent of GNP on military preparedness are given a weight of 1 on the grounds that together they represent a significant military capability. The other countries with military expenditures at the same level are rated at 0, along with other nations with lower levels of military effort. We make an exception in those few cases where the number of armed forces maintained by a nation is over 200,000 even though their defense programs constitute only 2-4 percent of GNP. These countries are assigned weights of 1 for perceived military effort.

Turning to the actual size of the armed forces maintained by the powerful nations of the world, a roughly similar picture emerges. The United States, the USSR, and China dwarf all the other countries in terms of deployed manpower, with (in 1974) 2,174,000, 3,525,000, and 3,000,000 respectively. The total of these three forces are approximately equal to the armed forces of all the rest of the world. Most of the forces with substantial combat capability are at a strength of 200,000 or more. Eleven nations with forces of more than 350,000 deserve 2 weights for perceived military power.

Military Strength:

Force Levels

In descending order of strength, the nations maintaining forces at the level of 200,000 or more but less than one million are:

	Country	*Armed Forces Strength (Rounded)*
1	**India**	956,000
2	**North Vietnam (Indochina)**	630,000
3	**South Korea**	630,000
4	**France**	500,000
5	**China/Taiwan**	490,000
6	**West Germany (FRG)**	490,000
7	**North Korea**	470,000
8	**Turkey**	450,000
9	**Italy**	420,000
10	**Pakistan**	390,000
11	**United Kingdom**	350,000
12	**Egypt**	320,000
13	**Poland**	300,000
14	**Spain**	280,000
15	**Indonesia**	270,000
16	**Portugal**	260,000
17	**Iran**	240,000
18	**Japan**	230,000
19	**Yugoslavia**	230,000
20	**Nigeria**	210,000
21	**Brazil**	210,000
22	**Czechoslovakia**	200,000

Armed forces of lesser size, for the most part, are only of local significance. Israel is of peculiar importance because its forces of about 145,000 can be effectively mobilized to a strength of 400,000 in 72 hours. This is a unique capability. Similarly, special notice must be given to the lesser East European Pact members because of their geographical contiguity with Soviet territory and their participation in an organized defense system. While the Democratic Republic of Germany has only 145,000 in its regular forces, Hungary 100,000, Rumania 170,000, and Bulgaria 150,000, their incremental capability in conjunction with Poland, Czechoslovakia, and the USSR is substantial. These countries are assigned a weight of 1 for perceived strength of armed forces along with the countries having more than 200,000 but less than 350,000 in their armed forces.

Control of the Seas and Global Reach[6]

It must be noted that the global reach credited to the United States derives primarily from its naval strength. The Soviet and U.S. navies, while they both have a share of responsibility for nuclear deterrence, were developed and deployed for essentially different purposes. U.S. naval forces are designed mainly to support distant U.S. forces overseas, and, when required, the armies of our allies. Because the United States, unlike the Soviet Union, is primarily and increasingly dependent on distant overseas sources of raw materials, the necessity of securing sea-lanes for commercial shipping and logistic transfers has strongly conditioned U.S. naval development and strategy. This means that the U.S. Navy, more than the Soviet Navy, must maintain forward defenses, sea control, and the ability to project power ashore.

The Soviet Union, as a traditional land power whose most vital interests are tied to Eurasia and whose global commitments have unfolded only gradually, has long tailored its navy to the primary purpose of preventing the U.S. Navy from carrying out its missions, that is, to counter U.S. deployed forces, especially submarines and aircraft carriers, and to obstruct sea-lanes. The original emphasis on preventing attacks on the Soviet homeland and adjacent areas and supporting Soviet ground and air forces has gradually given way to a global strategy, first in defensive capabilities and, increasingly, in offensive strength. The shift in emphasis was first evident in strategic attack (mainly submarine) capabilities, but now is extending to the capacity for waging conventional war as well. Only in recent years have Soviet planners assigned greater priority to the projection of their forces, especially air power, great distances from the homeland.

Furthermore, the USSR has increasingly designed and deployed its navy with a keen eye toward political objectives. This has become sharply evident since 1967 in Soviet ship design, naval exercises, and deployments. In times of crisis the USSR has often had more ships than the United States in the Mediterranean and it has begun routine deployments into the Indian Ocean. Admiral Gorshkov, who has commanded the Soviet Navy for many years, expressed Soviet policy most clearly when he said that the Soviet Navy now possesses the capability to demonstrate the economic and military power of the USSR beyond its borders during peacetime. This he attributes to the high mobility and endurance of the combatant vessels in the Soviet fleet and suggests it demonstrates readiness to take decisive actions, deter or suppress potential enemies, and to support friendly states. The highest Soviet officials since 1970 have commented frequently that no question of any importance in the world presently can be resolved without Soviet participation, or without taking into account Soviet economic and military might.

The Soviet Navy and the power it displays worldwide are politically exploited in a smooth and calculated way. Soviet sea power, deployed increasingly in foreign waters and visiting foreign ports, creates an image of great Soviet strength. This, because of its political impact, is influence acquired without firing a shot.

[6] This section is based on a research report prepared at CSIS specifically for this project. For the whole report, see Robert A. Kilmarx, *Soviet-United States Naval Balance,* May, 1975.

In line with the combined objectives of political impact and what might be termed "counterforce deterrence" *vis-à-vis* U.S. naval power, the USSR has optimized the design of its navy for strong initial striking power, with less emphasis on reload and endurance. It has tended to stress numbers of ships, especially submarines, with less tonnage per unit relative to the U.S. naval inventory. The Soviet ships generally boast more weapons and a greater variety of missile launchers than their U.S. counterparts.

By contrast, the missions of the U.S. Navy and the capabilities geared to those missions are much more variegated and complex. They reflect the differing geostrategic circumstances of the United States and its greater dependence on the seas, as well as the breadth of its global commitments. Given these asymmetries, an objective comparison of U.S. and Soviet naval capabilities becomes at best difficult, and cannot be focussed exclusively on such standard yardsticks as force levels, unit-tonnages, or weaponry.

The U.S. Navy in recent years has suffered a significant lessening of the capability to carry out its conventional missions—a trend that contrasts with the substantial and steady rise in Soviet sea power in recent years. The Soviet Navy also enjoys the advantage of less demanding missions.

Detente has not applied a brake to the sustained Soviet competition with the United States in naval power. Obviously, the United States still retains a superiority in the major categories of naval capability—for example, in aircraft carriers—that will have no counterpart in the Soviet Navy for many years. Our attack and ballistic missile submarines are qualitatively superior to those of the Soviet Union, and our strategic missile capability more widely deployed.

A simplistic war-fighting comparison of the naval inventories of the United States and the Soviet Union tends to be inconclusive. The Soviet Union is ahead of the United States in the size and composition of its submarine forces. The United States has 102 nuclear-powered submarines, while the USSR has 110.

The United States lags behind the Soviet Union in ballistic missile submarines, thanks partly to the SALT I agreement, and also in land-based naval aircraft. The two opponents are roughly balanced with respect to numbers of major surface ships, but here the Soviet Union has a strong lead in ships equipped with surface-to-surface missiles. The United States still has a clear lead in submarine warfare capabilities (ASW), but this advantage is vulnerable not only to the number of Soviet missile-carrying submarines but also to technological innovations. The United States is ahead in underway replenishment capability and its greatest advantage derives from its current force of 15 operational aircraft carriers. This strategic advantage conveys political benefits because of the high visibility of port calls and announced deployments of carrier task forces.

The USSR constructed over three times the number of naval ships that the United States did during the 1962-1972 period. The breakdown by ship category is as follows:

Naval Ship Construction 1962-1972

	USSR	U.S.
Major Surface Combatants	92	83
Ballistic Missile Submarines	32	32
Cruise Missile Submarines	51	—
Attack Submarines	54	43
Amphibious Warfare	80	51
Auxiliaries	42	37
Minor Combatants and Mine Warfare	560	17
Total	**911**	**263**

Projected deliveries of major combatant ships to the U.S. Navy, based on present contract commitments, are nine in 1974 and twelve in 1975. This will give a total of about 200 major combatant ships of the first four categories and a total U.S. Navy strength of 494 U.S. vessels at the end of FY-1975, a low point for the U.S. Navy. The record suggests that meanwhile the momentum of Soviet naval construction programs is continuing, not abating.

The impression resulting from patterns of U.S. and Soviet naval power confirms the image of an approximate parity for strategic deterrence and war-fighting, but with somewhat more global outreach and deployment flexibility accruing to the United States. Combined with greater and much longer-range U.S. airlift capabilities, this naval outreach exceeds Soviet capacity. Although the USSR is plainly moving in the direction of worldwide naval deployment, as of 1975 only the United States can be said to command a true global projection of its military strength.

NATO versus Warsaw Pact Balance

The only concentration of conventional military forces in the world which might upset these rather general calculations of relative capability are the opposing armies of the Warsaw Pact and NATO spread out over the northern plain of West and Central Europe. At present, these tremendous conglomerates of combat strength are roughly balanced. Neither could attack the other with the confidence of a quick victory without escalation to nuclear war. The tactical nuclear weapons on both sides are numerous enough so that only a truly crushing superiority in conventional arms would deny their effective use.

The NATO forces are not strong enough to mount such a blitzkrieg. The Soviet forces, with Warsaw Pact allies' support, could more readily stage a lightning assault which would sweep to the Rhine in a few days. Moscow has steadily increased the combat capability of its units along the NATO front, adding modern tanks, armored personnel carriers, artillery, and aircraft. The Warsaw Pact armies are nevertheless faced with a dilemma in preparing for a NATO assault. They would have to concentrate massively to launch an entirely conventional attack. Whereas, to anticipate the limited tactical nuclear counterattack which they have been warned may follow a successful initial NATO thrust, they would have to disperse. In the face of this dilemma, Warsaw Pact forces have remained inactive in spite of their slightly advantageous position *vis-à-vis* the NATO forces.

The main characteristics of these two great alliance armies in the central zone of potential combat are presented in tabular form below:

Central NATO and Warsaw Pact Forces*[7]

NATO Member**		Forces (thousands)	Main Battle Tanks	Tactical Aircraft
United States		190	2,100	240
United Kingdom		55	600	130
Canada		3	30	40
Belgium		65	375	140
Netherlands		77	500	160
West Germany (FRG)		340	2,950	600
	Total	730	6,555	1,310
Warsaw Pact Member				
Soviet Union		460	7,850	1,250
Czechoslovakia		155	2,900	500
East Germany (DRG)		100	1,650	330
Poland		220	3,100	730
	Total	935	15,500	2,810

* These forces are only the central ones in West Germany, the Benelux countries, East Germany, Poland, and Czechoslovakia.

** French forces of 58,000 in West Germany and France's 325 tanks and 400 aircraft are not shown in the table.

The two forces are unlikely in the near future to be used against one another and will remain a check on each other. Thus, despite their enormous political import, they do not affect the balance of military factors except as indicated above.

The U.S. military units shown in this table are the greatest concentration of force the United States deploys overseas. The United States keeps about 60,000 servicemen in naval forces at sea, has about 150,000 in the Far East—mainly in Japan, Okinawa, and South Korea—and an additional 75,000 in Europe outside Germany. Total U.S. military strength outside the continental limits of the United States is roughly one-half million. Only the United States keeps such large numbers of troops deployed at great distances from its own borders. The Soviet units in East Europe are contiguous to Soviet home defense commands.

The political payoff of U.S. ground and air deployments overseas has been significant in terms of alliance loyalties and guarantees of trade access, but it does not add additional tangible weight to U.S. military capability beyond the existence of the forces already noted. Such deployments are part of the global reach the United States possesses through its naval and air units.

[7] *The Military Balance, 1974-1975* (London: The International Institute for Strategic Studies, 1974), p. 101.

Conclusion

After this brief review of conventional military capability, it is possible to add up perceived power weights for those countries which have been singled out in the ways described above. Taking into account the level of effort in terms of GNP and the size of U.S. armed forces, as well as the special global reach of the United States, we can construct a ranklist of nations perceived to have conventional military capability of more than local significance. The list follows:

Military Capability: Perceived Power

	Country	Level of Effort	Armed Forces	Global Reach	Total
1	United States	2	2	1	5
2	USSR	2	2	0	4
3	China (PRC)	2	2	0	4
4	North Vietnam (Indochina)	2	2	0	4
5	China/Taiwan	2	2	0	4
6	North Korea	2	2	0	4
7	Pakistan	2	2	0	4
8	United Kingdom	2	2	0	4
9	India	1	2	0	3
10	South Korea	1	2	0	3
11	France	1	2	0	3
12	West Germany (FRG)	1	2	0	3
13	Turkey	1	2	0	3
14	Italy	1	2	0	3
15	Egypt	2	1	0	3
16	Portugal	2	1	0	3
17	Iran	2	1	0	3
18	Nigeria	2	1	0	3
19	East Germany (DRG)	2	1	0	3
20	Israel	2	1	0	3
21	Poland	1	1	0	2
22	Spain	1	1	0	2
23	Indonesia	1	1	0	2
24	Yugoslavia	1	1	0	2
25	Brazil	1	1	0	2
26	Czechoslovakia	1	1	0	2
27	Syria	2	0	0	2
28	Jordan	2	0	0	2
29	Saudi Arabia	2	0	0	2
30	Iraq	2	0	0	2
31	Yemen (Aden)	2	0	0	2
32	United Arab Emirates	2	0	0	2
33	Qatar	2	0	0	2
34	Somalia	2	0	0	2
35	Sudan	2	0	0	2
36	Albania	2	0	0	2
37	Cuba	2	0	0	2
38	Burma	2	0	0	2

	Country	Level of Effort	Armed Forces	Global Reach	Total
39	**Singapore**	2	0	0	**2**
40	**Mongolia**	2	0	0	**2**
41	**Japan**	0	1	0	**1**
42	**Canada**	1	0	0	**1**
43	**Greece**	1	0	0	**1**
44	**Netherlands**	1	0	0	**1**
45	**Belgium**	1	0	0	**1**
46	**Norway**	1	0	0	**1**
47	**Denmark**	1	0	0	**1**
48	**Hungary**	0	1	0	**1**
49	**Rumania**	0	1	0	**1**
50	**Bulgaria**	0	1	0	**1**

This chapter completes our survey of the basic elements of national power calculated in macrometric fashion. The remaining task is to combine these findings in national and politectonic zone totals. Only after we have done so can we proceed to considerations of strategy and national will as factors in our formula for perceived power.

CHAPTER SEVEN

Total Macrometric Power Pattern

$$Pp = (C + E + M) \times (S + W)$$

After consideration of strategic nuclear and conventional military capability (Chapters Five and Six), we are now able to add all the military value weights to the consolidated ranklist of nations with considerable perceived power. It is also necessary to adjust the order in which nations are listed to reflect perceived power in all categories: population, territory, economic capability, and military capability. A few nations are listed for the first time as having territorial critical mass despite a small population, because they carry either economic or military weight. The resulting consolidated list is as follows:

Total Weights (C + E + M)

	Country	Critical Mass	Capability Economic	Capability Military	Total
1	United States	10	20	20	50
2	USSR	10	16	19	45
3	China (PRC)	10	7	6	23
4	Canada	8	11	1	20
5	France	5	10	5	20
6	United Kingdom	5	8	6	19
7	West Germany (FRG)	5	10	3	18
8	Japan	6	10	1	17
9	Brazil	9	5	2	16
10	India	9	4	3	16
11	Italy	5	7	3	15
12	Iran	6	5	3	14
13	Australia	5	7	0	12
14	Indonesia	8	2	2	12
15	Nigeria	6	2	3	11
16	Mexico	7	4	0	11
17	South Africa	5	6	0	11
18	Poland	4	5	2	11
19	Pakistan	6	1	4	11

	Country	Critical Mass	Capability Economic	Capability Military	Total
20	Argentina	7	3	0	10
21	Spain	4	4	2	10
22	Turkey	5	2	3	10
23	East Germany (DRG)	2	5	3	10
24	Egypt	5	1	3	9
25	Netherlands	1	6	1	8
26	Yugoslavia	4	2	2	8
27	China/Taiwan	2	2	4	8
28	Rumania	3	3	1	7
29	Burma	5	0	2	7
30	Sudan	5	0	2	7
31	Saudi Arabia	3	2	2	7
32	Czechoslovakia	1	4	2	7
33	South Korea	3	1	3	7
34	North Vietnam (Indochina)	3	0	4	7
35	Zaire	6	0	0	6
36	Algeria	5	1	0	6
37	Venezuela	3	3	0	6
38	Colombia	5	1	0	6
39	Belgium	0	5	1	6
40	North Korea	2	0	4	6
41	Ethiopia	5	0	0	5
42	Philippines	4	1	0	5
43	Thailand	4	1	0	5
44	Sweden	1	4	0	5
45	Mongolia	3	0	2	5
46	Portugal	0	1	3	4
47	Bangladesh	4	0	0	4
48	Afghanistan	4	0	0	4
49	Peru	3	1	0	4
50	Libya	3	1	0	4
51	Denmark	0	3	1	4
52	Israel	0	1	3	4
53	Norway	1	2	1	4
54	Iraq	1	1	2	4
55	Morocco	3	0	0	3
56	South Vietnam	3	0	0	3
57	Tanzania	3	0	0	3
58	Switzerland	0	3	0	3
59	Austria	0	3	0	3
60	Chile	2	1	0	3
61	Finland	1	2	0	3
62	United Arab Emirates	0	1	2	3
63	Somalia	1	0	2	3
64	Hungary	0	2	1	3
65	Greece	0	1	1	2
66	Bulgaria	0	1	1	2
67	Sri Lanka	2	0	0	2
68	Kenya	2	0	0	2
69	Syria	0	0	2	2

Country	Critical Mass	Capability Economic	Capability Military	Total
70 **Jordan**	0	0	2	**2**
71 **Yemen (Aden)**	0	0	2	**2**
72 **Qatar**	0	0	2	**2**
73 **Albania**	0	0	2	**2**
74 **Cuba**	0	0	2	**2**
75 **Singapore**	0	0	2	**2**
76 **New Zealand**	1	1	0	**2**
77 **Nepal**	1	0	0	**1**
78 **Kuwait**	0	1	0	**1**
				Total 627

This comprehensive consolidated ranklist indicates that 78 nations have some claim to significant power. In some cases it is a claim based on a single valuable asset supported by little else in the way of strength. For example, Kuwait has only one economic asset: oil. Nepal, a different example, qualifies only because it sustains over 12 million people in its mountain realm. Some nations making major military expenditures in terms of percent of GNP are not able to support significant armed forces because their total GNP is not large. These cannot be taken as exercising formidable power if they have no other very valuable assets; Qatar, for example, is one of these.

Apparent anomalies in the ranklist can be explained; it must be remembered that each country is an individual case. Cuba, with limited national strength except for the military programs made possible by its status as the only Soviet client state in the Western Hemisphere, has had a great deal of impact on international affairs because of its highly visible military troublemaking potential. Similarly, Syria and Jordan, Israel's Arab neighbors possessing military programs rather than oil, receive a great deal of international attention.

In all, these 78 nations include over 85 percent of the peoples of the world and all of the powerful nations. Among them 25 to 35 overshadow the rest, and what happens to these leading nations will determine the trends in world power over the next 10 or 20 years.

Politectonic Distribution of National Power

The real advantage of a consolidated ranklist of this kind is to focus attention on the concentration of great power in the hands of a relatively small number of leading nations and to observe how this power is distributed geographically. The total number of weighted values, that is, units of perceived power in international affairs, is 627. The United States and the USSR alone have 95, which demonstrates once again that it is a bipolar world we live in; the next most powerful nations are only about half as strong as these two superpowers. Notwithstanding, if we concentrate our attention for the most part on the nations which qualify as having 8 or more units of perceived power on this ranklist, the number of nations is only 27 and they account for 425 of the 627—or about two-thirds—of the total weights on the whole list. These, on the basis of the macrometric analysis we have considered so far, are the nations that will tend to dominate world affairs, and they are distributed among the 11 politectonic zones as follows:

Politectonic Zones:

Importance of Powerful Nations

	Country	*Perceived Power*	*Total*
	United States	50	
I	Canada	20	81
	Mexico	11	
	USSR	45	
II	Poland	11	66
	East Germany (DRG)	10	
III	China (PRC)	23	23
	France	20	
	United Kingdom	19	
	West Germany (FRG)	18	
IV	Italy	15	98
	Spain	10	
	Netherlands	8	
	Yugoslavia	8	
	Iran	14	
V	Turkey	10	33
	Egypt	9	
VI	India	16	27
	Pakistan	11	
VII	Indonesia	12	12
VIII	Japan	17	25
	China/Taiwan	8	
IX	Brazil	16	26
	Argentina	10	
X	Nigeria	11	22
	South Africa	11	
XI	Australia	12	12
		Total	425

It is instructive to note that relatively little change occurs in the cumulative power weights among leading nations in the different zones through adding military capabilities to other elements of strength. A few nations have dropped off the list and China/Taiwan, with a strong defense program, has moved up decisively.

If we extend the list to include the nations with cumulative weight totals of 7 or more, then 7 extra countries would bring the total up to 34. The new additions would be Rumania and Czechoslovakia, Saudi Arabia and the Sudan, North Vietnam (Indochina), Burma, and South Korea. The adjusted table of total weights for perceived power in politectonic zones would change as follows:

Additional Nations of Importance

Zone	Additions	Total Perceived Power Weights
I		81
II	plus Rumania (7), Czechoslovakia (7)	80
III	plus North Vietnam (Indochina) (7)	30
IV		98
V	plus Saudi Arabia (7), the Sudan (7)	47
VI		27
VII	plus Burma (7)	19
VIII	plus South Korea (7)	32
IX		26
X		22
XI		12
		Total 474

This listing brings us immediately to our next task, which is the attempt to consider political and strategic factors in looking at these countries and zones. Obviously, as of 1975, Yugoslavia brings no useful increment of strength to West Europe, and Rumania is an unreliable asset for the USSR and its allies, since it is invariably the holdout for independence within the Warsaw Pact.

In Southeast Asia, Hanoi's victory is too recent for it to affect the real power factors of 1975 very much. In our next chart we will add to North Vietnam's index of national strength the weights appropriate for its control of the population and territory of South Vietnam, but only those weights. A period of organization and regimentation is inevitable before these strengths can be mobilized for Hanoi's strategic benefit. It will, in due time, be a power to be reckoned with in regional terms.

The possibility that North Vietnam, with prospects for command of all the people and resources of Indochina (Cambodia, Laos, and both Vietnams), might collaborate closely with Communist China represents a potential danger to the balance of power in both East and Southeast Asia. On the other hand, if Indonesia and Burma could join with the new Indochina dominated by North Vietnam and lean politically away from Communist China, a not very likely prospect, the chances of a coalescence of some kind of center of power in Southeast Asia would increase. Indonesia's strategic position commanding the Malacca Straits—along with Singapore—and other passageways between the Southwest Pacific and Indian Oceans makes this whole area a focal point of great power interest. For some time to come, the region will be a potential trouble spot inviting fragmentation, conflict, and national jockeying for influence.

The clear message for West Europe from our evaluation is that it could be the most powerful regional center in the world if its resources were successfully mobilized for a common political purpose. Since this is not now the case, the crucial question is whether West Europe becomes a rich prize for conflicting superpowers or whether the 25-year-old Atlantic Alliance will cohere sufficiently to make the two power centers in it (West Europe and North America) count as one strategic bloc internationally. This was truer in the 1950s and early 1960s than today, partly because the national political regimes involved do not exhibit an adequate need for cooperation in a period when their fear of Soviet military encroachment has lessened and detente with the USSR has become a worldwide goal.

Finally, the political fragmentation of the Mideast, South Asia, and Northeast Asia show how these regions run the risk of being dominated by better organized nations or alliances even though they are potentially very powerful in themselves. For example, the strategic triangle of countries in Northeast Asia —Japan, China/Taiwan, and South Korea—appear to be collectively capable of balancing off the still limited strength of Communist China only if the United States insures their strategic coherence through bilateral relations with all three to compensate for their limited political cooperation with one another.

The same problems explain why Central and South Africa, on the one hand, and Latin America, on the other, are only beginning to develop as great regional power centers. The two natural focal points in both of these continental regions are mutually antagonistic politically and strategically, Brazil *vis-à-vis* Argentina and Nigeria *vis-à-vis* South Africa.

These truths about the kaleidoscopic patterns of power in various global regions become even more apparent if the entire 78 nations (approximately one-half of the world total) whose perceived power we have rated as significant are divided among the politectonic zones to which they belong. The result of adding the remaining 44 nations would be:

Major Nations

Zone	*Countries*	*Perceived Power Weight*	*Total Perceived Power Weights*
	United States	50	
I	Mexico	20	81
	Canada	11	
	USSR	45	
	Poland	11	
	East Germany (DRG)	10	
	Rumania	7	
II	Czechoslovakia	7	92
	Plus		
	Hungary	3	
	Bulgaria	2	
	Mongolia	5	
	Cuba	2	
	China (PRC)	23	
	North Vietnam	7	
III	**Plus**		39
	South Vietnam	3	
	North Korea	6	

Zone	Countries	Perceived Power Weight	Total Perceived Power Weights
	West Germany (FRG)	18	
	United Kingdom	19	
	Italy	15	
	France	20	
	Spain	10	
	Netherlands	8	
	Yugoslavia	8	
IV	**Plus**		134
	Belgium	6	
	Sweden	5	
	Portugal	4	
	Denmark	4	
	Norway	4	
	Switzerland	3	
	Austria	3	
	Finland	3	
	Greece	2	
	Albania	2	
	Iran	14	
	Turkey	10	
	Egypt	9	
	Sudan	7	
	Saudi Arabia	7	
	Plus		
	Algeria	6	
	Libya	4	
V	Iraq	4	80
	Israel	4	
	Morocco	3	
	United Arab Emirates	3	
	Syria	2	
	Jordan	2	
	Yemen (Aden)	2	
	Qatar	2	
	Kuwait	1	
	India	16	
	Pakistan	11	
	Plus		
VI	Bangladesh	4	38
	Afghanistan	4	
	Sri Lanka	2	
	Nepal	1	

Zone	Countries	Perceived Power Weight	Total Perceived Power Weights
	Indonesia	12	
	Burma	7	
	Plus		
VII	Philippines	5	31
	Thailand	5	
	Singapore	2	
	Japan	17	
VIII	China/Taiwan	8	32
	South Korea	7	
	Brazil	16	
	Argentina	10	
	Plus		
IX	Venezuela	6	45
	Colombia	6	
	Peru	4	
	Chile	3	
	Nigeria	11	
	South Africa	11	
	Plus		
	Zaire	6	
X	Ethiopia	5	41
	Tanzania	3	
	Somalia	3	
	Kenya	2	
	Australia	12	
XI	**Plus**		14
	New Zealand	2	
		Total	**627**

Plainly Mongolia—locked between China and the Asian USSR—and Cuba—in the Western Hemisphere—are not so much additions of strength as potential conflict zones and threatening penetrations. China's relations with North Korea are shaky and its political foothold in Southeast Europe—Albania—is more liability than asset except in the sphere of communist ideology.

In West Europe, neutral Sweden and policy-straitjacketed Finland may indicate the wave of the future for the NATO powers rather than adding incremental strength.[1] Portugal may turn out to be a pro-Soviet penetration of NATO itself, whether it develops along Cuban communist lines or Stalinist Soviet lines and may weaken the Atlantic-Mediterranean flank of NATO crucially. Yugoslavia tries desperately to stay nonaligned between the Soviet bloc and West Europe, although it will have difficulty in doing so after Tito's death. In the Mideast, Israel exists among the Arab states in an equilibrium of military tension which has been and can again be shattered by war. Elsewhere diversity and disunity are the common rule, except in Zone XI, where New Zealand's strength combined with that of Australia creates a fairly homogeneous cluster of peoples of European origin in the Outer Ocean perimeter. This whole zone is vulnerable in view of the comparatively small population residing in it and disorder among the nations in neighboring Zone VII, Southeast Asia.

It is to reduce this chaotic picture to some semblance of order for purposes of strategic analysis that we have employed the concept of leading nations in the several zones. This clarity, gained by simplification, does not alter the fact that each politectonic zone has its own regional character, plus those anomalies in the distribution of power of the kind listed above.

There is one more useful way to look at the distribution of power among these 78 nations which register on the scale of international power according to our calculus. It is to classify politectonic zones on a broad political spectrum. Zones II and III contain the totalitarian states with closed societies and command economies. Due to China's vast population, about 35 percent of the world's population lives in these zones, but the total perceived power of nations in Zone II and Zone III is only about 20 percent of the world total as we have calculated it. Zone I, North America, and Zone IV, West Europe, add up to about 35 percent of the world total of perceived power. The United States, in combination with only the closest U.S. allies in other zones, possesses a preponderance of power as perceived according to the macrometric factors so far considered. The open societies and economies with substantial private enterprise and world trade are collectively very strong. Superficial examination of their share of world power suggests they should feel secure, not endangered.

For this reason it is essential to move on to political and strategic factors in the strength of nations and to look at clusters of powers associated or allied within and across the borders of the politectonic zones. These considerations

[1] *Pravda,* April 5, 1974, commenting on the anniversary of the Soviet-Finnish treaty of 1948, said: "The Soviet-Finnish treaty is confirmed by the whole course of history and, particularly, by the positive changes in the international situation in recent years as a model for the development of relations between states with different social systems. . . . The treaty is an important element of the system of all-European security, whose creation is the common cause of all states on our continent."

constitute the subject matter of our closing chapters. The key questions are: how do world leaders plan to exploit the power they are perceived to have and, how effectively can they organize national support for their broad strategic aims? Since our focus is on global strategy as a factor in the international balance of power, we will mainly deal in this context with the top ranking nations, the USSR, the United States, and China, each of which has a view of the way it would like the world to develop.

CHAPTER EIGHT

National Strategy and National Will

$Pp = (C + E + M) \times (S + W)$

All of the macrometric calculations reflected in the foregoing chapters provide a rough guide to the focal power points in the world today. From the beginning, however, we have indicated that our results would be modified by an estimate of the effectiveness of national strategies and national will. The formula calls for a coefficient, a multiplier, reflecting these two factors, S and W. As we now have rough quantifications for C + E + M, we can complete our assessment if we factor in the right coefficient to reflect the last part of the equation: $Pp = (C + E + M) \times (S + W)$.

People join together in a nation because they share common purposes over and above their individual goals in life. Not everyone in a nation need agree on all those broader purposes, but there is a general direction or trend discernible in every community, whether or not it is clearly articulated. Most national goals concern such domestic issues as the distribution of wealth and the balance between authority and civil liberty. In international affairs, the common purpose ought to include a strategy for dealing with other nations in ways that protect and enhance one's own goals. Strategy may sometimes be only a pattern of behavior reflecting cultural norms that are tacitly accepted by the citizenry. At other times, most especially in wartime, it is carefully articulated. In a dictatorship, policies can be worked out with precision and made mandatory. The range of possible international strategies runs from a total isolation from the affairs of other nations (Japan in the early nineteenth century) to carefully plotted campaigns of territorial conquest (Germany under Hitler).

A nation may be either efficient or inept in carrying out its policies, depending on the strength of the political will of the people as expressed in their national decision-making. National will may be unified and enthusiastic in support of a particular strategy or it may be sluggish and uncertain. The degree of energy and coherent behavior in a body politic is the main cause of its success or failure. Still, firmness of national will depends in part on whether strategic aims have been wisely formulated and skillfully explained in terms of national interest. This explanatory function is crucial in a representative government based on the consent of the governed.

With the consideration of these critical elements in national strength we enter a region where numbers can only be notations of subjective judgment, nothing more. Yet the judgments are critical and must be made, although reasonable men will differ on them. The task is simplified to some extent if it is recognized at the outset that most nations have only local or limited aims and are largely passive observers of strategic measures on a global scale.

Powerful nations need a global strategy to focus their great energies. Secondary and tertiary powers fashion their national policies in accordance with the associations they have formed with more powerful nations. In this situation the easiest way to deal with most countries is to assume that normally they are preoccupied with local and regional interests, but that they can summon up sufficient political and social cohesion to pursue their national purposes with reasonable effectiveness in the international arena if the need arises. In such cases, the index weight will be 1 for combined strategic purpose (S) and national will (W), that is, 0.5 for strategy and 0.5 for will. If the multiplier is 1, the value of the rest of the formula is unchanged. It is an arbitrary scale of measurement but it has the advantage of leaving most numerical weights unchanged, while focussing on deviations above and below the expected behavior pattern.

In the case of nations with clearcut strategic plans for international aggrandizement, a larger index number for the factor S may be assigned, up to an arbitrary maximum of 1. If, similarly, nations are unified socially, psychologically, and politically behind strategic aims, they also may be assigned a larger index number for the factor W, up to an arbitrary maximum of 1. Thus a perfect score would result in a multiplier of 2 for the term combining S and W. Other elements of national strength would be correspondingly magnified.

Conversely, if a nation is strategically confused and its will to pursue a policy is feeble, it may get a fractional index rating below 0.5 for one or for both factors. In that case the values for other elements of national power would be reduced. In an extreme hypothetical case, a zero multiplier would give a zero quantity of perceived power, regardless of other potential strengths that may exist; anything times nothing is nothing. A nation with no strategy at all and no will whatsoever could hardly exist, but at various times even the greatest of nations suffer from a confusion of strategic purpose or a weakening of national will. Hence the multiplier can be less than the normal index score of 1.

In the exercise of great power, standards must be rigorous because the competition is severe. Hence any falling off in these crucial matters of strategy and of strength of will is a severe handicap in the use of power for international purposes. Factoring in these elements of national strength therefore becomes the most important part of any net assessment of the world balance of power.

Only three nations in the recent past have had an integrated, truly global strategic concept in the conduct of their international affairs. They are the USSR, the United States, and the People's Republic of China. They are, of course, very large countries with tremendous strengths.

Other dynamic powers with positive strategic programs in the period prior to World War II were Germany and Japan, on the one hand, with France and the United Kingdom resisting them, on the other. All were nearly destroyed in the struggle and their strategic purpose over the past 30 years has been to regain strength and to reconstruct beneficial protective alliances. Other nations orient themselves around—or against—the very large and powerful countries, or in economic, political, and military combinations related to those three nations and to the four renascent secondary powers. Regional associations of nations and groups dedicated to "nonalignment" with any of the great powers have also been formed. In 1975 several newer nations of consequence are thrusting themselves into the ranks of the globally involved powers, but in discussing international strategy the field is comparatively small.

Soviet Strategy in a Global Perspective

Soviet strategic thinking reflects a consistent view of the evolving world situation—what Soviet ideologues call the "correlation of forces"—and a consistent operational code of international conduct designed to advance the interests of the Soviet Union within the constraints other nations impose on Soviet tactics and timing. Occasionally there are variations of language and tactics, but Soviet strategy has remained the same for a long time. At present Soviet officials repeatedly explain that they are following a policy of "detente", but this term can only be understood in the context of general Soviet political thinking about "peaceful coexistence" with capitalism.

Soviet strategy in all its basic features was formulated by Lenin and Stalin, although Khrushchev and Brezhnev have naturally adjusted some features of it to fit new conditions. Still, Brezhnev's detente is essentially Lenin's peaceful coexistence. The central thrust of Soviet policy is remarkably clear for those who read and listen, and it must be reckoned with by all who deal with the USSR.

The view from Moscow and the difficulties it presents for non-Marxists are revealed by the usage of the word detente, which has played such a large part in discussions of U.S.-Soviet relations in the United States in recent years. Detente[1] as employed in 1971 and 1972 in West Europe and the United States originally meant simply a relaxation of tension permitting Moscow and Washington to enter into a dialogue or negotiating process that might reduce confrontations and dangers of war. As time went on, the Nixon Administration claimed such enormous benefits from personal diplomacy in Moscow (and Peking) that the term came to carry with it a connotation of peace and international harmony favorable to U.S. security and welfare. By 1975, many people in the United States had come to think that detente means 1) a guarantee of peace, in the sense of avoidance of all kinds of war; 2) stability in the international relations of governments and in social order; 3) coordination and friendly cooperation between great powers, including the United States and the USSR; and 4)

[1] The term detente is, of course, ambiguous, and its usage has become almost mindless in many intellectual circles in the United States. Detente literally means simply a stopping or release of tension. The word in French means a "stop" or holding device, a kind of trigger associated with a weapon, such as a medieval crossbow, and later a pistol. The concept derived from the old crossbow where the bow was bent as it was put under tension by drawing it. The string was then permitted to rest against the "stop" or "detente" to hold it in a somewhat reduced tension which could easily be released, either to fire an arrow or to return the bow to its normal relaxed state. Perhaps this "trigger" or "release" connotation is not a bad usage for the wary adversary relationship that actually exists between the USSR and the United States, when it is used in its original sense.

tolerance of differing social systems, even as different as those in the United States and the USSR.

Unfortunately, this widespread U.S. understanding of detente conflicts with the basic interpretation which the USSR has always had of what it originally quite scrupulously referred to as peaceful coexistence. From the very beginning, Soviet doctrinal literature explaining to the cadres and officialdom, as well as to the people of the Soviet Union, what peaceful coexistence meant, took a quite different line.[2]

The USSR puts a heavy emphasis on "peace"—even as the United States does—but Soviet leaders obviously mean by it only the avoidance of total nuclear war between the United States and the Soviet Union. This meaning was especially clear during the many years of U.S. weapons superiority. Soviet leaders did not want international issues settled in a contest in which the USSR was the weaker nation. The partial coincidence of their interest with the U.S. view cloaked the fact that the remaining connotations of peaceful coexistence or detente in the USSR were quite contrary to the vibrations which the term aroused in the United States.

Soviet leaders have always espoused the right to fight a "just war" of "national liberation", that is, to assist a country to shake off external domination, as they would say they were doing in Vietnam. Beyond that, they have made it painfully clear, especially for the benefit of their own citizenry, that peaceful coexistence, in addition to avoiding total war, means 1) unrelenting class struggle; 2) worldwide support of the forces of revolution by the ballot if possible and by violence if necessary; 3) diplomatic moves to bring about political realignments in non-Communist areas so as to restrict the parts of the world open to U.S. influence, trade, investment, and procurement of economic raw materials; and 4) permanent positive antipathy between the communist and capitalist social systems, the latter of which, according to Soviet doctrine, is still supposed to perish in the ultimate and long-heralded "world crisis of capitalism".

Soviet statements for the past several years have carefully restricted the meaning of peaceful coexistence to fit this classical Marxist-Leninist theory of social conflict. Their purpose is to preserve and strengthen the one-party dictatorship in the Soviet Union, which insists on the total compliance of Soviet officials and the Soviet citizenry with doctrinal edicts on international strategy as well as with day-to-day administrative commands of the totalitarian government.

Lenin stated in 1919 the classic world view of the generation of Bolshevik rulers who had seized power in 1917:

> We are living not merely in a state, but in a system of states and the existence of the Soviet Republic side by side with imperialist states for a long time is unthinkable. One or the other must triumph in the end.

[2] Many of the citations in this chapter are from a Miami University monograph by Foy D. Kohler, *et al.*, *Soviet Strategy for the Seventies*, 1973. The interpretation of Soviet doctrine presented here corresponds closely with the findings of Ambassador Kohler and his colleagues.

Brezhnev set forth the same idea explicitly in his report to the 24th Soviet Party Congress, March 30, 1971:

> In recognition of its international duty, the CPSU will continue to pursue a line in international affairs which promotes the further activation of the world anti-imperialist struggle and strengthens the combat unity of all its participants. The total triumph of Socialism the world over is inevitable. And for this triumph, for the happiness of the working people, we will fight, unsparing of our strength.

There are many classic formulations of this central idea, but a good one was made December 21, 1972, not long after President Nixon's euphoric summit visit to Moscow, when Brezhnev explained that the Soviet Communist Party

> . . .has always held and still holds that the class struggle between the two systems—the capitalist and the socialist—in the economic, political and also, of course, in the ideological spheres will continue. It cannot be otherwise, because the world outlook and class aims of socialism and capitalism are opposed and irreconcilable. But we will strive to shift this historically inevitable struggle onto a path which will not threaten wars, dangerous conflicts, an unrestricted arms race.

The clearest theoretical pronouncement on Soviet world strategy came from Stalin shortly before his death in March 1953:

> The disintegration of a single universal world market must be considered the most important economic consequence of the Second World War. . . . This circumstance determined the further aggravation of the general crisis in the world capitalist system. . . . It follows . . . that the sphere of exploitation of world resources by the major capitalist countries (USA, Britain, France) will not expand but contract, that the world market conditions will deteriorate for these countries and that the number of enterprises operating at less than capacity will multiply in these countries. It is this essentially which constitutes the aggravation of the general crisis in the world capitalist system due to disintegration of the world market. . .

Since the mid-1950s, under Khrushchev's leadership, military assistance and economic aid on a massive scale to countries which the USSR hoped could be won away from economic and political relations with the United States or West European "capitalist" powers have poured out in a mighty flood. While not quite so generous or ebullient as Khrushchev, Brezhnev has continued to use arms and money to gain influence over peripheral areas and to deny them to the West. Particularly in the Mideast, Soviet policy has brought a major change in the patterns of stability in this region and jeopardized the access of the United States, West Europe, and Japan to the oil which is vital to their industries.

The heady impression Moscow gained from watching the removal of a U.S. president and the diffusion of leadership in the United States has provided the strategic underpinning of the entire peaceful coexistence or detente policy of the 1970s. The Soviet Union insists that the change in the "correlation of forces" in the world, not any increased virtue in capitalist society, has caused the United States to adopt what Soviet leaders call a more realistic policy.

Moscow's official newspaper, *Pravda*, said flatly in August 1973, after the touted summits held in Moscow and Washington:

> Peaceful coexistence does not mean the end of the struggle of the two-world social system. The struggle between the proletariat and the bourgeoisie, between world socialism and imperialism, will be waged right up to the complete and final victory of communism on a world scale.

This extraordinary frankness on the part of Soviet leaders seems somehow to escape most U.S. observers, who would like to think that peaceful coexistence is the same as their concept of detente and will certainly lead to "a generation of peace", as President Nixon promised.

Soviet world view and strategy have been consistent down to the present day. A Plenum of the Central Committee of the Communist Party of the Soviet Union met in Moscow, April 16, 1975, and reiterated basic Soviet strategies in the context of detente. An authoritative *Pravda* editorial of April 18 and a parallel *Isvestia* statement on the same day hailed detente as having brought about a "significant breakthrough" in "relations between the USSR and the U.S.", and "a positive turning point in relations". The pre-eminent old Bolshevik theoretician, Suslov, gave the Lenin anniversary address at the April Plenum, striking many familiar notes. His main theme was:

> Life convincingly confirms Lenin's forecast on the intensification of the general crisis of capitalism, and the victorious growth of the forces of socialism, peace, and national liberation. . .

In this context he also stressed that:

> The prevailing line in the development of the present international situation is the strengthening and deepening of the reduction of tension, the translation into life of the principles of peaceful coexistence.

Suslov drew the conclusion from the viewpoint of Moscow that:

> Under the conditions of detente and the further intensification of the general crisis of capitalism, the role of the international Communist movement as the most influential and active political force of our time is increasing.

There is a relentless consistency and clarity in Soviet thought about supporting revolutionary class warfare against non-Communist governments and aiding national wars of liberation from "imperialist", i.e., U.S. influence, as the "correlation of forces" in the world shifts in favor of the USSR. An international atmosphere of peaceful coexistence is understood by every Marxist-Leninist student to contribute to the conditions in which conflict remains below the dangerous intensity of total war and yet weakens capitalism, i.e., the United States and its allies, and strengthens the USSR.

These ideological concepts are taught throughout the USSR and they constitute part of the furniture of the minds of those Soviet leaders in the Communist

Party bureaucracy who control foreign policy and make all strategic decisions. Brezhnev and his most influential colleagues in the Soviet Politburo are the last legatees of the grim decades of Stalinist rule, all men in their late sixties or early seventies. Brezhnev is not very healthy and may step down in the next year. His successors almost certainly will come from a small group of bureaucratic loyalists nurtured in the same ideas and policies. Some years hence, younger generations may have different ideas, but for the present this national strategy of fundamental hostility to the non-Communist world provides the best clue there is to Soviet behavior in international affairs for a number of years to come. Detente is, and is likely to remain, a strategy by which the USSR expects ultimately to gain total strategic superiority over the United States.

Strategic Thinking in the United States

In contrast with Soviet strategic consistency, the United States in the past five years has been moving steadily away from the policies which dominated U.S. thinking about international affairs for the preceding quarter century. U.S. strategic thinking in 1975 exhibits a confusion about national purposes which has not existed since the breakdown of neutrality and isolation in the period prior to World War II. Strategy in any nation under a system of representative government and multi-party elections is bound to be more diffuse than it is in a totalitarian dictatorship where a comparatively small number of leaders are able to make secret and authoritative decisions. The strategy of the United States must be approached through its history of conducting international affairs much more than in its pronouncements of political purpose, which are usually designed to win the widest possible popular support rather than to delineate future national action. Moreover, much of U.S. policy is reactive, designed in response to situations created by other nations. Therefore, over the past 30 years U.S. strategy has been defined through a pattern of actions and goals worked out within the framework of relations with the USSR, the only power competing with the United States on a more or less equal basis.

The United States relied during most of its history on a policy of avoiding entangling international commitments, counting on the vigor of the nineteenth-century British Empire to protect the Western Hemisphere from hostile intrusion. Despite a brief emergence into a wider world in World War I, the United States still clung to hemispheric isolation and neutrality with regard to international conflicts through the 1930s. There was a strong tendency to accept purely declaratory assurances like the Kellogg-Briand Pact of 1928, which renounced war as an "instrument of policy" but provided no sanctions to guarantee compliance. All of this ended abruptly in 1941 when Pearl Harbor vividly confirmed the argument of the interventionists of the period that the United States could not stay out of world conflicts but had instead an obligation to protect the interests of U.S. citizens through positive action.

Formulations of national interest are usually ambiguous. The democracy for which President Wilson said World War I would make the world safe, is somewhat misleading as a term for describing the U.S. system of representative government, free elections, constitutional checks and balances, and guarantees of individual and minority rights in a pluralistic society. The choice of political systems in our time is between pluralism and totalitarianism. In a pluralistic society like that of the United States, individual rights and the privileges of minority groups are protected insofar as they do not impinge on the rights of others. Under such a system, an economy with great latitude for free enterprise and private decision-making becomes possible.

In a totalitarian state, an effort is made to direct and control every aspect of the life of every citizen to facilitate state-directed goals, and there is no political process for representing the wishes of the governed. The economy is centrally controlled and there is little room for private initiative and innovation.

Modern democracy is a far cry from the town meeting or the Greek city-state, but it is also plainly quite different from the one-party, non-parliamentary political process and state-owned or -managed economic structure of totalitarian regimes. Right-wing or left-wing totalitarianism is a twentieth-century phenomenon. Absolute monarchies and authoritarian tyrannies of many varieties have abounded throughout history, but it is only the technology of modern communications that enabled first Hitler and Mussolini, and then Stalin and Mao, to try to establish total control over the thoughts and actions of their citizens. Most arbitrary governments have been content with passive submission and obedient action. Stalin and Mao demanded positive thinking and abdication of privacy and individual rights.

To preserve the U.S. plural system, open society, and the prosperity based on free-enterprise economics has been the bedrock of U.S. strategy. President Kennedy put it succinctly when he said repeatedly in the last year of his life that the United States was striving for a world safe for diversity as distinct from totalitarianism. If there is a moral element in U.S. policy, it is a determined preference for the open, pluralistic society and an affirmation of the right of individuals to determine the kind of society they want. This political philosophy implies resistance to the spread of totalitarianism, whether by direct or by indirect aggression.

Evolution of U.S. Strategic Concepts in the "American Age"

U.S. national strategy since 1945 has tended to be dominated by U.S. concern about the hostile intentions of the USSR. There has, however, also been a strong positive strand of strategic thinking about the importance of our allies and of worldwide economic stability. Professional critics of U.S. policy, led by Soviet ideologues and U.S. "revisionist" historians, have portrayed the United States in an imperial role. This interpretation is fictitious, because the United States in most cases has been drawn into world responsibility only reluctantly and for the past five years has undergone a phase of voluntary withdrawal and retrenchment from international commitments unprecedented for so powerful a nation.

In fact, the domination of world events in the past 30 years by the United States resulted largely from its virtually unscarred position at the end of World War II. The era which can be dubbed the "American Age" of the twentieth century—leaving aside the delicate question of whether it is over—was marked by almost incidental accretions of U.S. influence in regions of the world which wanted assistance because the local leaders feared military domination or internal political subversion sponsored by the USSR or, later, by Communist China. The United States has exhibited little appetite for seizing and holding real imperial power.

Nevertheless, the United States was so powerful in the late 1940s and 1950s that it inspired fear and envy as well as admiration. The paranoia of the Stalinist regime almost inevitably clouded the Soviet view of U.S. intentions. Soviet leaders invariably said and quite possibly believed that the United States was bound by the "objective" Marxist-Leninist laws of political behavior to build an empire that would "encircle" the Soviet Union and try to destroy it.

This view, whatever Stalin and the old Bolsheviks may have thought, is a myth. The United States arrived at its powerful position almost entirely because of the vast mobilization of economic strength required to fight and win World War II, a conflict which the United States avoided unconscionably long after its interests were plainly at stake. It maintained its strength in good part out of concern over Soviet behavior in the immediate post-war time of troubles of 1946 and 1947—the time of the formulation of the Kennan theory of "containment" of Communist Russia, the enunciation of the Truman Doctrine, and the evolution of the Marshall Plan for the economic recovery of Europe.

The United States clearly demonstrated its anticipation of peace rather than war in the early post-war era by reducing U.S. armed forces from their level of more than 12 million men in 1945 to less than 2 million men in 1947. At that time, the United States had a complete and unequivocal monopoly on atomic weapons. While these were few in numbers, their destructive capacity was so enormous and had been so devastatingly demonstrated at Hiroshima and Nagasaki that U.S. military strength was unquestionably perceived as superior to that of any other nation. Yet no responsible thought was ever given to using this naked military power for outright national aggrandizement. The United States was preoccupied at the time with "bringing the boys home" and converting to a peacetime economy.

Gradually, in 1947 and later, U.S. leaders, rightly or wrongly, thought that the great danger of this period lay in the establishment of a permanent controlling influence in many foreign countries by Soviet-dominated Communist regimes. East Europe soon became a belt of nations ruled by one-party Communist dictatorships committed to cooperation with the policies of the Soviet Union. The economically devastated nations of West Europe were not secure against the same political evolution. Consequently, the United States under President Truman decided it was necessary to engage in diplomatic programs designed to stop unilateral moves by the Soviet Union to increase Soviet political control in the nation-states of East Europe, particularly Poland and Czechoslovakia, and to maintain or increase the influence of West Europe and the United States in Iran, Turkey, and Greece.

In the beginning, most U.S. citizens did not feel any serious fear of war, but they did worry that the political and economic conditions in West Europe would create a power vacuum tempting to the Soviet Union under Stalin. Increasingly the USSR came to be viewed as a threat to the security of West Europe because of active Soviet support of Communist Parties in East Europe.

In this situation, a deep impression was made by the forceful Communist coup in Czechoslovakia in February 1948, and the beginning of the Soviet blockade of Berlin on June 21 in that year. At the time of the crystallization of the containment policy, the United States felt fairly confident of its own position in the world. After all, the total economic activity in the United States (GNP) was 480 billion U.S. dollars (rounded, in 1973 dollars). In the same terms, the Soviet Union's GNP was approximately 150 billion (1973) U.S. dollars. This comfortable margin of superiority of more than three to one in gross measurement of economic strength supplied the United States with a surplus which enabled it to raise the standard of living of its own people rapidly—something the Soviet Union was quite unable to do—and at the same time to disperse its money in vast amounts to restore and stimulate economic production in West Europe and elsewhere. Here was a situation of strategic superiority based on economic strength which clearly could be used, and was used, to exercise U.S. influence in Europe in ways designed to prevent major aggrandizement by a large and increasingly hostile power, the USSR. At the same time, the humane instincts of the U.S. people were satisfied with respect to restoring civilized life in an area of the world from whose cultures most citizens of the United States had come.

The "Containment" Strategy

What was to become the classic text of U.S. strategic policy for many years was published in July 1947 as a magazine article by "Mr. X," who was George Kennan, then State Department policy planner for Secretary of State George C. Marshall. While it is very simply stated, most of the Kennan essay still provides a coherent rationale for U.S. international behavior from that time into the late 1960s.

The "Mr. X" article summed up the U.S. view of Stalin's USSR.[3]

> Stalin, and those whom he led in the struggle for succession to Lenin's position of leadership, were not the men to tolerate rival political forces in the sphere of power they coveted. Their sense of insecurity was too great.
>
> The men in the Kremlin have continued to be predominantly absorbed with the struggle to secure and make absolute the power which they seized in November 1917. They have endeavored to secure it primarily against forces at home, within society itself. But they have also endeavored to secure it against the outside world. For ideology, as we have seen, taught them that the outside world was hostile and that it was their duty eventually to overthrow the political forces beyond their borders.

Kennan noted that the "innate antagonism between capitalism and socialism" is a concept that led to

> . . . many of the phenomena which we find disturbing in the Kremlin's conduct of foreign policy: the secretiveness, the lack of frankness, the duplicity, the war suspiciousness, and the basic unfriendliness of purpose.

[3] George F. Kennan, "The Sources of Soviet Conduct," *Foreign Affairs*, XXV, No. 4 (July 1947).

Kennan recommended adoption of a U.S. "policy of firm containment, designed to confront the Russians with unalterable counter-force at every point where they show signs of encroaching upon the interests of a peaceful and stable world."

Finally Kennan made his famous estimate that

> The United States has it in its power to increase enormously the strains under which Soviet policy must operate, to force upon the Kremlin a far greater degree of moderation and circumspection than it has had to observe in recent years, and in this way to promote tendencies which must eventually find their outlet in either the break-up or the gradual mellowing of Soviet power.

The leaders in the Kremlin after Stalin turned out to be precisely those men who were Stalin's colleagues at the time of which "Mr. X" was writing. They continued in absolute power in the Party Politburo, jostling one another for relative position in the group, co-opting a few new members as old ones died or were discarded. They remained secretive, suspicious, and hostile toward the outside world. The last of this group is only now in 1975 reaching the age of retirement from the seats of power they fought so hard to hold. The big five of the Politburo, Brezhnev, Kosygin, Podgorny, Suslov, and Kirilenko, are all from 68 to 72 years old. Their ideology never changed except in the direction of less stress on the inevitability of war and more stress on peaceful coexistence. As Khrushchev once rashly put it, there might not need to be a "frightful collision" between the two systems, but eventually the Communists would "bury" the capitalists. Brezhnev is shrewder and does not use words like "bury", but his regime still talks of the ultimate triumph of the Soviet system everywhere.

In the face of the collective Soviet personality described by Kennan, the United States adopted a firm strategy of containment. It was not difficult to enlist public support of a policy for opposing the expansion into Europe of left-wing totalitarianism in the same way the United States had so lately—and belatedly—fought against control of Europe by German right-wing totalitarianism.

Within this context, in my view the best succinct formulation of U.S. strategy and national purpose for the period 1947-1968 would be something along the following lines:

> The United States should protect the security of its people and society by preventing a potentially hostile nation from establishing either political or military control over the heartland of Eurasia, the entirety of the great central plains from the Rhine across the Urals and West Siberia.

A corollary of this strategic formulation is:

> Vigilance should be redoubled to prevent such a development if the hostile nation represents a totalitarian society with great military power at its command.

A second strategic corollary is:

> Expansion of the political or military power of such a hostile totalitarian

> nation anywhere in the world ought to be prevented because it undermines the sense of security and the unity of economic and political cooperation among the non-Communist countries which stand in the way of domination of the Eurasian heartland by a single power.

Most people in the United States who had lived through the 1930s and 1940s thought they had learned the need for early resistance to a dangerous aggressor because it had cost the world so much to let Manchuria be occupied by Japan, Ethiopia by Italy, and Austria and Czechoslovakia by Germany, prior to World War II. Allowing small nations to be toppled one by one by forces external to the nation had only made the ultimate showdown harder. For a long time, until the fall of South Vietnam, corollary number two was an integral part of U.S. strategy.

The "Free World" Alliance Strategy

This containment policy soon developed a positive or free world alliance content as its vital obverse side. The economic spread of Soviet influence could best be stopped in Europe by the economic rebuilding of Germany, Italy, France, and the other nations close to the USSR. It was perceived that West Europe had to be helped to become socially stable in order to resist internal subversion by Communist Party or other pro-Soviet organizations. Hence the Marshall Plan. In the military sphere, a parallel move set up the North Atlantic Treaty Organization to stiffen military defense of the area and relieve fears that the massive conventional Soviet armies in East Germany might suddenly roll toward the Rhine. In 1948 the decision was made to ask the Central Intelligence Agency to take covert political action to bolster center and non-Communist left parties against clandestine assaults by Soviet-financed left-wing factions in Italy and other nations of West Europe where parliamentary systems were still shaky. With this economic, military, and political support from the United States, the countries of West Europe began to stabilize and in time to prosper.

By 1950, after mainland China had been conquered by a Communist regime, had signed a treaty with the USSR, and had poured its armies into Korea, few in the United States doubted that a united Communist bloc of nations constituted a real and present danger to the safety of the non-Communist nations on both the Pacific and Atlantic flanks of Eurasia. Efforts to prop up non-Communist regimes around the entire periphery of the Sino-Soviet area were undertaken with varying degrees of success, but without any expansion of the area under Communist control in the 1950s.

Military and economic aid worked miracles eventually, especially in Germany and Japan and China/Taiwan. It was not unrealistic to speak of a non-Communist world—a Free World—tied together by interlocking U.S. alliances and by sea-lanes across the Atlantic, Pacific, and Indian Oceans. Naval power, airbases, and steadily expanding commerce provided the skeleton of contact and common interests for this Free World of the 1950s.

Containment in this era seemed to require a global trading network that strengthened every nation not already under a Communist regime, particularly all of those in the U.S. alliance system. U.S. aid strengthened and protected vast areas sheltering under the umbrella of U.S. commitments. It is hard to say whether fear of the USSR and mainland China held this loose association of nations together or whether the positive economic benefits of trade and aid were responsible. Almost certainly both aspects contributed to the cohesion of the U.S. alliance system. Containment and alliance building were two sides of the same coin of U.S. strategy in this era. The facing down of the USSR over the clandestine introduction of nuclear weapons into Cuba in 1962 marked the high point of U.S. power and prestige in pursuit of this strategy in this century.

Khrushchev was humiliated by being forced to withdraw Soviet missiles from the Western Hemisphere. On the other hand, the USSR gained a new member in the cluster of Communist states dominated by Moscow. The Monroe Doctrine became obsolete. The Kennedy era rhetoric, which sounds somewhat highflown today, captured a spirit of vigor, confidence, and ready response to all global challenges. The containment-Free World strategy enjoyed wide popular support in the United States during the early 1960s.

In his inaugural address, President Kennedy was widely cheered when he said that he represented

> . . . a new generation of Americans, born in this century, tempered by war, disciplined by a hard and bitter peace, proud of our ancient heritage, and unwilling to witness or permit the slow undoing of those human rights to which this nation has always been committed, and to which we are committed today at home and around the world.

In this context he went on to say:

> Let every nation know, whether it wishes us well or ill, that we shall pay any price, bear any burden, meet any hardship, support any friend, oppose any foe to assure the survival and success of liberty.
>
> Now the trumpet summons us again—not as a call to bear arms, though arms we need; not as a call to battle, though embattled we are; but a call to bear the burden of a long twilight struggle year in and year out, 'rejoicing in hope, patient in tribulation,' a struggle against the common enemies of man: tyranny, poverty, disease, and war itself.

This was the language of containment and commitment to the defense, economic freedom, and social well-being of the Free World. The ring of assurance was at the time not unjustified. U.S. superiority in economic strength and military capabilities was so clearcut that Kennedy did not hesitate in 1962 during the Cuban missile crisis to challenge the USSR to a crucial showdown. He said in his October 22 speech revealing the existence of the Soviet missiles in Cuba:

> It shall be the policy of this nation to regard any nuclear missile launched from Cuba against any nation in the Western Hemisphere as an attack by the Soviet Union on the United States, requiring a full retaliatory response upon the Soviet Union.

The existing balance of military power permitted this unequivocal extension of the nuclear umbrella. Since the United States also had a vast superiority in conventional armed forces in the Caribbean area, the USSR backed down. Most

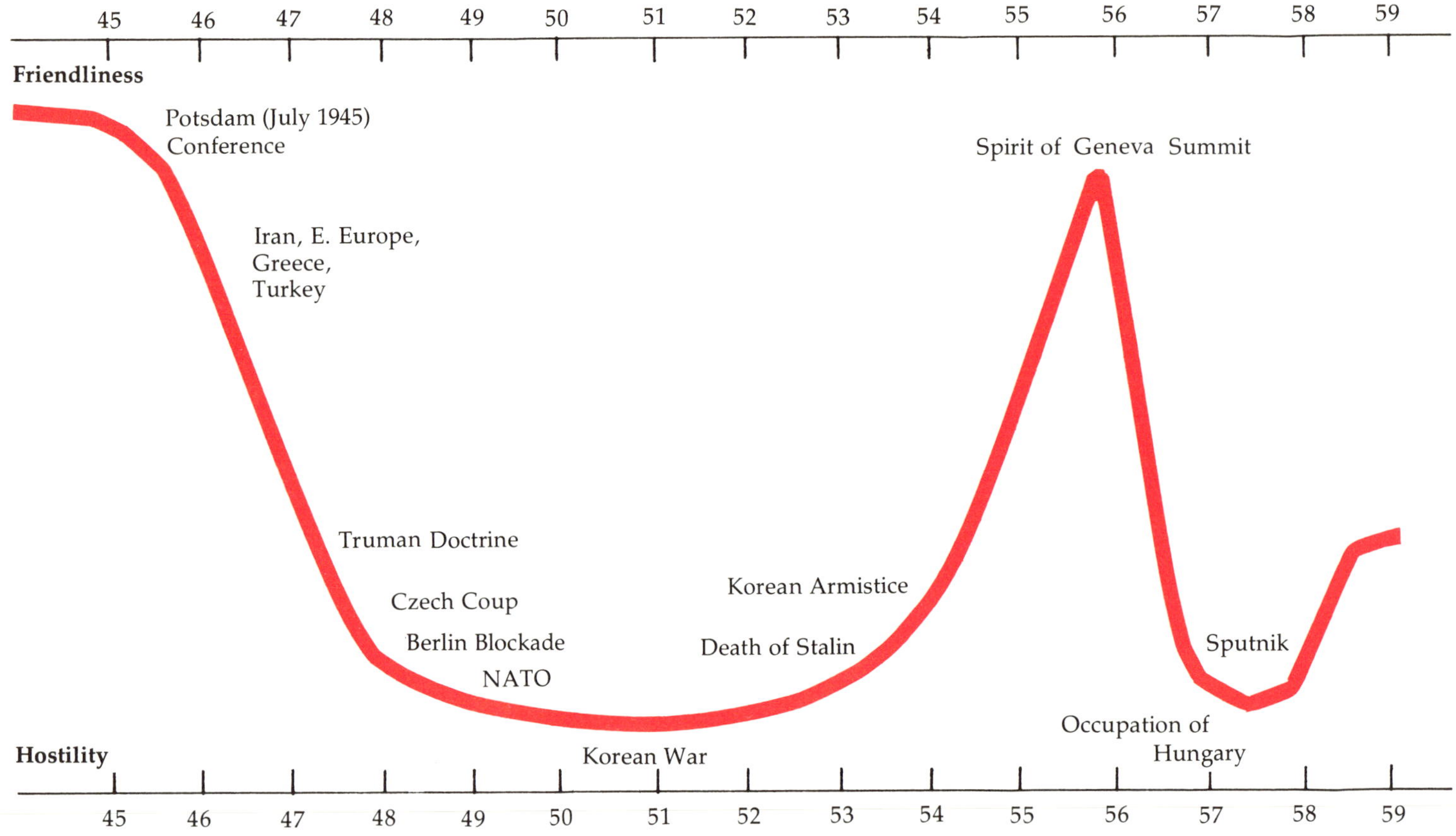

countries allied with the United States assumed this umbrella also covered them, although doubts about the total protection it afforded were soon to grow. A Soviet official returning from Cuba in 1962 said the USSR would never again face a showdown with the United States anywhere until military parity had been achieved. The Soviet Union set out immediately in its weapons-building program to achieve it.

The United States, despite the triumph of the Soviet missile withdrawal, paid a price by tacitly acquiescing in the establishment of an avowedly Communist, pro-Soviet, revolution-exporting regime in the Western Hemisphere. The Cuban missile crisis was a turning point in several ways. It was a strategic victory for the United States in the military sense, but a political loss in that the Soviets were able to extend their influence to a country only 90 miles from U.S. shores. It was also the starting point for a ten-year Soviet drive to reach military parity.

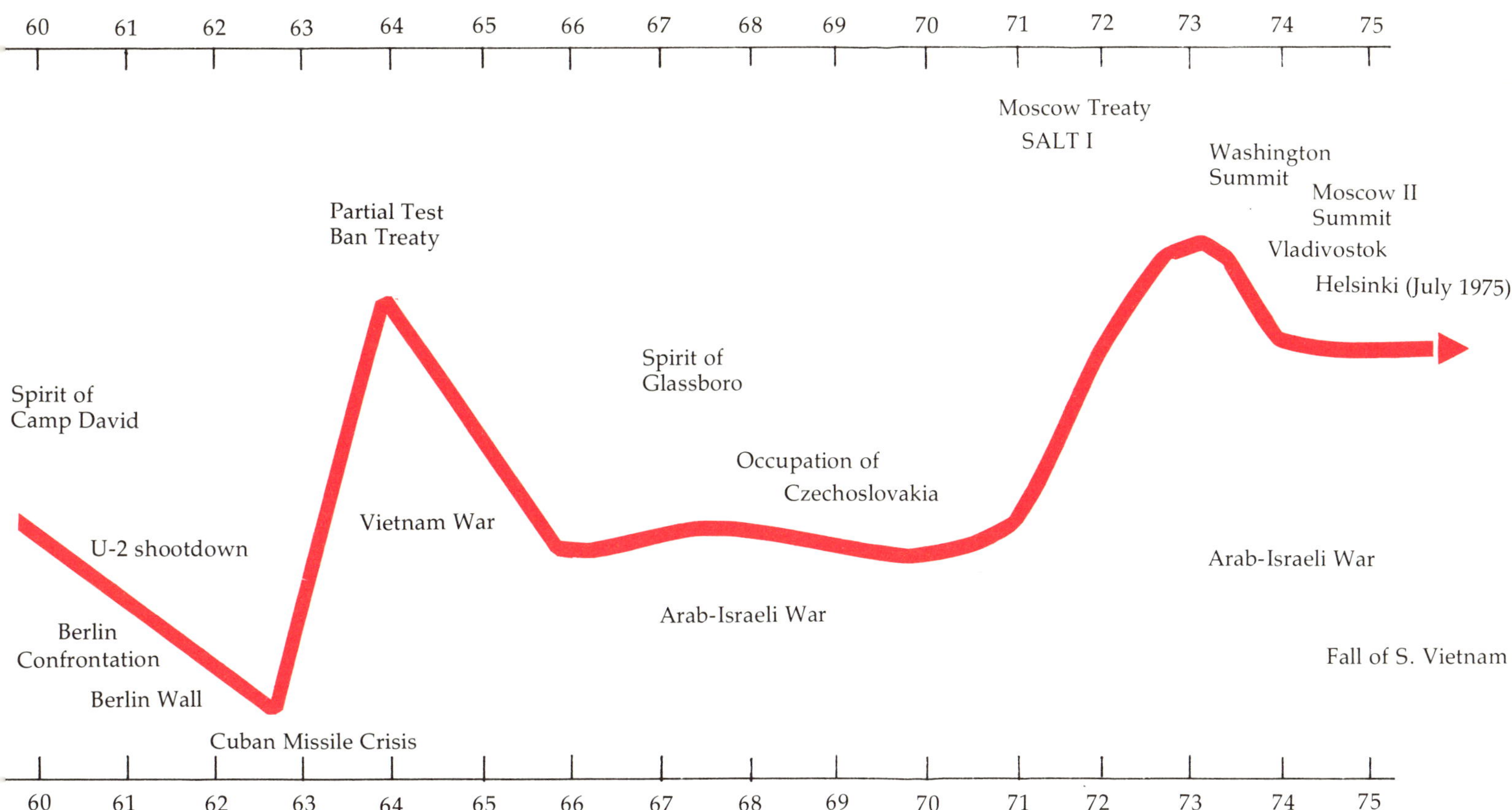

U.S.-Soviet Diplomatic Atmospherics

Pursuit of the Free World alliance strategy of containment brought relative security and prosperity to the United States for many years. For one thing, it made strong U.S. allies out of its World War II enemies, Germany and Japan. Throughout this period, however, attention focussed on the crucial bilateral U.S.-Soviet relationship, and the theatrics of this great power rivalry tended to obscure the real strategic competition, as well as the vital character of the U.S. alliance system. These atmospherics, which Moscow is able to turn on and off on short notice, are illustrated above.

The Cuban missile crisis of 1962 shocked and disturbed people almost as much as the occupation of Hungary and the Korean War. In its aftermath, however, there developed a brief relaxation of tension—relaxed because of Soviet recognition of the clear-cut strategic superiority of the United States and the demonstration that, in a serious confrontation, the government in Washington had the courage and skill to face down the Soviet Union with force. At the time it seemed in the United States a marvelous clearing of the air, and provided the opportunity for the greatest diplomatic breakthrough in U.S.-Soviet relations in the post-war era, the negotiation of the Partial Test-Ban Treaty of 1963 with the USSR.

This success in Cuba may later have given an impetus to the overcommitment of U.S. resources and the slow escalation of fighting in Vietnam. U.S. and Soviet policy-makers were soon caught up in the struggle for control of the Indochina peninsula. In 1965 and 1966, both great powers were supporting opponents in what looked like another "proxy war" of the Korean type but was in fact complicated by the cross-currents of Indochinese politics. It ended up with massive U.S. forces fighting with indifferent success an enormous guerrilla army directed from Hanoi and supported economically and logistically by both China and the USSR.

The hostility generated by the Vietnam situation was aggravated in some ways by the Arab-Israeli War of 1967. An attempt to re-establish an atmosphere of friendliness by the meeting of President Johnson and Prime Minister Kosygin gave only a brief respite—a shallow, insubstantial "Spirit of Glassboro" —punctuating the atmospheric trend.

Hostility soon reached another high point as a result of the Soviet decision to occupy Czechoslovakia in 1968 and prevent the "Prague Spring", with its enthusiasm for bringing forward the "human face" of Communism, from getting out of hand and compromising Soviet control in the most progressive and sophisticated of the East European nations.

Soviet strategic policy was thenceforth crystal clear, in accordance with the "Brezhnev doctrine" that the USSR would send military forces to police any country ruled by a Communist Party if Moscow foresaw a danger of the "restoration of the capitalist order". Brezhnev declared that a threat to "the cause of socialism" in any country was a "threat to the security of the socialist (i.e., Communist) community as a whole" and therefore became "no longer a problem for the people of that country but also a common problem, a concern for all socialist states". In other words, the USSR gave what seemed to be an iron-clad guarantee that there was no going back when any country adopted a Soviet-oriented Communist form of government. The guarantee certainly applies where Soviet armies are adjacent in East Europe; it is ambiguous with respect to the more remote communist states—Cuba and Yugoslavia.[4]

The Age of Detente, 1969-1975

Strangely, the occupation of Czechoslovakia and the Brezhnev security guarantee of the "socialist community" did not seem to generate the same indignation as the occupation of Hungary had more than a decade earlier, and, beginning in 1969, the hostility curve slowly began to descend in the wake of a determined Soviet campaign emphasizing peaceful coexistence and the relaxation of international tension—which gradually came to be called by the more ambiguous term detente. The waning of public support in the United States for the Vietnam War paralleled and partially caused U.S. adoption of detente as its foreign policy.

The latest phase of U.S.-Soviet relations has brought the diplomatic atmosphere in which these relations are conducted closer to the "Spirit of Geneva" than at any other time in the post-war period. This change was accomplished

[4] Comments and suggestions from Dimitri Simes, CSIS Senior Research Fellow, and Kenneth Myers, CSIS Director of European Studies, were of great assistance in preparing this section on the USSR.

principally through the deliberate policy of the Nixon Administration of endorsing the Soviet concept of peaceful coexistence. The strong U.S. expression of interest in restricting the further growth of costly strategic weapons systems, very congenial to Moscow, reinforced the new U.S. foreign policy trend.

The comparative harmony of 1972 and 1973 saw the Moscow Treaty and Moscow Summit Meeting, the conclusion of SALT I, and the Washington Summit in the summer of 1973. This harmony was widely acclaimed in the United States as leading to a "generation of peace" and closing out the Cold War forever.

The USSR, discovering that the people of the United States enjoyed the word detente very much, whatever it might mean, did everything possible to suggest to the outside world—as distinct from its own officials—that a new era was at hand quite different from the period of twenty-odd years when containment was the keynote of U.S. policy. The momentum toward improved relations was hard to maintain, however, because of very real continuing conflicts of interest between the USSR and the United States.

The most significant clash of recent years came in the Mideast when the Arab-Israeli War broke out in October 1973, with an attack by Egypt and Syria. Massive amounts of modern Soviet weapons were employed by the two Arab states and it became necessary for the United States to resupply Israel on a crash basis to insure its survival.

Nevertheless, the governments in both Moscow and Washington forged ahead in an effort to maintain that detente was a unique and valuable accomplishment of Nixon-Kissinger/Brezhnev collaboration and that it would persist in bringing the United States and the USSR closer together. In fact, it is hard to plot a curve of relationships between the USSR and the United States without turning it away from cooperation in the fall of 1973, on through 1974, and into 1975. Not the least of the difficulties in the way of amicable U.S.-Soviet relations was the preoccupation of the Nixon Administration with Watergate.

A somewhat ambivalent state of affairs, with protestations of good intentions coming from both capitals but with very little solid progress being made, set in during the summer of 1974 when the highly advertised Moscow II Summit Meeting and SALT II deliberations produced almost no results whatever. Perhaps a modest gain was registered as a result of an agreement on equivalence of numbers of strategic weapons (at very high levels) at President Ford's meeting with Brezhnev in Vladivostok, but this still has to be translated into concrete details and, in any case, leaves more strategic questions open than settled.

Continued tension, plus danger of war, in the Mideast have somewhat clouded the atmosphere of detente. So has the final collapse of the U.S. position in Vietnam in the face of a military assault spearheaded by Soviet tanks, artillery, and other military equipment. At this stage, it is impossible to tell whether the determination of the two governments to maintain the atmosphere of comparative cordiality will be able to dominate events despite crucial strategic conflicts of interest. The airy language of the odd assortment of agreements and undertakings on European security and economic cooperation signed in Helsinki at the end of July 1975 is too insubstantial to do more than keep the curve of hostility from moving farther downward.

The Nixon-Kissinger Strategy

In the beginning the Nixon-Kissinger approach toward improving relations with the Soviet Union was quite cautious. When the President and his entourage travelled to Europe shortly after taking office in 1969, they explained to our major West European allies that they were uncertain how successful they would be in starting an "era of negotiation" which would result in a relaxation of tension. The U.S. position was quite plainly based on the proposition that our national strength was so great that we could comfortably deal with the USSR and try to win it over to a policy of non-confrontation and hence relaxed tension. The payoff for the United States was thought to be reduced needs for armaments and possibly cooperation from Moscow in ending the Vietnam War with some kind of compromise solution. Out of these cautious statements later came much less equivocal claims of the positive advantages of the improved relationship which gradually came to be summed up in a loose way as detente.

After the spectacular Nixon trip to Peking in February 1972, Nixon and Kissinger became intent on creating a "linkage" of detente with both the USSR and China upon achieving a Vietnam peace settlement. Unhappily in 1972 and 1973 the rational underpinnings of the negotiations changed into an increasingly euphoric interpretation of detente which extolled Soviet-U.S. summitry and those broad treaty commitments alleged to have created the framework for a "generation of peace". This loose language oversimplified and oversold detente. U.S. views tended to narrow down to a singular emphasis on the one word "peace" which figured in both Soviet and U.S. characterizations of detente. With Kissinger's endless travels in the news, U.S. foreign policy turned into something of a spectator sport on the part of the U.S. public. It is small wonder the thread of U.S. strategic thinking was lost.

When hostilities broke out in the Mideast in October 1973, some observers questioned the compatibility of Soviet behavior in massively arming the Arabs to attack the Israelis with linkage and detente. This implicit criticism of Soviet behavior motivated Kissinger, by this time Secretary of State as well as Assistant to the President for National Security Affairs, to restate some of his views on detente on December 27, 1973.

Recognizing that considerable international conflict and hostility had been taking place despite the detente, Kissinger commented specifically on the Mideast War, albeit only in answer to a question. He said:

> There are two schools of thought about Soviet objectives in the Middle East. One school of thought is that the Soviet Union has an interest in maintaining the tension because that will guarantee permanent Arab hostility to the United States, and enhances the possibilities of Soviet influence. The other school of thought is that while this may have started out to be the Soviet policy in the 1950s there have been since then three wars which have consumed a great deal of Soviet resources and whose outcome has been inconclusive. It has been demonstrated that the conflict in the Middle East can bring the superpowers into positions of potential confrontation. And it is therefore at least possible that the Soviet Union now has an interest in contributing to the stabilization of the situation in an area which neither superpower can really control by itself.

As far as the United States is concerned we will deal with the Soviet Union as long as its actions are consistent with the second interpretation.[5]

Very little has been said in Washington since about the first interpretation. The second interpretation, if looked at worldwide rather than merely in the Mideast, is the essence of the Nixon-Kissinger detente strategy.

Later on, President Nixon—under heavy domestic political criticism—became more extravagant in his claims that the personal relationships established between the President and his Secretary of State with the principal leaders in the Kremlin were indispensable to world peace. While Kissinger was usually more cautious in his formulations, he tended at that time to sound terribly sanguine. For example, after the sterile Moscow II Summit Meeting in 1974, Secretary Kissinger explained:

> Two nations capable of destroying humanity . . . have a special obligation to prevent conflicts caused by inadvertence, by miscalculation, by misassessment of each other's motives, with examples of which history is replete.

Kissinger said the purpose of detente and the many diplomatic arrangements with the USSR was to

> . . . construct a network of positive relationships that will provide an incentive for moderation and for a beneficial and humane conduct of foreign policy . . .
>
> The . . . goal is to identify those areas of common interest, either produced by the non-military aspects of technology or by others, or by the nature of modern life in which the Soviet Union and the United States can cooperate and thereby create a perspective on world affairs that recognizes the interdependence of events and the fact that isolation and confrontation are, over a period of time, inimical to progress and inconsistent with human aspirations.[6]

The line of reasoning which holds out hope that continued discussion with the USSR will bring about reorientation of Soviet thinking away from conflict and toward cooperation is an entirely legitimate hope. It is not a certainty. It became less promising as tension in the Mideast continued, as a squabble over the right of Soviet citizens to emigrate prevented trade expansion between the USSR and the United States, and as the Vietnam peace treaty collapsed in a total victory for Hanoi.

After the USSR had moved in 1974 to re-arm Syria massively and give generous support to the Palestine Liberation Organization, the hope of linkage and a reduction of tension seemed more and more remote. The architecture of detente and its overselling to the U.S. public and to U.S. allies came under increasing criticism. It has been suggested in Washington that for the United States detente is a policy of placating enemies by alienating allies.

[5] Henry A. Kissinger, Bureau of Public Affairs, Department of State news release, December 27, 1973, p. 6.

[6] Henry A. Kissinger, Bureau of Public Affairs, DOS news release, July 3, 1974, p. 1.

The Ford Administration has undertaken a partial return to some of the strategic concepts of earlier years, stressing U.S. alliances and refusing to cut defense expenditures on the basis of hopes about the fruits of detente. The climate of detente lingers on, however, and Kissinger is still defending its benefits, no matter how limited, by saying there is no alternative except nuclear war. Of course there is an alternative, and that is the kind of continuous political and economic conflict of lower intensity visualized by the USSR as the essence of peaceful coexistence. In view of these ambiguities, it is not surprising that the present confusion of Congress, the people, and the opinion-makers has never been so great since the isolation-intervention debates just before Pearl Harbor.

Since there has been so little clarification of national strategy and since the Watergate political tragedy taught the U.S. public to be suspicious of authoritative leadership, there existed no consensus in mid-1975 as to what the goals of U.S. relations with the USSR and China, or of U.S. alliance commitments, should be. It was not clear what the United States stood for and would fight for. Strategically, the United States was drifting.

The Strategic Concepts of Communist China (PRC)

Both U.S. and Soviet strategic planners must, whether they like it or not, fit the Chinese puzzle into their thinking. The existence of the People's Republic of China complicates every calculation in Moscow and Washington. In terms of the foregoing elements of national power, Mao Tse-tung's China is not an equal of the United States or the Soviet Union. As a nuclear military threat it is more in a league with France and the United Kingdom. Nevertheless, the tradition of China as the Celestial Central Kingdom lingers on in the thinking of Mao and his colleagues. Communist China considers itself the ultimate central kingdom of world communist states, and as such, the greatest power on earth. The Oriental time frame is long and Chinese patience and endurance are great. Still, within its limited capacities, Peking acts even now as the main strategic antagonist of the USSR and the United States. Communist China's global strategy must be understood if we are to assess perceptions of the world balance of power accurately.

As in the case of the USSR, there are serious doubts as to how and when Communist China will be able to reach the ambitious goals it has set for itself. Tactical caution and restraint are often dominant in Peking's policy, but the ultimate aim of the Chinese Communist Party is clear. Mao himself has pronounced the word and it is taught throughout China as infallible wisdom—what they call "Mao Tse-tung thought". The Chinese claim that Mao has made a crucial contribution to modern Communist doctrine and that the USSR under Khrushchev and Brezhnev is no longer a true communist state but is instead a "social imperialist" society as bad as, or worse than, the United States, the archetype of capitalist imperialism. This charge has made present-day China anathema to Soviet Communist Party leaders, who compare Mao to Stalin in his most savage days and counter-charge that Mao's China does not properly belong to the communist camp at all but instead has turned into a nationalist military dictatorship.

The crucial elements of Mao Tse-tung thought were collected in the famous "little red book" which was issued by the now discredited Lin Piao, intended successor to Mao, at the beginning of the cultural revolution of 1966-1968. While Lin has fallen from grace and the "little red book" has been withdrawn from circulation, for a time it was waved by millions of "Red Guard" revolutionaries and recited by rote at countless meetings as the revealed truth for China and the world. Its doctrine is still valid because it is vintage Mao served up in convenient capsule form, and as long as Mao lives he remains an idol virtually deified by the Party.

The crucial concepts of Mao Tse-tung thought on class conflict and war are similar to those of Lenin and Stalin, both of whom Mao retains in the Communist pantheon:[7]

> Classes struggle, some classes triumph, others are eliminated. Such is history, such is the history of civilization for thousands of years. (1949)
>
> The enemy will not perish of himself. Neither the Chinese reactionaries nor the aggressive forces of U.S. imperialism in China will step down from the stage of history of their own accord. (1948)
>
> A revolution is not a dinner party, or writing an essay, or painting a picture, or doing embroidery; it cannot be so refined, so leisurely and gentle, so temperate, kind, courteous, restrained and magnanimous. A revolution is an insurrection, an act of violence by which one class overthrows another. (1927)
>
> When politics develops to a certain stage beyond which it cannot proceed by the usual means, war breaks out to sweep the obstacles from the way . . . When the obstacle is removed and our political aim attained, the war will stop.
>
> But if the obstacle is not completely swept away, the war will have to continue until the aim is fully accomplished . . . . It can therefore be said that politics is war without bloodshed. (1938)
>
> Every Communist must grasp the truth, 'political power grows out of the barrel of a gun'. (1938)
>
> The seizure of power by armed force, the settlement of the issue by war, is the central task and the highest form of revolution. This Marxist-Leninist principle of revolution holds good universally, for China and for all other countries. (1938)

Mao's views on the United States prior to the diplomatic about-face which led him to accept detente and to welcome Nixon in Peking were extremely hostile:

> Riding rough-shod everywhere, U.S. imperialism has made itself the enemy of the people of the world and has increasingly isolated itself . . . . The raging tide of the people of the world against the U.S. aggressors is irresistible. (1964)

[7] These quotations are from Mao's works found in *Quotations from Chairman Mao Tse-tung,* Foreign Languages Press, Peking, 1966 (First Edition).

If the U.S. monopoly capitalist groups persist in pushing their policies of aggression and war, the day is bound to come when they will be hanged by the people of the whole world. The same fate awaits the accomplices of the United States. (1958)

It is my opinion that the international situation has now reached a new turning point. There are two winds in the world today, the east wind and the west wind. There is a Chinese saying, 'Either the east wind prevails over the west wind or the west wind prevails over the east wind.' I believe it is characteristic of the situation today that the east wind is prevailing over the west wind. That is to say, the forces of Socialism have become overwhelmingly superior to the forces of imperialism. (Moscow, 1957)

Mao's rhetoric about U.S. imperialists was incendiary at the time of the Korean War, as might be expected, and it had not fundamentally changed ten years later:

However many years U.S. imperialism wants to fight we are ready to fight up to the moment when it is willing to stop, right up to the moment of complete victory for the Chinese and Korean people. (February 1953)

People of the world, unite and defeat the U.S. aggressors and all their running dogs! People of the world, be courageous, dare to fight, defy difficulties and advance wave upon wave, then the whole world will belong to the people. Monsters of all kinds shall be destroyed. (1964)

The Chinese were still painting over wall slogans about "U.S. aggressors and all their running dogs" when Nixon arrived in Peking in 1972.

Probably the most romantic and yet authentic Maoist explanation of the long-term strategy of Communist China since it has consolidated its power position was given by Lin Piao when he was Defense Minister and aspirant for the position of heir-apparent. In 1965 he made a policy statement called "Strategy and Tactics of a People's War," which was published in the Peking newspaper *Renmin Ribao* on September 3, 1965.[8] Some of the passages require a great deal of explication to be understood and, of course, relate very directly to the internal argument in China at the time about the proper reaction to U.S. intervention in the Vietnam War. Needless to say, the upshot of the policy debate was to support the Vietnamese but not to become directly involved in a conflict with the United States. After a long preamble discussing the twenty-year period since the victory of the Chinese "People's War of Resistance" against Japan, Lin Piao took up the international significance of Mao's thinking:

The Chinese revolution and the October Revolution have in common the following basic characteristics: Both were led by the working class with a Marxist-Leninist Party as its nucleus . . . . In both cases state power was seized through violent revolution and the dictatorship of the proletariat was established. . . . Both were component parts of the proletarian world revolution.

Comrade Mao Tse-tung's theory of People's War solves not only the problem of daring to fight a people's war, but also that of how to wage it.

[8] Reprinted in full in Martin Ebon, *Lin Piao*, (New York: Stein and Day, 1970), pp. 197-243.

> It must be emphasized that Comrade Mao Tse-tung's theory of the establishment of rural revolutionary base areas and the encirclement of the cities from the countryside is of outstanding and universal practical importance for the present revolutionary struggles of all the oppressed nations and peoples, and particularly for the revolutionary struggles of the oppressed nations and peoples in Asia, Africa, and Latin America against imperialism and its lackeys.

Mao's disciple then laid out that extraordinary vision of Chinese leadership of the Third World against the industrial superpowers which seems to be the ultimate goal of the Mao generation of Chinese Communist leaders:

> Taking the entire globe, if North America and Western Europe can be called 'the cities of the world', then Asia, Africa, and Latin America constitute 'the rural areas of the world'. Since World War II, the proletarian revolutionary movement has for various reasons been temporarily held back in the North American and West Europe capitalist countries, while the people's revolutionary movement in Asia, Africa, and Latin America has been growing vigorously. In a sense the contemporary world revolution also presents a picture of the encirclement of cities by the rural areas. In the final analysis, the whole cause of world revolution hinges on the revolutionary struggles of the Asian, African, and Latin American peoples who make up the overwhelming majority of the world's population. The Socialist countries should regard it as their internationalist duty to support the people's revolutionary struggles in Asia, Africa, and Latin America.
>
> History has proved and will go on proving that people's war is the most effective weapon against U.S. imperialism and its lackeys. All revolutionary people will learn to wage people's war against U.S. imperialism and its lackeys. They will take up arms, learn to fight battles, and become skilled in waging people's war, though they have not done so before. U.S. imperialism, like a mad bull dashing from place to place, will finally be burned to ashes in the blazing fires of the people's wars it has provoked by its own actions.

This vision, no longer publicized in the era of detente, appears to explain the efforts which Peking has made to place itself at the head of the states representing the populous, poor, and colored peoples of the world since the United States acquiesced in the entry of the People's Republic into the United Nations.

It is not that Peking expects these dreams to materialize immediately but that it wants to make the Chinese Communist Party the wave of the future, displacing present-day Soviet Communism as a model for revolution and gradually tightening the strategic encirclement of both the United States and the USSR.

Chinese strategy began to change in one respect in the 1960s, as a result of the Sino-Soviet split. This bitter antagonism between the two ideological rivals is crucial in the power equation for the 1970s. It is not immutable although it stems from deep cultural and political antipathies.

Whether or not the rift will be papered over so that the two nations can cooperate in working against the interests of other states is one of the great imponderables of the post-Mao world. The competitive way in which Moscow and Peking approached the Vietnam War and yet gave Hanoi the military and economic support it needed, gives some disturbing evidence of the trend in the future. Nevertheless, as long as Mao lives and Moscow continues to revile him, the Sino-Soviet split divides much of Eurasia between these two hostile giants and the United States remains a lesser enemy, although still an enemy. This fact constituted the basis for Mao's and Chou En-lai's latter-day strategy of a limited accommodation with the United States and permitted Nixon and Kissinger to claim triumphs for detente on both sides of the world.

One premise of Chinese Communist strategic thinking must have done much to frighten Khrushchev and to begin the alienation of the Sino-Soviet leaders. In November 1957, less than a year before Peking launched an attack on the Quemoy and Matsu Islands in an effort to destroy the relatively tiny Chinese Nationalist government residing in Taiwan, Mao, according to Khrushchev, startled Communist delegates at a conference in Moscow by declaring:[9]

> We shouldn't fear war. We shouldn't be afraid of atomic bombs and missiles. No matter what kind of war breaks out—conventional or thermo-nuclear—we'll win. As for China, if the imperialists unleash war on us, we may lose more than 300 million people. So what? War is war. The years will pass, and we'll get to work producing more babies than ever before.

Khrushchev was not so dull-witted as to miss the point that there might not be any Russians left to reproduce after such a war. He refused to be of direct assistance during the Quemoy crisis of 1958, when Peking failed in its goals. He was not reassured by Mao's suggestion in 1958 that the USSR start a war of its own. Mao said, again according to Khrushchev, "All you have to do is provoke the Americans into military action, and I'll give you as many divisions as you need to crush them—a hundred, two hundred, one thousand divisions."[10]

By 1960 the USSR and China had drawn apart, to become ideological rivals and strategic adversaries. By 1970 territorial disputes and actual clashes along the 4,500-mile Sino-Soviet border had made Peking more frightened of Moscow than of Washington, which was signalling its intentions of withdrawing from South Vietnam. By 1971 Chou En-lai agreed with Kissinger to play the detente game and smooth over Sino-U.S. strategic conflicts so that Nixon could stage his visit to Peking.

Since 1972 Communist China has attempted to stand between the two superpowers, playing them off against each other while trying to solve its own difficult problems of economic growth and of orderly political succession to the elderly, failing Mao Tse-tung. Because this temporizing phase fitted in with the Nixon-Kissinger detente phase of U.S. policy, things have until now gone smoothly for Peking.

Chou En-lai, the public apologist for accommodation with the United States in this period, has made it very clear that China still considers the United States

[9] Strobe Talbott, ed., *Khrushchev Remembers* (Boston: Little, Brown, 1974), p. 255.

[10] *Ibid.*

an enemy—merely a less dangerous one than the USSR. On March 24, 1974, Chou gave a speech in Peking establishing the strategic line his colleagues are following to this day:

> Friends and comrades, at present the international situation is characterized by universal great disorder. It is developing in a direction ever more favourable to the peoples of the world and unfavourable to imperialism and reaction, particularly to the two superpowers which are contending with each other in a vain attempt to seize world hegemony. One of the superpowers, beset with troubles both at home and abroad, is having a hard time. The other superpower entertains wild ambitions but lacks the strength to achieve them; it reaches out in all directions but runs up against the wall everywhere; it is in a dire predicament. The two superpowers at times talk about detente, but in actuality they are engaged in an intense rivalry.
>
> At present, the struggle of the Third World countries and peoples to safeguard or win national independence and oppose the power politics and hegemonism of the superpowers, and the struggle of the masses of people in the capitalist countries against monopoly capital's exploitation and shifting of the burdens of economic crises onto them are supporting each other and developing in depth and breadth, which presents an excellent revolutionary scene of 'the wind sweeping through the tower heralding a rising storm in the mountains.'

These cheerful Chinese sentiments about the future are repeated over and over, with only minor variations in terminology, by all of Mao's and Chou's senior colleagues. Vice-Premier Teng Hsiao-ping said at banquets for African visitors in the spring of 1975:

> Like a torrential tide the anti-imperalist, anti-colonialist, and anti-hegemonic struggle of which the Third World is the main force is pounding away at the old world.
>
> Imperialism of all descriptions will inevitably be buried once and for all. (March 1975)
>
> Whether war gives rise to revolution or revolution prevents war, in either case the future of the world will be bright. (February 1975)

This "bright" future was linked specifically to Third World economic resources by Vice-Premier Li Hsien-ning in a speech made in April 1975:

> The international situation characterized by great disorders under heaven is continuing to develop in a direction favorable to the people. Countries want independence, nations want liberation and the people want revolution. This tide of struggle is surging forward irresistibly and pounding away at colonialism, imperialism, and big power hegemonism. The Third World countries are uniting ever more closely and playing an increasingly important role in international affairs . . . The Third World countries are winning great victories in their struggle to protect national resources and oppose superpower plunder and exploitation.

In recent months Peking has tried further to isolate the United States and the USSR by urging other industrial states (Japan and the West European countries) to join China and the Third World in opposition to both superpowers. The opportunity to publicize this message on a global basis was part of the price paid to Peking at the time of the People's Republic of China's admission into the UN, in exchange for Mao's acceptance of peaceful coexistence with the United States. West Europeans, skeptical about the support they will receive from the United States if the "great disorders under heaven" get worse, joke about optimists learning Russian while pessimists are learning Chinese.

If the power position of Mao's China were equivalent in economic strength and modern weapons-technology with its self-esteem and ambition, Peking would have greater effect with this heavy class-war revolutionary rhetoric. Since the power base is weak and Communist China will do well to feed its burgeoning population during the next 10 or 20 years, China must be perceived as having a clear national strategy but one that presently functions more in the realm of propaganda than of action outside the regional Asian context. Moreover, uncertainty about the succession to Mao and Chou, both of whom are aged and frail, leaves quasi-independent military leaders, practical managerial bureaucrats, and visionary Maoist revolutionary ideologues to work out a political *modus vivendi.* Strategy could move in almost any direction when Mao dies. At present, then, China has the strategic concepts and political ambition of a great global power, but it does not yet have a unified national will to support its long-range revolutionary goals.

The Rest of the World

It is a reflection on the way global power is perceived in this era that we can turn from the three nations with pretensions to a broad, world-encompassing strategy to observe that the other 149 independent nations and more than two and one-half billion people are pursuing regional strategies and trying to manipulate to advantage one way or another relationships with the USSR, the United States, and China (PRC). This psychological-political phenomenon complicates the life of policymakers in Moscow, Washington, and Peking and makes international forces extremely fluid. The balance of power is changing from a period of U.S. dominance and is unstable. A few sudden key shifts could cause a movement of politectonic power clusters from one zone of influence to another. In these concluding paragraphs on national strategy and will we deal first with the 27 nations on our high priority ranklist. (See page 90.)

In North America the two large neighbors of the United States have enjoyed reasonably close relations with Washington, but this is less true now than in the day of clearer articulation of U.S. strategy. Both Canada and Mexico at present strongly stress independence from the United States despite geographically-determined economic and military interdependence. This strategic inconsistency requires a reduction in the coefficient for this factor. On the other hand both countries have fairly stable and efficient political systems. In a reading of national will we should assess the normal rating. Thus the increment to power of North America is close to what is implied by the size and economic strength of the two nations. Their military power is limited because they do not feel the need to invest large percentages of GNP in defense while they remain under the U.S. military deterrent shield.

In East Europe, Poland and East Germany are subject to the political discipline of police states occupied by massive Soviet armies. Because they are required to follow Soviet strategy without question and because public consent does not play a large part in decision-making, the power of these states is enhanced by a comparatively high coefficient for strategy. The national will is somewhat reduced, however, because the people in countries that are virtually occupied states most often lend fairly lethargic support to Soviet goals.

West Europe is not a unity in any true strategic sense, although each nation in NATO feels some lack of coherent national strategy as a result of reduced clarity in strategic leadership by the United States. The national will in these countries varies according to the domestic political situation. Both Spain and Yugoslavia are unique, with reasonably clear strategies (to stay close to the United States in the case of the former and to stay non-aligned and independent in the case of the latter). In both of these nations, the domestic political situation is sufficiently unsettled to raise grave doubts about a future political consensus.

In the remaining rimlands of Eurasia, the key countries from Egypt and Turkey around to Japan are all uncertain about their strategic future and about the degree of political consensus in their conduct of foreign affairs.

Finally, the outer circle of states geographically more remote from the great-power conflicts is taking advantage of this distance to pursue almost exclusively regional policies. These states differ in their clarity of strategic purpose and internal political structure. Brazil, Nigeria, and Australia are dynamic economically and psychologically, but are largely regional in their strategic and political ambitions in this decade. South Africa and Argentina have such serious domestic, social, and political problems that they are on the defensive internationally.

Final Ratings of Major Nations

Judgments about this final factor in the formula we have been using are bound to be entirely qualitative, rather than precise and quantitative. It would be unproductive to describe and defend in detail the coefficients assigned.[11]

Prudence suggests that no attempt be made to rate most of the less powerful nations of the world for national strategy and national will. A few exceptions, however, are rather compelling. Some smaller powers with strong governments, whether democratic or totalitarian, and clear national goals, must be rated and ranked anew so they can be added to the 27 most powerful nations already described. Some, like Rumania, Cuba, Israel, Singapore, and New Zealand, are added because of special strategic significance accruing to their geo-

[11] If this approach to rating individual nations for national strategy and will seems Olympian or magisterial, the only defense is to point out that it is impractical within the confines of this book to give each country the close political and sociological analysis it deserves. Therefore the coefficients listed below reflect only the author's personal evaluation based on long experience and extensive research in the field of foreign affairs. This is plainly a game that any number can play; if readers disagree with the coefficient assigned, they can substitute their own and adjust the arithmetic or the reasoning reflected in the concluding chapter. If the conceptual framework is valid, all reasonable men can write their own conclusions.

graphic locations. Rumania is on the edge of the Soviet-dominated zone, maneuvering for independence; Cuba is in the U.S. zone of influence but presently committed to the USSR. Israel is virtually a U.S. outpost in a dangerous sea of Mideast states. Singapore is a key commercial entrepôt and—with Indonesia—a co-custodian of the Malacca Straits. New Zealand is culturally and strategically tied to Australia and, to some extent, to the United States.

On this basis, 13 nations are ranked and added to the original 27 in the following table. This table gives final ratings for perceived power under our formula for 40 nations.

Strategy and Will:

Perceived Power for Major Nations

Zone	Country	Elements of Perceived Power	National Strategy	National Will	Total Coefficient	Total
I	United States	50	0.3	0.4	0.7	35.0
	Canada	20	0.3	0.6	0.9	18.0
	Mexico	11	0.5	0.4	0.9	9.9
II	USSR	45	0.8	0.7	1.5	67.5
	Poland	11	0.8	0.2	1.0	11.0
	East Germany (DRG)	10	0.8	0.2	1.0	10.0
III	China (PRC)	23	0.7	0.3	1.0	23.0
IV	West Germany (FRG)	18	0.7	0.8	1.5	27.0
	France	20	0.4	0.8	1.2	24.0
	United Kingdom	19	0.6	0.4	1.0	19.0
	Italy	15	0.5	0.3	0.8	12.0
	Netherlands	8	0.7	0.8	1.5	12.0
	Spain	10	0.6	0.2	0.8	8.0
	Yugoslavia	8	0.5	0.2	0.7	5.6
V	Iran	14	0.9	0.5	1.4	19.6
	Egypt	9	0.7	0.4	1.1	9.9
	Turkey	10	0.2	0.6	0.8	8.0
VI	India	16	0.5	0.3	0.8	12.8
	Pakistan	11	0.5	0.5	1.0	11.0
VII	Indonesia	12	0.5	0.5	1.0	12.0
VIII	Japan	17	0.5	0.5	1.0	17.0
	China/Taiwan	8	0.6	0.9	1.5	12.0
IX	Brazil	16	0.5	0.8	1.3	20.8
	Argentina	10	0.3	0.2	0.5	5.0
X	Nigeria	11	0.5	0.5	1.0	11.0
	South Africa	11	0.6	0.4	1.0	11.0
XI	Australia	12	0.4	0.7	1.1	13.2

EXCEPTIONAL CASES

II	Rumania	7	0.5	0.5	1.0	7.0
	Czechoslovakia	7	0.8	0.2	1.0	7.0
	Cuba	2	0.8	0.8	1.6	3.2
III	North Vietnam (with South Vietnam)	10	0.8	0.6	1.4	14.0
	North Korea	6	0.8	0.8	1.6	9.6
IV	Portugal	4	0.1	0.2	0.3	1.2
V	Saudi Arabia	7	0.6	0.8	1.4	9.8
	Israel	4	0.9	0.9	1.8	7.2
VII	Singapore	2	0.7	0.8	1.5	3.0
VIII	South Korea	7	0.8	0.5	1.3	9.1
IX	Venezuela	6	0.7	0.8	1.5	9.0
X	Zaire	6	0.5	0.5	1.0	6.0
XI	New Zealand	2	0.7	0.8	1.5	3.0

The striking fact that emerges from this table and from the entire method of analysis followed in this book is that national purpose and national will make a critical difference in the relative power of nations. A totalitarian system has many shortcomings and its suppression of individual freedom and initiative cripples the development of a high level of achievement within a society. Nevertheless, the fact that the USSR has a coherent strategy and a tightly controlled population multiplies the brute power it projects into the international arena. The high rating of 1.5 derives from the efficiency of Soviet decision-making and the discipline enforced on the Soviet people.

The Chinese system has some of the same advantages, but it lacks a truly coherent national policy at this juncture, despite its ambition, because Chinese leaders are jockeying for position in preparation for the succession to power after Mao's death. The nation is not yet unified in pursuit of its long-range strategy and hence its coefficient for national will is lower than that of the USSR.

Clarity of national purpose and coherence of disciplined political will also show up in the ratings of countries like West Germany, Iran, China/Taiwan, and Israel. Most of the coefficients for the nations rated can be derived fairly readily from their current history.

For the United States a low coefficient for strategy and will must be assigned as of mid-1975. The political malaise left as a legacy of Watergate, Vietnam, and the illusions of detente has yet to be dispelled. The debilitation of the National Security Council decision-making system under Nixon and the breakdown of Congressional-Presidential cooperation in strategic and international policy formulation are still grave handicaps.[12] Only President Ford's preferences for caution, candor, simplicity, and loyalty to alliances holds out hope that the United States will move in the right direction.

The best thing that can be said today is that U.S. political moods are volatile and its people are resilient. The United States is capable of formulating anew a reasonable strategic policy and building a consensus in support of it. If this occurs, U.S. power would again rise to high levels. National purpose and national will are the most critical factors in determining power. The tremendous power potential of a country like the United States can be fully achieved only when its political leadership is unified and crystal clear in explaining national security strategy and foreign policy. In these circumstances, as the highpoints of World War II and the late 1950s-early 1960s show, an open society with the support of the governed becomes virtually invincible.

[12] For damage done to the National Security Council and the failure to use fully the analytical and estimative capabilities of the Intelligence Community, see an article, ''Policy Without Intelligence,'' by the author of this book, in *Foreign Policy*, Number 17, Winter 1974-1975.

III: Politectonic Assessment

Final Assessment

$Pp = (C + E + M) \times (S + W)$

The calculations of perceived national power in accordance with our macrometric measurement formula are now complete, including subjective judgments about national strategies and national will. At this point it is possible to complete a final table showing 40 nations of high strategic priority in 1975. The table on the following page is arranged in order of politectonic zones, and within the zones in order of total weights of perceived power.

This table allows some useful insights into the distribution of international power. First, there are enough nations with clearcut strategic aims, and disciplined national support for those aims, to raise the total number of weighted units to a perceived power above the total based on size, economic strength, and military capability alone—that is, from 495 to 531.7.

Second, a loss of coherent strategic direction changes power totals drastically. Politectonic Zone I, North America, is approximately equal with Zone II, the Soviet bloc, in the more quantifiable forms of power, but the coefficient for strategy and national will reduces perceptions of U.S. and North American power while it multiplies perceptions of Soviet bloc power.

Third, by all calculations West Europe remains the politectonic zone with the highest total of perceived power. Even discounting non-aligned Communist Yugoslavia and politically endangered Portugal, this zone is still perceived as having more power than either North America or the USSR and East Europe when viewed as a unit. The leading individual states in West Europe still play primary roles in international affairs. There would be a drastic change in the world balance of power if West Europe drifted away from its strong historic ties to North America as these were set forth in the Atlantic Community concepts of the 1950s and 1960s.

Fourth, the control of vast oil supplies and political tensions in the Mideast make this politectonic zone the most potentially volcanic region in the world. The tremors of dislocations in this unstable area spread immediately all over the globe. They have special impact upon the industrial economies of Northeast Asia and West Europe. The present trend is toward division along a political

Perceived Power = (C + E + M) × (S + W)

Zone	Country		Elements of Perceived Power	Coefficient for National Strategy and Will	Total Weighted Units of Perceived Power	Politectonic Zone Totals
I	United States		50	0.7	35	
	Canada		20	0.9	18	
	Mexico		11	0.9	9.9	
		Subtotal	81			62.9
II	USSR		45	1.5	67.5	
	Poland		11	1.0	11	
	East Germany (DRG)		10	1.0	10	
	Czechoslovakia		7	1.0	7	
	Rumania		7	1.0	7	
	Cuba		2	1.6	3.2	
		Subtotal	82			105.7
III	China (PRC)		23	1.0	23	
	North Vietnam (Indochina) (with South Vietnam)		10	1.4	14	
	North Korea		6	1.6	9.6	
		Subtotal	39			46.6
IV	West Germany (FRG)		18	1.5	27	
	France		20	1.2	24	
	United Kingdom		19	1.0	19	
	Italy		15	0.8	12	
	Netherlands		8	1.5	12	
	Spain		10	0.8	8	
	Yugoslavia		8	0.7	5.6	
	Portugal		4	0.3	1.2	
		Subtotal	102			108.8
V	Iran		14	1.4	19.6	
	Egypt		9	1.1	9.9	
	Saudi Arabia		7	1.4	9.8	
	Turkey		10	0.8	8	
	Israel		4	1.8	7.2	
		Subtotal	44			54.5
VI	India		16	0.8	12.8	
	Pakistan		11	1.0	11	
		Subtotal	27			23.8
VII	Indonesia		12	1.0	12	
	Singapore		2	1.5	3	
		Subtotal	14			15
VIII	Japan		17	1.0	17	
	China/Taiwan		8	1.5	12	
	South Korea		7	1.3	9.1	
		Subtotal	32			38.1
IX	Brazil		16	1.3	20.8	
	Venezuela		6	1.5	9	
	Argentina		10	0.5	5	
		Subtotal	32			34.8
X	Nigeria		11	1.0	11	
	South Africa		11	1.0	11	
	Zaire		6	1.0	6	
		Subtotal	28			28
XI	Australia		12	1.1	13.2	
	New Zealand		2	1.5	3	
		Subtotal	14			16.2
		Totals	495		531.7	531.7

fault line with Iraq and Syria leaning toward the Soviet zone and most of the other states leaning toward the United States or West Europe.

Fifth, the militant communist regimes of East Asia are not yet formidable enough to challenge the superpowers effectively on a global front, but the perceived power of China, North Korea, and Vietnam is causing their Asian neighbors deep concern over their own security and independence. The romantic promises of revolutionary Maoist doctrine appeal to the young and underprivileged everywhere, causing present disorders motivated by dreams of the future.

Sixth, the clusters of power in all of the other peripheral Eurasian politectonic zones (South, Southeast, and Northeast Asia) are not strong enough to resist outside pressure from either the USSR or the Asian communist nations without substantial reliable political and economic support from the United States and West Europe. Without such help political instability in Asia is virtually inevitable.

Seventh, the outer circle zones (South America, Central and South Africa, and the Australia-New Zealand ocean area) are not yet powerful enough and are still geographically too remote to affect the world balance of power in the 1970s. Their present regional policies and their future strategic importance are important for longer-range U.S. policy planning, which should aim at persuading nations in these zones to support the independence of peripheral Eurasian nations from communist domination.

Eighth and finally, the power position of the United States as perceived in 1975 remains strong. With key alliances in other regions and with the survival of present international trade patterns, the United States with its existing alliance system is superior in potential power to any likely adversary or combination of adversaries. Yet the United States is having difficulty in maintaining this power position. There has been a failure of U.S. political leadership to lead in a clear national strategic direction. The people of the United States do not know for sure who our enemies are, what dangers to the United States they represent, or what is worth fighting for abroad. This situation has caused a loss of confidence among those nations dependent on U.S. security guarantees and the complex structure of U.S. overseas alliances is crumbling. The global balance of power is, in this context, at best in rough equilibrium, and dangerously unstable.

Clear and Present Danger

There is no need to dwell on the situations around the globe, touched on in our earlier analysis of national power, which so encourage the classical Marxist-Leninists in Moscow to believe that their concept of detente is correct and that a new crisis of capitalism is at hand. The same situations encourage Maoist thinkers to look forward in the distant future to crushing the U.S. and Soviet world cities with the aid of the revolutionary countryside.

The major industrial nations of the world other than the USSR and China have managed in the mid-1970s to arrive at the same time at a cyclical dip into inflation, unemployment, and reduced economic output and trade. The oil embargo and sudden price rise of 1973-1974 contributed substantially to this economic recession. Beyond that, the Mideast has remained a general focus of

Arab-Israeli tension and Soviet-U.S. diplomatic confrontation from which only the Soviet Union reaps benefit.

On the other side of the world, full-scale organized military hostilities brought North Vietnam victory and political domination over the non-communist states of Cambodia, South Vietnam, and Laos. Not only did local military aggression pay, it paid handsomely in the face of U.S. efforts to prevent it. Communist-dominated regimes have taken over control of these three states in the first successful communist territorial expansion in 25 years, apart from Cuba. Hanoi sees itself as the cutting edge of the communist future.

Finally, in Europe two NATO allies, Greece and Turkey, have threatened to leave the alliance because of a local Mediterranean conflict. Another NATO ally, Portugal, is in the hands of a revolutionary-minded military dictatorship and may become the first nation in Europe since Czechoslovakia, in 1948, to be taken over politically by a Communist party, in this instance without benefit of Soviet armed forces nearby.

The fall of South Vietnam is a major shift away from U.S. influence and economic access at the fractured edge of one of the politectonic zones. The shock waves have made a deep global impression. Perceptions of power have changed. This expulsion of U.S. power is the intended Chinese and North Vietnamese pattern for conflicts of the future.

If revolution or war brings a similar strategic movement away from the United States and its allies in the Mideast, a tremendous shift in politectonic structure would ensue. To put the matter simply, the USSR is engaged in a long-term effort to gain sufficient political influence over parts of the Mideast to endanger access by the international free market economies to its valuable economic resource, oil. Soviet leaders feel that they can create disorder in the area even without necessarily controlling it. Since Mideast oil is crucial to economic and socio-political stability in West Europe and Japan for the next decade, such a gain for the USSR would result in economic insecurity for the trading nations of the Northern Hemisphere. Such political and economic turmoil would entail a crucial shift in the "correlation of forces" and a fracturing of key politectonic zones. In the strategic tensions of the Mideast we see the preferred pattern Moscow envisages for confrontations under the conditions of detente.

It is essential, if the current unfavorable and unstable drift in the balance of power is to be avoided, that the nations allied at present by cultural, political, military, and economic links recognize that the trend of events in the world of detente is not altogether benign. They must be prepared to prevent or to hold their own in conflicts short of total nuclear war. Neither the USSR nor China intends to let the balance of power remain in its present rough equilibrium. Their efforts must be countered.

The so-called American Age of the post-World War II era may have had its shortcomings and its unrealistic idealism. The concept of U.S. responsibility for security and freedom in every part of the world is unviable. The containment-Free World strategy nevertheless offered to defend a non-totalitarian way of life that would be endangered if the world power balance shifts decisively to the

USSR or China, separately or collectively. It is hard to believe that the sense of self-preservation and self-interest of the people and leadership of the United States and its closest allies are so enfeebled as to permit further major gains by the great totalitarian regimes. Stopping the drift of the last few years in U.S. foreign policy is essential, however, if politectonic shifts are not to cause whole regions to slide away from the present alliance structure that makes U.S. security and economic prosperity possible.

U.S. Policy: An Analogue from History

Reasonable men will differ over what to do in these circumstances. How to restore U.S. foreign policy to vigor and coherence is something that only the whole people of this nation can accomplish by an increased understanding of trends in the world balance of power.

One idea worth thinking about is an old but still valid definition of a sound foreign policy. In a book written during World War II, Walter Lippmann laid down as a "fundamental principle" the need in foreign policy of "bringing into balance, with a comfortable surplus of power in reserve, the nation's commitments and the nation's power."

Lippmann went on to say that "the true statesman" must be sure that commitments concerning "ideals, interests, and ambitions which are to be asserted abroad" are covered or balanced by adequate support at home "combined with the support he can find abroad among other nations which have similar ideals, interests, and ambitions."[1]

If the United States is to balance its foreign policy commitments with its national power, alliances with overseas nations are crucial, as the analysis of the world balance of power in earlier chapters of this book indicates. Key strong nations in the whole politectonic structure must be preserved lest the crumbling of some destroy the foundations on which others rest.

Every man will have his own prescription for a redefined U.S. strategy that would win national support and permit the United States to conduct a foreign policy in pursuit of a favorable balance of world power. From my viewpoint, the most promising strategic blueprint of the 1970s and 1980s would be a limited system of core alliances formed or reconfirmed on a voluntary basis by strong nations strategically linked by common political, economic, and security interests with the United States. The model ought to be the Athenian League of the fifth century B.C. which defeated the onslaught of the armies sent by Persian tyrants to conquer Greece. The Athenian League's use of seapower and the voluntary fiscal contributions, as well as the ships and fighting men, of allied Greek city-states permitted the mobilization of military forces which were more dynamic and better led than those of the much more powerful absolute monarchy the Greeks were fighting.

For many years the Athenian League experienced a period of remarkable success in keeping peace and protecting commerce in the whole Eastern Mediterranean. The wellsprings of what we consider civilization stems from this

[1]Walter Lippmann, *U.S. Foreign Policy* (London: Hamish Hamilton, 1943).

era. Only later the states of the League fell to bickering among themselves over burden-sharing, and Athens attempted to use naked force against her own allies to hold them together rather than working out clear common policy purposes. In these circumstances the alliance fell into disrepair and its ill-conceived and badly managed military ventures eventually destroyed it, along with the fortunes of all the member states.

A New National Strategy

What is needed now in the aftermath of the American Age of the 1950s and 1960s is to reconstitute a pattern of key alliances—a kind of latter-day Athenian League—on the basis of informed common understanding of the problems ahead. Such a group must be strong enough to counter hostile moves by potential totalitarian adversaries. The aim of the United States should be to select and work closely with the main allies with whom we share interests and strategic aims. The ultimate goal is not imperial hegemony but a common dedication to insuring the safety and desired way of political and social life of these nations' respective citizens. To evoke the best and most realistic aspirations of the people in each society is the real role of national strategy.

Today what the United States needs is a consensus in support of a non-totalitarian alliance capable of maintaining an approximation of the present balance of world power. The right alliance at this time can stop unfavorable trends. It can only be a strictly voluntary association of a core group of friendly states, committed to a mutually beneficial cooperation with each other, in economic relations, in military burden-sharing, and in political planning. Its goals would embrace the essential purposes of the North Atlantic community, but its scope would be broader geographically and its functions not limited to military planning.

Other states should be viewed as potential associates of such a core group, and not as adversaries, unless they choose to be. The numerous nations of the Third World may join such an alliance if they accept the common strategy. Economic aid to all needy nations on a humanitarian basis ought to be one of the stabilizing policies of the alliance. It is unrealistic, however, to expect the less powerful nations to carry the burden or take the risks of major allies. Many political and social changes will disrupt the power potential of the hundred-odd weaker states. Not all of today's nations will survive, since local and tribal loyalties are strong and divisive in many regions. The leading nations, however, the core group, must stick together firmly in maintaining something close to the balance of power of the mid-1970s since all of them will otherwise suffer individual losses of security and influence adding up to an irreparable shift toward totalitarian domination.

The best name for such an association of independent nations might be "Oceans Alliance", in reference to the Atlantic and Pacific seaways which link these states. The many international associations in which the United States participates could continue as at present. The core group of nations in an Oceans Alliance structure would simply have to bind themselves to cultivate economic interdependence and cooperation in support of a common strategy.

Such a strategy is implicit in the situation described in preceding pages of this book and is closely related to the old strategy of the 1950s and 1960s. The new strategy might be formulated along these lines:

> The United States should protect the security of its people and society by maintaining an alliance system which will prevent a hostile totalitarian nation or combination of such nations from establishing political or military control over central Eurasia *plus* any substantial parts of the Eurasian peripheral rimlands.

To translate this strategy into the politectonic terminology employed in this book, this strategy would mean: the USSR and China could expect completely peaceful relations with the United States provided they did not try to dominate from their central (heartland) position in Eurasia any of the major countries identified as leading nations in the peripheral Zones IV through VIII, West Europe, North Africa and the Mideast, South Asia, Southeast Asia, and Northeast Asia. In the case of direct or indirect aggression against any of these major nations which voluntarily join an Oceans Alliance, the United States would render political, economic, logistic, and, if necessary, military assistance to the extent that circumstances required. Such commitments would have to be guaranteed by agreements or treaties approved by the U.S. Senate.

Existing U.S. alliance commitments would not necessarily be dropped if the President and the Congress could agree on a new affirmation of strategic purpose and invite the major nations to shoulder special responsibility in pursuit of this strategy. The NATO alliance could continue in being as an overlapping security system. Such members of NATO as Belgium, Greece, the Scandinavian countries, and Iceland, regardless of size and power, would be eligible to join the Oceans Alliance if they chose to adopt its purposes.

In any case, decisive leadership in the United States in pursuit of a clearly articulated goal of this kind could bring together an association of nations worthy of the description of a new Athenian League and capable of preventing the spread of Soviet or Chinese totalitarianism. It is clear that at this state of historical evolution it is not possible to "leave it to the UN" or to other existing international organizations to preserve a stable world order.[2] The United States must instead implement the purposes of the UN Charter—which are excellent as abstract goals—with the moral force, political purpose, and military power necessary to protect the way of life of the non-totalitarian regions of the world.

An Oceans Alliance

The first choices for membership in the core group of a new Oceans Alliance are bound to consist of the major states with common political and social processes, as well as shared goals and views about international dangers: the United States, Canada, the United Kingdom, West Germany (FRG), France, Italy, the Netherlands, Israel, Japan, China/Taiwan, Australia, and New Zealand. These 12 nations collectively possess about 40 percent of the perceived power of the entire 40 nations we have singled out (page 130) as being of highest international

[2] A majority vote in the UN can be carried by 70 states representing less than 5 percent of the population of the world and virtually none of the significant power and international responsibility.

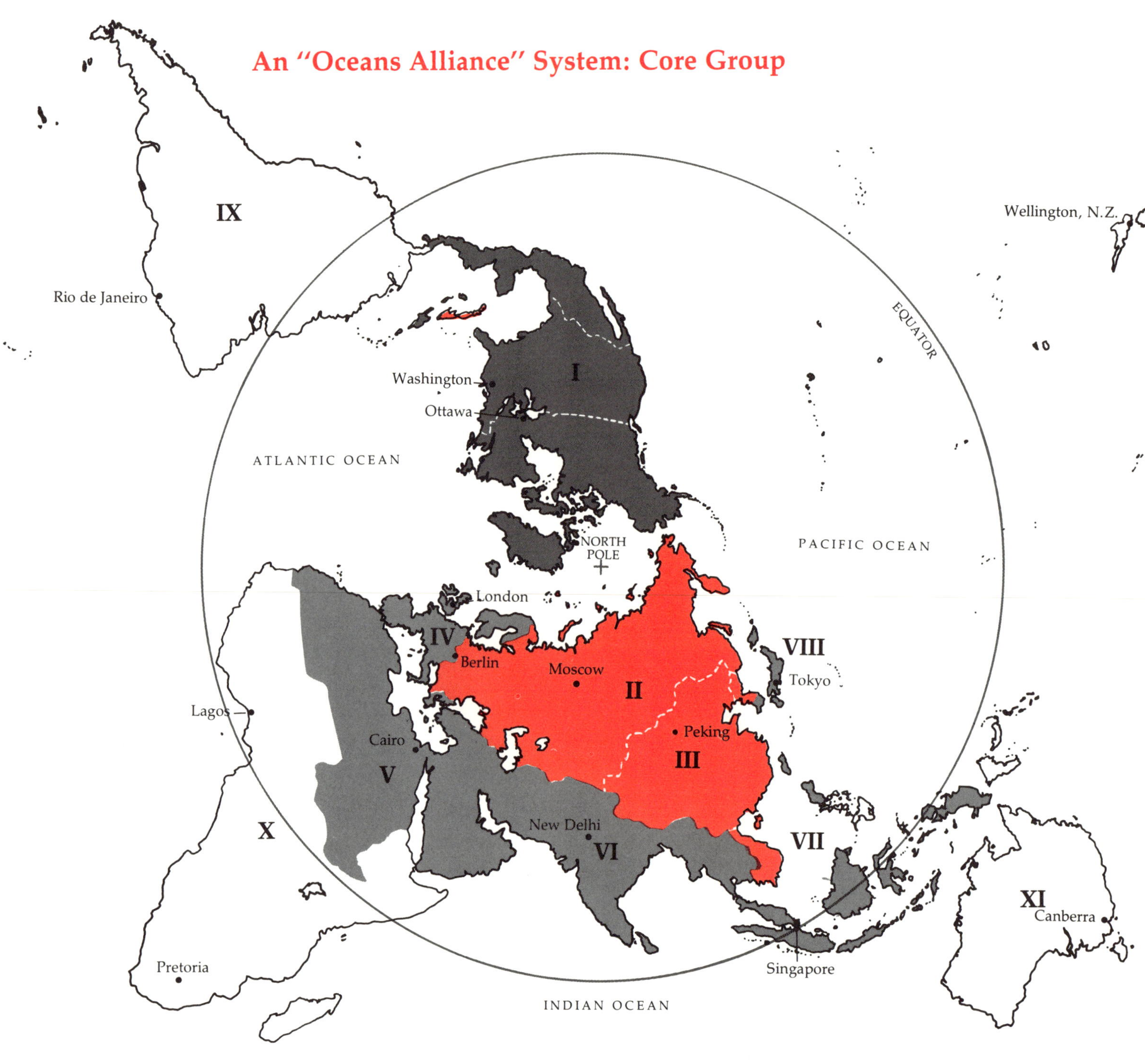

POLITECTONIC ZONES

I
Canada
United States
Mexico

IV
United Kingdom
Germany
France
Netherlands
Italy
Spain

V
Israel
Iran
Turkey
Egypt
Saudi Arabia

VI
India
Pakistan

VII
Indonesia
Singapore

VIII
Japan
China/Taiwan
South Korea

IX
Brazil

X
Nigeria
South Africa

XI
Australia
New Zealand

importance. This group of 12 tends to set the strategic pattern in four politectonic zones containing more than 850 million people, 14 million square miles of territory, and most of the world's advanced technology.

Substantial ethnic groups in the United States have emigrated from all of the dozen countries selected above, bringing their cultural contributions to U.S. society. All have parliaments, relatively open electoral processes, and economic systems based on comparatively free international trade. It is easy to quibble about the effectiveness of national democratic procedures, including those in the United States, but these countries represent open societies operating under rules of law with substantial concern for civil rights and the consent of the governed.

The English-speaking nations have a long history of special bonds with one another and with the United States. Israel is a unique case, a country created by the United Nations and sustained by support from the United States and West Europe for a quarter-century of turbulent existence. Its close cultural and religious ties with Jewish communities in the United States are comparable to the ties of U.S. citizens of Chinese, Japanese, German, and Italian descent, and all the rest, with their ethnic homelands.

Since World War II, Japan and China/Taiwan have closely associated themselves with the United States, the most advanced nations in East Asia to do so. They are almost totally dependent on U.S. treaties to guarantee their security against domination or conquest by mainland China. The Government of the Republic of China in Taipei claims it is *de jure* the government of all China, but it is as the *de facto* government of the island of Taiwan and of the Pescadores that it has a defense treaty with the United States. Its island position, its modern export-oriented economy, and its political progress toward democratic government in Taiwan in the face of still serious military threats from Peking, qualify it along with Japan as an Asian strong point in an Oceans Alliance. Japan represents the only large population unit in Northeast Asia and the leading proponent of modern economic technology based on world trade. The inclusion of these Asian states in the core group extends its reach from Northeast Asia and the Pacific across North America to connect with the leading nations of West Europe.

These dozen nations can accomplish prodigies by working closely together. In terms of global strategy and geography, however, there is a dangerous gap on the periphery of Eurasia between Northeast Asia and West Europe—a gap that has to be filled by leading nations interested in maintaining the independence and freedom of their own regions from Soviet and Chinese domination. An Oceans Alliance must be sure its members are able to move and trade along routes running around the world through the Pacific, Indian, and Atlantic Oceans.

Consequently, beyond the dozen already mentioned, equally close alliances should be built up with other friendly nations, some of whom may have political traditions or social structures different from those of the United States. The strategic power of the Oceans Alliance has to include at least one strong point in every politectonic zone in the Eurasian rimlands.

There is a great difference between an authoritarian political regime with a regard for the welfare of its citizens, and a rigidly totalitarian state determined to control the minds and actions of every person within its borders. The United States should welcome into the Oceans Alliance nations which at present have compelling reasons to follow political processes that do not fully qualify them as democratic, providing they have enough political support to govern in their own countries and do not emulate Soviet or Chinese models of totalitarianism. If nations have substantial elements of power, appear to have general support of their people, and look to trade and to political contacts with the United States and its allies for future security and economic prosperity, they belong in the Oceans Alliance core group.

Nations which are suitable candidates for inclusion, in addition to those already mentioned, based on the calculus in this book, would be: Mexico, Spain, Iran, Turkey, Egypt, Saudi Arabia, India, Pakistan, Indonesia and Singapore, South Korea, Brazil, Nigeria, and South Africa. This list is not necessarily meant to exclude others and some of these will not at present be able or willing to join. India, South Korea, and Nigeria are in some political disarray at the moment, for example. The list simply indicates which of the 40 most consequential nations are logical candidates for U.S. guarantees and can be expected to support U.S. strategic aims.[3]

Such an Oceans Alliance, or new Athenian League, if all of these countries should join, would contain 26 nations possessing about 70 percent of the perceived power of the 40 ranking nations. If these 26 nations were members, the Alliance would have one or more strategic strong points in every politectonic zone except the Soviet and Asian Communist Zones, II and III. They would tend to shore up the spirits and enterprise of people in an area containing the non-totalitarian 65 percent of the world's population. To guard against hostile totalitarian inroads into this entire core group of 26 would be a clear and reasonable national strategy for the United States. If all or most of these nations joined the United States in a system of bilateral but mutually supporting alliances, many of them reaffirming other alliance bonds, the world balance of power would gain enormously in stability. This does not mean the United States would try to preserve a frozen *status quo* in world affairs, which is impossible, but simply that it would work for orderly economic, social, and political evolution without destructive spasms of violence.

Some observers would subtract a few of these nations from a list of major allies; others might add a few. There is nothing final about the selection made above. The basic pattern is sound, however, and if fully understood by U.S. citizens it would provide the nucleus of a national consensus on U.S. strategic purpose. The main concept should be that key nations whose interests are compatible with U.S. purposes be included, and that at least one strong nation from each politectonic zone on the periphery of Eurasia be represented. Preven-

[3] Reasoned differences of view will arise as to the suitability of choices for the core group of an Oceans Alliance. As with assigning coefficients for national strategy and will, this is also a game any number can play. Readers are invited to select their own alliance membership provided they accept the strategic concepts outlined in this book.

tion of the domination of any substantial parts of the Eurasian rimlands by totalitarian powers would be a unifying strategic goal for an alliance extending through the Atlantic, Pacific, and Indian Oceans. Some of the major nations in the Outer Ocean circle ought to support this goal and probably will.

Detente in the literal sense of taking every reasonable step to avoid war would, of course, continue. The leaders of the United States should, however, plainly recognize and explain to the people of this country, that crucial short-of-war conflicts over political influence and economic resources in the rimlands of Eurasia are likely to continue so long as governments in Moscow and Peking sponsor revolution, class warfare, and guerrilla liberation movements in other nations. U.S. defense policy and national strategy ought to focus on this danger, not on superficial diplomatic atmospherics in the conduct of relations with the totalitarian nations.[4] Civility and fair dealing toward all nations are entirely in the U.S. interest. Confrontations would occur only if interventions by totalitarian states occur in areas vital to leading nations in the U.S. alliance system. The United States would continue to try to resolve all conflicts peacefully, but it would not avoid confrontations by making concessions at the expense of its allies or its own strategic interests. This new strategy would do more to stabilize international relations and permit a realistic *modus vivendi* with the totalitarian nations than bushels of detente rhetoric. It would also recommit this country to the political and economic ideals in which most people in the United States believe.

At present, the power of the United States is declining, not because it has become a weak nation, but because it is strategically muddled and because the number of its reliable allies is declining. The United States has untold strength. It has immense economic wealth. What it needs is the kind of straightforward, candid leadership that deserves to be followed at home and abroad in pursuit of a sensible strategy.

The United States must organize its own efforts along these lines. Otherwise the trend toward further decline in others' perceptions of U.S. power cannot be halted. The remedy lies in a renaissance of energetic alliance-building efforts. Not only would the United States and its allies benefit but so would those nations low on the scale of present international power rankings whose future fate will be determined largely by the evolution of the balance of power in the 1970s and 1980s. The United States must offer credible security guarantees to a core group of allies in order to prevent totalitarian control of Eurasia. It must also provide imaginative, farsighted economic policies that will bring mutual benefits to the Oceans Alliance nations, tied one to another by the sea-lanes of the world and a sense of common purpose. The United States then can act firmly and honorably to oppose totalitarianism as a way of life and to create an international environment safe for diversity, free international exchange of economic goods and services, political pluralism, orderly social change, and the nonviolent resolution of conflicts.

[4] President Ford seems to be moving in this direction as indicated in his post-Helsinki speech in Minneapolis on August 19, 1975.

Appendices

A Closer Look at Recent Economic Trends

The analysis in Chapter Four of main elements of economic power and its distribution in strategic zones of the world is static. To indicate long-term trends in international economics and to pinpoint some of the changes during the past year (1974), we have examined the record of the growth of the world's GNP over a quarter century and have translated the statistics into a series based on the value of 1974 U.S. dollars in order to make them more easily comprehensible today. Naturally, because of inflation, the figures are different (10.2 percent above) from those based on 1973 dollars as presented elsewhere in this book.[1]

The GNP yardstick has serious shortcomings for comparative purposes, owing to the sharp differences between advanced economies like that of the United States, in which consumer goods and services bulk large, and the more traditional or more autarkic economies. It is for this reason that we recognized at the outset that the USSR must be given special added weight for its economic power at any given time because it is focussed so exclusively on industrial production and military support items at the expense of the consumer society. The *potential* strength of a post-industrial economy on the U.S. pattern is greater but enormous domestic consumption of bottled beverages and huge domestic sport and entertainment expenditures, for example, do not immediately and readily equate to effective power in the international arena.

Despite all of these limitations on the meaning of GNP data, economic exploitation of resources, labor, and technology are fundamental in providing the muscle for international power. The following observations on economic output allow a more precise evaluation of major regional, political, and economic trends. The critical data are presented in tabular form (page 145).

The most notable trend shown by this series of statistics is the surge of growth worldwide that occurred in the last 25 years. While there has been international tension and conflict and even limited wars throughout this period,

[1] This appendix is based on a special unpublished research report prepared for this specific purpose by Herbert Block, economic consultant at the Department of State. For his basic methods, as explained in connection with similar 1973 series used elsewhere in this book, see Block, *Political Arithmetic.*

the economies have grown prodigiously. Populations have grown as well, and in many poorer regions of the world this growth has outstripped economic development. Until 1974, when a cyclical peak of inflation and record unemployment hit most of the industrial nations at the same time, the people of the advanced industrial world have enjoyed steadily increasing material prosperity beyond anything dreamed of in the past. Small ruling or aristocratic groups may have lived better before, but never have so many produced and consumed so much. This sustained economic growth trend is most apparent if absolute quantities are translated into average annual percentage increases as shown. (See page 146.)

The beneficiaries of this extraordinary wealth are in the nations where birth rates have been reduced to a level below that of economic growth. Comparable statistics on population in the nations and groups of nations whose economic growth we have sketched are presented in the table. (See page 147.)

The unequal distribution of material goods in the world as a result of the concentration of industry and technology in the Northern Hemisphere and the enormous pressure of population on resources in many other regions is better shown by per capita GNP figures. A preliminary analysis based on our 1974 dollar series tells the story for the particular groupings of nations categorized in this chapter. (See page 148.)

Negative Growth for 1974

Looking at the world in the light of all these statistics, we see that economic growth slowed down from a record 6.8 percent in 1973 to 2.6 percent in 1975. Given a population increase of about 1.9 percent, the latter rate still implies a modest growth per capita for mankind of 0.7 percent.

The developed non-communist nations, containing 18 percent of the world's population and more than three-fifths of the world's economic output, experienced a real GNP growth of 6.3 percent in 1973, a rate that had been reached only once in the preceding quarter of a century (in 1964). A letup had become visible even before OPEC quadrupled oil prices and hit the highly industrialized world in its vulnerable energy solar plexus. An economic syndrome dubbed slump inflation, or recession plus inflation, spread and produced in 1974 an overall standstill.

In fact, GNP fell in the U.S. (by 2.1 percent), in Japan (by 1.8 percent), and in the United Kingdom (by 0.2 percent) while other nations stagnated (the Federal Republic of Germany had a growth of only 0.4 percent), or expanded moderately (France by 3.9 percent, Norway—despite an oil boom—by 3.7 percent). The combined growth of the advanced non-communist world has been a negative 0.1 percent except for those newly rich OPEC members which, by creating some of the dislocations, were able to benefit sufficiently to join the club of the developed countries. The exact 1974 growth score for developed non-communist countries, including oil-rich newcomers to affluence, was a plus of 0.5 percent, a precision that is a little unrealistic in a year of rapid inflation.

For simplicity in this statistical series we use the per capita GNP of 1,500 U.S. 1974 dollars as the dividing line between developed and less developed

World Product: Selected Years 1950-1974

(In Billions of 1974 Dollars)

	1950	1960	1970	1973	1974
World	1,767.8	2,791.0	4,642.6	5,424.6	5,563.3
Developed	1,458.2	2,278.7	3,784.3	4,434.5	4,489.9
Less Developed	309.6	512.3	858.3	990.1	1,073.4
Non-Communist Countries	1,405.5	2,148.5	3,613.5	4,230.8	4,322.6
Communist Countries	362.3	642.5	1,034.4	1,193.7	1,240.7
Developed Non-Communist Countries	1,187.2	1,800.1	3,007.4	3,493.0	3,510.2
United States (50 States)	604.1	829.2	1,229.3	1,428.1	1,397.4
United States (Puerto Rico, outlying territories)	2.0	3.4	6.5	7.7	8.1
Total United States	606.1	832.6	1,235.8	1,435.8	1,405.5
West Europe	430.6	702.8	1,172.5	1,350.6	1,379.4
West Germany (FRG)	93.0	197.9	319.4	358.0	359.4
France	84.2	130.9	231.1	273.7	284.4
United Kingdom	96.9	127.0	168.1	186.6	186.2
Italy	43.4	76.2	131.6	146.6	151.5
Other					
Canada	40.3	64.5	107.1	128.0	132.8
Australia	22.5	33.0	56.8	65.4	65.8
New Zealand	n.a.	6.9	10.0	11.3	11.8
Japan	50.1	120.9	341.0	438.4	430.7
Less Developed Non-Communist Countries	218.3	348.4	606.1	737.7	812.4
OPEC (OAPEC)				113.8	157.4
India	46.9	70.6	103.9	114.7	115.8
Brazil	17.7	34.2	61.0	83.6	91.6
Communist Countries	362.3	642.5	1,029.6	1,193.7	1,240.7
USSR	201.0	362.4	608.1	687.6	709.6
Six East European Countries	83.5	141.3	214.4	253.8	270.1
China (PRC)	54.0	109.2	170.7	199.8	205.3
Special Groupings					
NATO	1,035.0	1,532.9	2,362.4	2,724.3	2,721.2
European NATO	390.6	639.2	1,026.0	1,168.2	1,191.1
Warsaw Pact	284.5	503.7	822.5	941.4	979.7

Growth Rates: Annual or Average Annual

(in Percent)

	1950-55	1955-60	1960-65	1965-70	1970-74
World	4.8	4.5	5.0	5.4	4.7
Developed	4.6	4.5	5.0	5.4	4.4
Less Developed	5.6	4.7	5.1	5.5	5.7
Non-Communist Countries	4.4	4.2	5.1	5.5	4.7
Communist Countries	6.1	5.6	4.6	5.1	4.7
Developed Non-Communist Countries	4.3	4.2	5.0	5.4	4.0
United States (50 States)					
United States (Puerto Rico, outlying territories)					
Total United States	4.3	2.2	4.8	3.2	3.2
West Europe	5.3	4.8	4.9	5.6	4.2
West Germany (FRG)	9.4	6.3	5.0	4.8	3.0
France	4.3	4.7	5.8	5.9	5.3
United Kingdom	2.7	2.7	2.2	2.4	2.1
Italy	6.0	5.6	5.3	5.9	3.6
Other					
Canada	5.5	4.1	5.7	4.7	4.4
Australia	3.7	4.1	5.2	6.0	3.7
New Zealand	n.a.	4.3	4.7	2.9	4.2
Japan	9.2	9.2	10.0	11.9	6.0
Less Developed Non-Communist Countries	4.9	4.5	5.4	5.9	6.0
OPEC (OAPEC)	n.a.	n.a.	n.a.	n.a.	n.a.
India	4.0	4.4	3.3	4.6	2.8
Brazil	6.8	6.8	4.5	7.4	10.3
Communist Countries	6.2	5.6	4.7	5.0	4.8
USSR	6.2	5.9	5.1	5.6	3.9
Six East European Countries	5.3	5.4	4.0	4.6	5.7
China (PRC)	10.9	3.8	3.9	5.2	4.7
Special Groupings					
NATO	4.8	3.3	4.9	3.9	3.6
European NATO	5.4	4.7	4.9	4.7	3.0
Warsaw Pact	5.9	5.8	4.7	5.3	4.5

World Population

(in Millions)

	1950	1960	1970	1974	*Percentage of Population Growth* 1970-74
World	2,510.6	3,044.9	3,689.0	4,010.3	2.1
Developed	746.0	862.0	987.8	1,086.5	2.4
Less Developed	1,764.6	2,182.9	2,701.2	2,923.8	2.0
Non-Communist Countries	1,668.3	2,012.8	2,460.2	2,659.2	2.0
Communist Countries	842.3	1,032.1	1,228.8	1,351.1	2.4
Developed Non-Communist Countries	504.0	577.3	670.8	729.0	2.1
United States (50 States)	152.3	180.7	204.9	211.9	0.9
United States (Puerto Rico, outlying territories)	2.0	2.5	3.1	3.4	2.3
Total United States	154.3	183.2	208.0	215.3	0.9
West Europe	242.1	269.8	315.3	333.8	1.4
West Germany (FRG)	50.0	55.4	60.7	62.1	0.6
France	41.7	45.7	50.8	52.5	0.8
United Kingdom	50.6	52.6	55.4	56.0	0.3
Italy	47.1	50.3	53.7	55.4	0.8
Other					
Canada	13.7	17.9	21.3	22.5	1.4
Australia	8.2	10.3	12.5	13.3	1.6
New Zealand	1.9	2.4	2.8	3.0	1.7
Japan	83.8	94.1	104.3	109.7	1.2
Less Developed Non-Communist Countries	1,164.3	1,435.5	1,789.4	1,928.9	2.5
OPEC (OAPEC)	n.a.	n.a.	n.a.	318.7	—
India	359.1	432.6	539.9	586.1	2.1
Brazil	52.8	71.8	94.7	104.2	2.5
Communist Countries	842.3	1,032.1	1,228.8	1,351.1	2.4
USSR	180.1	214.3	242.8	252.1	0.9
Six East European Countries	85.5	96.7	103.0	105.5	0.6
China (PRC)	547.0	684.5	836.7	920.1	2.4
Special Groupings					
NATO	419.0	477.0	532.0	548.2	0.8
European NATO	243.0	278.0	305.8	314.8	0.7
Warsaw Pact	265.6	311.0	345.8	357.6	0.8

GNP: Per Capita
(In U.S. 1974 Dollars)

	1950	1960	1970	1974
World	703	916	1,258	1,387
Developed	1,963	2,641	3,827	4,125
Less Developed	175	235	318	367
Non-Communist Countries	842	1,066	1,465	1,625
Communist Countries	430	623	842	919
Developed Non-Communist Countries	2,352	3,114	4,470	4,804
United States (50 States)	3,967	4,589	6,000	6,594
United States (Puerto Rico, outlying territories)	1,000	1,360	2,097	2,396
Total United States	3,928	4,555	5,953	6,528
West Europe	1,779	2,605	3,513	4,133
West Germany (FRG)	1,860	3,572	5,262	5,793
France	2,019	2,864	4,549	5,416
United Kingdom	1,915	2,414	3,029	3,125
Italy	921	1,515	2,451	2,737
Other				
Canada	2,942	3,603	5,028	5,907
Australia	2,744	3,204	4,544	4,930
New Zealand	n.a.	2,875	3,571	3,906
Japan	598	1,285	3,269	3,927
Less Developed Non-Communist Countries	188	243	339	421
OPEC (OAPEC)	n.a.	n.a.	n.a.	494
India	131	163	192	198
Brazil	335	476	644	879
Communist Countries	430	623	838	919
USSR	1,116	1,691	2,505	2,815
Six East European Countries	977	1,461	2,082	2,561
China (PRC)	99	132	204	223
Special Groupings				
NATO	2,470	3,214	4,441	4,955
European NATO	1,544	2,300	3,355	3,784
Warsaw Pact	1,071	1,620	2,379	2,740

countries.[2] As a result of near zero growth, which was generally decried rather than hailed despite the earlier popularity of advocacy of "limits of growth" economics, the share of the developed non-communist countries in the world product, counting the affluent OPEC countries, dipped from 64.4 to 63.1 percent. The changes in the past year for those countries on which we have sufficient 1974 data to make preliminary calculations are set forth in the following table:

GNP: 1974

(in U.S. 1974 Dollars)

Area or Country	*GNP (Billion $)*	*% of World*	*GNP per capita ($)*
World	5,563.3	100.0	1,387
Developed	4,489.9	80.7	4,125
Less Developed	1,073.4	19.3	367
Non-Communist World	4,230.8	78.0	1,625
Developed Countries	3,510.2	63.1	4,804
GNP per capita $4,500 or more	2,517.7	45.3	6,126
United States (50 States)	1,397.4	25.1	6,594
Canada	132.8	2.4	5,907
Australia	65.8	1.2	4,930
West Europe:	903.5	16.2	5,580
Sweden	55.4	1.0	6,790
Switzerland	42.9	0.8	6,634
West Germany (FRG)	359.4	6.5	5,793
Denmark	27.9	0.5	5,530
France	284.4	5.1	5,416
Luxembourg	1.8	0.03	5,223
Norway	20.4	0.4	5,099
Belgium	49.4	0.9	5,040
Netherlands	61.9	1.1	4,568
OPEC:	18.2	0.4	13,700
United Arab Emirates	5.8	0.1	25,000
Kuwait	10.6	0.2	11,400
Qatar	1.8	0.03	10,600
GNP per capita $3,001-$4,500	683.3	12.3	3,727
Japan	430.7	7.7	3,927
New Zealand	11.8	0.2	3,906
West Europe:	233.8	4.2	3,415
Iceland	0.9	0.02	4,064
Austria	29.3	0.5	3,878
Finland	17.5	0.3	3,757
United Kingdom	186.2	3.3	3,322

[2] See Block, *Political Arithmetic*, pp. 66-79 and Tables I and II, where the same approach in 1973 dollars is used, although the dividing line was then $1,300 between developed and less developed countries.

Area or Country	*GNP (Billion $)*	*% of World*	*GNP per capita ($)*
OPEC:			
Libya	7.0	0.1	3,125
GNP per capita $1,501-$3,000	309.2	5.5	2,267
Puerto Rico, U.S. Territories	8.1	0.1	2,396
West Europe:	240.8	4.3	2,345
Italy	151.5	2.7	2,737
Ireland	6.9	0.1	2,226
Spain	66.9	1.2	1,899
Greece	15.5	0.3	1,717
OPEC (OAPEC):	33.6	0.6	1,855
Saudi Arabia	13.4	0.2	2,350
Venezuela	18.7	0.3	1,604
Bahrain and Gabon	1.5	0.02	1,970
Others	26.7	0.5	2,190
Less Developed	812.4	14.6	421
OPEC (OAPEC)	157.4	2.8	494
Non-OPEC (OAPEC) Countries:	655.0	11.8	407
India	115.8	2.0	198
Brazil	91.6	1.7	879
Others	447.6	8.1	487
Communist World	1,240.7	22.4	919
Developed Countries	979.7	17.6	2,740
GNP per capita $3,001-$4,500	107.8	1.9	3,411
East Germany (DRG)	59.8	1.1	3,536
Czechoslovakia	48.0	0.9	3,268
GNP per capita $1,501-$3,000	871.9	15.7	2,675
USSR	709.6	12.8	2,815
Poland	76.1	1.4	2,259
Hungary	23.5	0.4	2,247
Bulgaria	19.4	0.3	2,235
Rumania	43.3	0.8	2,059

Area or Country	GNP (Billion $)	% of World	GNP per capita ($)
Less Developed Countries	261.0	4.8	2,263
Yugoslavia	30.8	0.6	1,456
Mongolia	1.3	--	929
Cuba	8.2	--	902
Albania	2.0	--	833
North Korea	10.0	--	645
North Vietnam	3.4	--	142
China (PRC)	205.3	3.7	223
Memoranda Items			
European Community	1,129.4	20.3	4,381
European NATO (including Portugal and Turkey)	1,191.0	21.4	3,784
Total NATO (including Portugal and Turkey)	2,721.2	48.9	4,955
European OECD (including Portugal and Turkey)	1,409.9	25.3	3,711
Total OECD (including Portugal and Turkey)	3,448.3	62.0	4,658
Portugal and Turkey	31.7	0.6	677
Six East European Warsaw Pact Countries	270.1	4.9	2,561
Total Warsaw Pact	979.7	17.6	2,740
OPEC and OAPEC developed	58.8	1.1	2,710
less developed	157.4	2.8	494
Total	216.2	3.9	635

The recent changes in patterns of economic activity take on much more meaning if viewed in the perspective of the general framework of economic growth over a number of years. The trends since 1950 show that the extraordinary concentration of economic strength in the developed nations of the West Europe-North American-West Pacific belt is still the paramount fact of economic life. The number of developed nations has steadily increased over the years as the trading nations worked out mutually advantageous exchanges of goods and services and standards of living gradually increased. Thus according to our calculations Spain became a developed country in 1970, Greece in 1972, and several OPEC countries in 1973 and 1974.

It is hard to judge what is "normal" or "natural" in economic history and what is out of the ordinary. Spain's ascent to a developed status appears normal, as does Venezuela's, which came partly as a result of the 1973 oil price increase. The conversion of a backward sheikdom, like Abu Dhabi, into a nation that claims to be the richest community on earth in per capita terms ($50,000) is utterly abnormal or unnatural. Yet it happened.

Japan's recovery from its World War II defeat (with a share of only 2.8

percent of the world product in 1950) was to be expected, but the speed of its growth (to a share of 8.1 percent in 1973) is unique. The United Kingdom declined from 5.3 to 3.3 percent between 1950 and 1974. The U.S. share (50 states) declined from 32.7 percent in 1950 to 26.3 percent in the boom year 1973 and 25.1 percent in the recession year 1974.

Much of this was simply a "return to normalcy" from a condition after the war when the United States was—some small neutrals excepted—the only intact economic structure in the world. Part of the change was due to an unprecedentedly generous and enlightened U.S. economic foreign policy which restored West Europe to economic health and converted defeated enemies to flourishing allies. U.S. technical progress in recent years (e.g., in aircraft, nuclear power, and electronics) shows that the country's innovative spirit has not diminished despite deceleration in productivity increases.

In the same quarter century the USSR's share in world economic output rose from 10.9 to 12.7 percent. It need hardly be added that Hanoi would have proved less aggressive and OPEC less troublesome had it not been for the USSR's support.

The OPEC Apex

Economically, the OPEC collaboration between the very rich and very poor members has been eminently successful in siphoning off wealth from the industrial nations. The oil-rich states have also succeeded in spending their money in the industrial developed states to an astonishing extent thus avoiding so far the fiscal crunch many bankers feared from the accumulation of petrodollars. Actually the members of OPEC are in part newly developed and in part still underdeveloped. Their combined GNPs rose in 1974 by an estimated 43 percent (on the basis of preliminary reporting) and their share in the world product from 2.8 to 3.9 percent of the world total. The entire cartel group, with its glaring differences in affluence—between countries and within each country—as well as its divergences of political outlook and regional interests, is none too stable as a power grouping. Its ability to upset the economies of the mighty industrial nations in the past 20 months has been an extraordinary accomplishment that may be difficult to repeat.

The world will never be the same as it was before the oil crunch of 1973, but the shock has been absorbed without basic change in the structure of world power to date. The future of oil economics will depend on supply and demand in different parts of the world, which we take up in the next chapter, and on the strategic play of political forces in the Mideast in the next few years—now far from clear to foresee.

The Rest of the Third World

From the point of view of international politics the most interesting development in recent economics is an attempted alliance between oil-rich and underdeveloped countries against the advanced West. With Algeria serving as the rallying point, the less developed nations have come out with a radical Declaration on the Establishment of a New International Economic Order (September 1973). It is the quintessence of the "redistribution of wealth" economic policy on the international scale which appears to be a third alternative between the U.S. and Soviet economic systems. Communist China is seeking to identify itself with this potential alliance of the poor against the international rich, and the proliferation of weapons worldwide plus the strength of guerrilla warfare tactics and urban terrorism may bode ill for the future. At this moment, however, the economic strength available to animate this group of nations is not adequate to change the pattern of economic power we described in the preceding chapter.

Statistics for GNP in less developed countries are beset with problems. Suffice it to say in this context that during the past quarter of a century the less developed world has grown faster than the non-communist developed nations as a whole, at times even faster per capita despite the higher population increase in underdeveloped countries. This growth was on the order of 5 percent in 1974. The remarkable performance of the developing world—after centuries of stagnation—does not solve a number of complicated problems of an international character within this less developed world. First, the developing nations are undergoing severe social growing pains inevitable in the mechanization, industrialization, urbanization, and monetization of traditional societies. Second, the absolute gap is increasing between rich and poor within the less developed countries and between developed and developing countries, a politically unsettling fact in a world full of rising expectations and strong egalitarian tendencies. Third, a conflict (possibly a long one) is emerging over which communities should be allowed to consume scarce resources (raw materials, foodstuffs, technical skills) and which will fall behind. These tensions create enormous possibilities for violence, domestic and international. They could bring about dislocations and sudden shifts in the present economic power structure. They are almost bound to do so through "rich-poor" and "north-south" conflicts at some time in the future, particularly if they can be exploited politically by either Soviet or Chinese egalitarian revolutionary propaganda.

The spirit of Algiers is both intensely nationalistic and dogmatically socialist. It is closer to right-wing totalitarianism than to the humane instincts of welfare states in Western Europe. This Third World of the underprivileged often harbors resentment against alien "haves", is frequently willing to spend limited resources on national military purposes, and at times shows a disposition to employ terrorist means in internal and foreign conflicts. The economic trend among these ambitious members of the Third World is favorable enough to constitute real strength and at the same time so unsatisfactory as to guarantee ceaseless pressure for radical change for a long time to come.

Special Trends in International Economics: Oil[1]

Of all the specific elements of economic power that serve as instruments of international policy in the 1970s, oil is one of the most crucial, not only in the Mideast, where it overshadows every other consideration, but worldwide. Industrial production, conventional military power, and agricultural activity have all to a large extent become dependent on access to oil. For this reason we have already rated the oil-producing states as deserving special "bonus" units of perceived power. Yet this static measurement does not do justice to the far-reaching influence of oil and oil politics as of 1975.

The Oil-Producing Countries

The major oil-producing and oil-exporting countries fall into three groups:

1. OPEC (Organization of Petroleum Exporting Countries), which was founded in September 1960, now has as its members Saudi Arabia, Iran, Venezuela, Kuwait, the United Arab Emirates, Libya, Iraq, Algeria, Qatar, Indonesia, Nigeria, Ecuador, and Gabon, an associate member.

2. OAPEC (Organization of Arab Petroleum Exporting Countries), set up in 1968, includes the Arab members of OPEC (Saudi Arabia, Kuwait, Iraq, the United Arab Emirates, Libya, Algeria, and Qatar) plus three other Arab states with minor oil resources (Egypt, Bahrain, and Syria).

3. Other major oil producers and exporters, in neither OPEC, nor OAPEC, are the United States, the USSR, Canada, and the People's Republic of China.

The perceived power which accrues to oil exporters in international affairs was dramatically demonstrated by OAPEC's embargo of oil in 1973, following the Arab-Israeli War, an embargo directed against the United States and the Netherlands, which supported Israel. This power was further enhanced by subsequent cutbacks in most oil production and sharp increases in oil prices. These price increases have benefited not only OPEC and OAPEC members, but also Canada, the USSR, and the People's Republic of China.

[1] The data in this chapter are taken from a research report prepared specifically for this project by Dr. Sevinc Carlson, Director of Legal and Energy Studies at CSIS, June 1975.

This sudden (approximately five-fold) increase in oil prices in international commerce caused a shift in wealth and economic power away from the oil consumers and the industrial countries toward the producers of oil. Initial projections of the revenue and financial reserves likely to be accumulated by the oil producers, of a size that staggered the financial institutions of the world free market, have been revised downward. The present consensus is that the peak investment accumulation of the OPEC countries will be on the order of 200-300 billion U.S. 1974 dollars rather than twice or three times that amount, as had been predicted would occur about 1980. The 1974 total accumulation was about $50-$60 billion and the absorption of this sum in trade and investment has been surprisingly smooth. Less than $1 billion entered the United States in the form of long-term private investment, and the private banking system handled it without any disruption.

Nevertheless, the total deficits on this order in the balance of payments of the industrialized countries have placed these countries in unfavorable economic positions through acceleration of inflation and economic recession aggravated by higher energy costs. Moreover, vast short-term deposits of petrodollars in European, particularly British, banks create a sense of economic and political instability and dependency, since these funds can be withdrawn at will.

The Arab nations have used these economic facts of life to pressure Israel's friends to oblige Israel to withdraw from the territories it occupied in the 1967 war. Many consuming countries responded with a reassessment of their Mideast policies and the adoption of a more pro-Arab or at least a less pro-Israeli stance. For example, Japan, in November 1973, and South Korea, in December 1973, called upon Israel to withdraw from all Arab territory it had occupied since 1967. Japan also declared that it would have to reconsider its policy toward Israel depending upon future developments. Many of the other consumer countries aligned themselves with the Arab position, making an effort to establish or strengthen their political and economic relations with the Arab and other oil-producing countries.

In spite of a recent oil glut which has resulted mainly from the decreased consumption due to economic recession, the leverage of the oil producers has not yet appreciably diminished. Countries such as Kuwait, Libya, and Saudi Arabia, with large oil reserves and a limited need for revenues, have been able to cut back their oil production without immediate adverse effects on their economies. Others, such as Venezuela, which have a greater need for the revenue from their oil exports, have also cut down production to preserve their remaining resources for sale at high prices. The result is that these oil-producing countries, especially the Arab states which are members of OAPEC, have had an unprecedented influence on world events through the control of a single economic resource, upon which the wealth, security, and life-style of the industrialized world depend. By 1980 or 1985 alternate sources may relieve this situation; for the time being, the Mideast region as a whole and the oil-producing Arab states have special clout and are being courted by nearly every other state.

The United States

The United States is the world's largest importer and consumer of oil. It is also the second largest producer (the USSR overtook it in 1974) and has about 5 percent of world proved oil reserves. Estimates of the recoverable part of these reserves range from 72 to 400 billion barrels.

At the time of the 1967 Arab-Israeli War it was claimed that the United States was capable of self-sufficiency in oil. However both U.S. proved reserves and oil production reached their peak in 1970 and have declined since, while domestic consumption and imports have continued to rise. At the time of the 1973 embargo, the United States was importing 31 percent of its oil needs; in 1975 it expected to import 39 percent, with 22 percent coming from the Mideast and Africa, a shift away from its traditional sources in Canada and Venezuela, which remain important suppliers. At the present rate, the United States will have to import 8 million barrels of oil a day by 1977 and 13 million per day by 1985. The cost of this imported oil to the United States has already risen from $3 billion in 1970 to an estimated $26 billion in 1974.

To assess the impact of even a partial cutoff of these oil imports, one can look at the effects of the 1973 OAPEC embargo on the United States which resulted in a shortage of between 2 and 3 million barrels of crude oil and refined petroleum products a day. The United States had been importing crude oil directly from the Arab countries and refined petroleum products from European, Canadian, and Caribbean refineries, whose oil originated in the Mideast. Although the embargo lasted only from October 1973 to March 1974, it had a tremendous impact on U.S. military preparedness and on the U.S. economy in general.

Military readiness and mobility were impaired when Arab oil producers prevented U.S. forces from acquiring fuel from the refineries of those countries which obtained their crude oil from the Arabs. Singapore stopped fueling the Seventh Fleet and the U.S. air bases in Thailand. The Philippine government cut off petroleum supplies to the Subic Bay base. Spain, Bahrain, and even Aramco, at the behest of the Saudi government, stopped fueling the U.S. forces. This meant that the Defense Department lost access to foreign oil supplies, which amounted to nearly half of its total current requirement of about 650,000 to 750,000 barrels a day (about 3.6 percent of the total U.S. oil consumption). The deficit in oil supplies to the U.S. fleet was made up through use of war reserves and through oil sent from the United States.

This growing dependence on oil imports has made the United States increasingly vulnerable to political leverage by the oil-producing countries. Because the political, military, and economic power of the United States is the basis of the Western security system, that system is in turn threatened by energy shortages. The U.S. government is attempting to alleviate this situation by decreasing oil imports from the 1974 level of 36 percent of total consumption to a more bearable 25 percent, while increasing its stockpile of oil to meet emergencies. This problem will continue well into the 1980s.

NATO

The United States is nonetheless in a far more favorable energy position than most of its NATO allies, although Canada, the United Kingdom, and Norway also have substantial reserves. With strictly applied energy conservation measures and a greater effort to develop alternative energy sources, the United States can survive a crisis period with relative impunity. Most of the other NATO countries are almost totally dependent on imported oil. West European countries consumed 15 million barrels of oil a day in 1973 while producing only 445,000 barrels. The United Kingdom and the Federal Republic of Germany, with their rich coal resources, and the Netherlands, with its natural gas, are potentially less dependent on oil than the other NATO nations, as are Canada and Norway.

Canada, which was eleventh in world oil production in 1974 with about 1.7 million barrels per day, produces enough oil to be self-sufficient. However, since most of this is produced in the Western provinces and there is no pipeline from the West to the Eastern market regions, Canada exports more than half of its oil to the United States, which makes it one of the largest U.S. suppliers. The oil requirements of the Eastern provinces of Canada are met with imports from foreign sources, largely Venezuela and the Mideast; only a very small amount is sent from Western to Eastern Canada via the Panama Canal and the St. Lawrence Seaway.

In November 1973, the Canadian government decided to decrease its oil exports to the United States gradually with a view to phasing them out completely by the end of 1982. This decision was made when the government realized that Canada's proved oil reserves of only 9.4 billion barrels would be exhausted in about seven years at the current production rate. Plans are also being made to extend the Western Canadian pipelines to Eastern Canada. Canada has potential reserves of 121 billion barrels of crude oil, in addition to what can be extracted from the Athabasca tar sands, which may eventually produce 125,000 barrels per day of synthetic crude oil. This increased oil production may keep Canada self-sufficient for a long time to come, although the "Canada First" oil policy, if continued, will force the United States to find a replacement for its former largest foreign oil source.

The United Kingdom and Norway are the other NATO members which have the potential for oil self-sufficiency in the 1980s, stemming from their proved reserves in the North Sea, now about 18 million barrels but which may reach 42 billion. The United Kingdom owns 62 percent of the North Sea fields and their production, which is estimated at 3.5 million barrels per day by 1980, is expected to provide the bulk of its oil needs in the last two decades of this century. Nevertheless, the United Kingdom currently relies on oil for 52 percent of its energy requirements and imports 99 percent of that oil. Exploration has been less intense in the Norwegian sector of the North Sea, but Norway is already receiving North Sea crude and expects to be a net exporter of oil during 1975. This oil should earn over $2.5 billion for Norway in that year.

As indicated above, other NATO countries have very little or no domestic oil and have to import most of their oil needs. All are adopting conservation policies. West Germany uses oil for 58.6 percent of its energy needs and now imports nearly 96 percent of this oil. In August 1973, it adopted an energy plan according to which it will purchase natural gas from the Soviet Union, the Netherlands, Norway, and Algeria, thus increasing the share of natural gas necessary for its overall energy needs from 10 to 17 percent. In the next 12 years West Germany will build 100 more electric-power stations based on nuclear power (aiming at an increase from 1 to 14 percent of its total needs), increase its production of natural gas and brown coal, and make efforts to invest in oil production in other countries.

France depends on oil for 72.5 percent of its energy needs. In September 1974, the French government put a $10.1 billion absolute ceiling on the amount to be spent on oil imports in 1975. This means that France would be importing at least 10 percent less oil than in 1973. At the end of January 1975, the French government announced a ten-year program aimed at reducing the country's dependence on imported fuel from the current 75 percent to 55-60 percent and is also making a concentrated effort to develop alternative energy sources. It is emphasizing the development of nuclear energy and hopes that by 1985 this will represent 20 percent of the total.

The Netherlands depends on oil for only 54.1 percent of its total energy needs. Domestic natural gas makes up 42.2 percent of its total energy consumption and surpluses of this natural gas are exported to Belgium, West Germany, France, and Italy. Although the Netherlands was faced with a total embargo of Arab oil exports in 1973, the economic life of the country was not severely affected as its oil stocks were high and oil companies were able to divert oil to it. The Netherlands plans to purchase additional natural gas from Algeria, Iran, and the USSR as well as coal from Australia, Poland, China, and the United States to avoid rapid depletion of its domestic natural gas reserves.

Italy presently needs oil to meet 78.8 percent of its requirement, and 99.1 percent of this oil must be obtained overseas.

Japan

Japan is one of the industrialized countries most dependent on foreign energy sources. In 1973 oil accounted for 80.4 percent of Japan's total energy consumption and 99.6 percent of it was imported; over 80 percent of these imports came from the Mideast.

Japan has large coal reserves but has shifted from coal to oil over the past 30 years because of the cheapness and easy availability of oil; coal, which provided 35 percent of Japan's primary energy supply in 1960, yielded only 5.4 percent at the end of 1973. Japan is now attempting to increase its coal production again and is also emphasizing research and development in nuclear energy. It already has five commercial nuclear power plants in operation, 17 under construction, and several more planned.

International Energy Agency

Because of the overdependence of U.S. allies on foreign energy sources, the 1973-74 oil embargo, subsequent cutbacks, and higher prices had a severe impact on the economies of the NATO countries and Japan. Because of these economic difficulties, NATO and the European Economic Community (EEC) unity suffered a severe setback. Most of the NATO countries and Japan adopted a pro-Arab stance. Many of them also made bilateral arrangements with OAPEC and OPEC countries for uninterrupted oil supplies.

As a result of diplomatic pressure by the United States, the Organization for Economic Cooperation and Development (OECD) formed the International Energy Agency (IEA) in November 1974. Its members are Austria, Belgium, Canada, Denmark, West Germany, Ireland, Italy, Japan, Luxembourg, the Netherlands, Spain, Sweden, Switzerland, Turkey, the United Kingdom, and the United States. Norway, with its oil export potential, did not join; nor did France, as a result of its decision to pursue an independent policy. The IEA countries plan to cooperate on a scheme for emergency allocation and mandatory demand restraint; to create an extensive information system on the international oil market; and to consult with the oil companies. The plan calls for long-term cooperation on energy, an exchange of information with producer countries, a series of coordinated programs in the fields of energy conservation, and the exploitation of alternative energy sources.

The Warsaw Pact

Warsaw Pact countries depend on the USSR to meet their energy needs, which vary in accordance with each country's resources. The USSR's oil reserves were estimated to be 83.4 billion barrels as of January 1, 1975, although many specialists doubt this high figure. It became the world's largest producer of oil in 1974 with over 9 million barrels a day, surpassing the United States and Saudi Arabia. In 1973 the Soviet Union was exporting 1.3 million barrels a day to Communist countries, including those of East Europe, Cuba, Mongolia, North Korea, and North Vietnam, and 1 million barrels daily to West Europe and other areas of the world.

Soviet exports of oil to East European and other Communist countries are politically as well as economically motivated. Although the USSR advised these governments as early as 1969 to find additional sources of oil, such as the Mideast, it would still like to maintain its role as their main supplier. The Soviet Union sells oil and gas to its COMECON partners under special trading arrangements in which it takes soft currencies and manufactured products. Although it did not increase the price of its oil to its East European allies in 1973 and 1974, the Soviet Union doubled the price in January 1975, going from about $3.20 a barrel to about $7.50 a barrel, an amount which still remains substantially lower than the price charged West European buyers.

The USSR has recently been emphasizing long-term economic cooperation in COMECON, especially in energy matters; because the other COMECON countries are dependent on the USSR for their oil and gas needs, they are obliged to cooperate. This cooperation includes joint planning in geological prospecting and developing enterprises for coal, oil, and gas extraction and processing. As production in extractive industries is highly capital-intensive, the East European countries are expected to share the costs by granting extensive credits to the USSR. From 1976 through 1980, the duration of their next national year-plans, all East European countries are expected to cooperate in energy programs and preferential development of oil and other fuel resources, as well as in the construction of installations and pipelines.

The USSR exports oil and gas to West Europe as a principal means of obtaining large-diameter pipe and the hard currencies which are important to the USSR in the purchase of Western technology. In 1973 the price of Soviet oil to West Europe was increased between 3.5 to 4 times the old rate, to nearly $11 per barrel. Soviet oil earnings increased by around 50 percent, to about $3 billion, up from about $1.2 billion in 1972. Total Soviet exports increased in value from almost $5 billion in 1973 to an estimated $7.5 billion in 1974.

Although the USSR wants convertible currencies and claims to have vast oil and gas reserves, it has not been able to keep up either with its own target figures set for production or with its domestic consumption and export commitments. For example, it promised to supply West Germany with 68,000 barrels per day of oil in 1973, but actually delivered only 57,200 barrels. There also have been shortages in the deliveries of its crude oil, high-octane gasoline, and light and heavy industrial fuels to France. It seems clear that the availability of the USSR's oil for export to the West will be declining because of Soviet and East European needs. What the USSR obviously wants is to increase its capacity over a long term through U.S. or Japanese investment in Siberian development projects. It also hopes gradually to insert itself through special arrangements with Mideast states into a future trade pattern which lets the USSR import oil and gas from Iran, Iraq, and other nearby producers and pass along to West European countries some of the surplus thus acquired.

Consumption of energy, especially of oil, is one of the key yardsticks of economic development. The USSR's current per capita consumption of oil is less than that of the United Kingdom and the Democratic Republic of Germany and only about 40 percent of that in the United States, but Soviet domestic consumption is increasing rapidly and the Soviet Union is developing a vast petrochemical industry. Since the more accessible sources of oil in the western part of the USSR are being depleted, more remote sources must be tapped to meet needs even though they involve high development and transportation costs and require advanced technology for exploitation. This is the main reason that, since 1965, the USSR has increasingly turned to the United States and Japan in attempts to get technical help and investment capital.

To make up the difference between lagging production, increasing domestic consumption, and commitments to its allies and other associates, the USSR will have to increase its imports of oil from the Mideast. In 1973 the USSR imported 294,000 barrels of oil a day from the Mideast, and 402 billion cubic feet of gas from Iran and Afghanistan. These imports allowed the USSR to sell 240 billion cubic feet of gas to West Europe. The USSR has been buying Mideast oil and gas in return for military hardware, industrial products, and technical assistance.

Soviet imports of oil have been steadily increasing and are projected to be much larger in the next decade. The USSR did not suffer directly from either oil cutbacks or the 1973 oil embargo, which Soviet broadcasts encouraged. Currently the oil it buys from Libya and Iraq comes from nationalized fields. Because Soviet policy has been consistently pro-Arab, the USSR and East Europe stand to gain, not lose, from any future oil embargo.

The People's Republic of China

The People's Republic of China has just emerged as a force in international oil economics and politics. As of January 1, 1975, its oil reserves were estimated to be 25 billion barrels. Its oil production in 1974 was approximately 1.2 million barrels per day and the 1975 projection was for 1.4 million barrels. China has only a limited refining capacity, and, since production has been growing faster than this capacity, Peking plans to export the excess of about 10 to 20 percent of total production.

Crude oil exports are the means by which China expects to reduce its international trade deficit, which was almost $1 billion in 1974. In addition, the Chinese leaders consider these exports a step toward undercutting Soviet influence and increasing their own in East Asia. China accused the Soviet Union of profiting from the oil crisis of 1973-74, but it also increased the price of Chinese oil sold to Japan from $4.59 per barrel in 1973 to $14.80 per barrel in early 1974. China was forced to reduce the price to $12.10 at the end of February 1975 because of a worldwide increase in the availability of oil. Due to transportation cost differentials, Japan still profits by buying at this price.

China's exports to Japan were expected to reach about 36 million barrels in Japanese fiscal year 1974 and will reach about 40 million barrels in 1975. Peking also promised to provide Hong Kong with oil and is selling oil to Thailand and the Philippines. Although China has had to import chemical fertilizers for agriculture as well as some refined products from the Mideast, the oil crisis has given Peking new leverage with Japan and potentially with energy-importing Third World countries.

Conclusion

This detailed review of the world oil situation is designed to answer the question raised in many minds as to whether the OPEC oil cartel represents a new and lasting international power structure. Our tentative finding is that it does only marginally. In the final analysis, the major oil producers of the world are unified by their desire for economic improvement, and this purpose would not be served by the disruption of the world's trading system. They hope rather to profit within it. Certain of the OAPEC and OPEC countries will emerge as major powers in their own right and, as such, play a proportionately larger role in world councils, but collectively the oil producers are not likely to affect major power alignments. Moreover there is nothing in the oil situation that cannot be worked out by skillful diplomacy and orderly marketing arrangements.

The worst blow to the consuming nations from the oil crunch of 1973 seems to have been weathered. A second embargo would not be as burdensome as it was in 1973, having lost the element of surprise, and oil reserves are substantially higher than at that time. While some oil prices may rise by one or two dollars above the Saudi benchmark price of $10.46 for a barrel of crude, other prices ostensibly tied to this indicator may be adjusted downward rather than upward as a result both of higher reserves in the industrial countries and of reduced consumption, either through policy decision or sluggish economies. Consumption of oil in the non-Communist world in mid-1975 is averaging 46.5 million barrels per day, less than the average of 47.8 million barrels per day in 1973.

In spite of the rise in oil prices, commerce between the industrialized world and the Mideast has expanded tremendously. Exports to the Mideast are mopping up most of what was once thought to be a dangerously destabilizing surplus of OPEC money available for banking or investment in the West. For example, U.S. trade in 1974 in the petrodollar market doubled over trade in 1973. U.S. imports, practically all petroleum or petroleum products, rose to a value of $4.3 billion in 1974 because of higher prices. These costs were almost exactly offset, however, by a doubling of U.S. exports in 1974, reaching the same total—$4.3 billion. (These calculations exclude Israel but include Iran as well as the Arab states). U.S. exports were led by passenger cars, air conditioning equipment, rice, construction and mining machinery, and farm tractors.

The financial structures of the international trading community have proved to be stronger than many bankers and businessmen believed last year. This does not negate the economic strength accruing to oil producers in national-power terms, already noted, or of oil as a source of energy. Long-term trends indicate future increases in energy demand and reluctance on the part of democratic governments to restrict consumer use of oil and gas in industrial nations. Although the future is clouded because of the possibility at any time of renewed Arab-Israeli fighting, from this survey we can conclude that the much-advertised OPEC leverage will not be as destabilizing as was expected by many.

Oil Production[2]

(In Million Barrels)

	1960	1965	1970	1974	% of World Total 1974
OAPEC					
Saudi Arabia*	1.2	2.0	3.4	8.4	
Kuwait*	1.6	2.1	2.7	2.6	
Iraq*	.955	1.3	1.5	1.8	
United Arab Emirates* (Abu Dhabi, Dubai & others)			.640	1.9	
Libya*		1.2	1.0	1.7	
Algeria*	.180	.550	.984	.888	
Qatar*	.175	.230	.353	.546	
Egypt			.328	.118	
Bahrain			.076	.068	
Syria			.050	.119	
Neutral Zone*** (Kuwait & Saudi Arabia)	.135	.355	.485	.485	
Other Mideast					
Iran*	1.0	1.9	3.7	6.1	
Oman			.339	.297	
Israel (Includes captured Sinai fields)			.093	.100	
Other OPEC					
Venezuela	2.8	3.4	3.6	3.0	
Indonesia	.414	.520	.861	1.4	
Nigeria	.020	.275	1.0**	2.3	
Ecuador			.004**	.232	
Gabon (Associate Member)			.106**	.182	
Other					
United States	7.0	7.8	9.5	8.9	
USSR	2.9	4.8	7.1	9.4	
Canada	.520	.925	1.2	1.7	
China (PRC)		.203	.400	1 or 1.2	
West Europe	.300	.440	.356	.381	
World Total	**22.0**	**31.7**	**44.9**	**56.7**	
Total OAPEC			**11.6**	**18.3**	**32.3**
Total Mideast	**5.3**	**9.2**	**18.3**	**22.6**	**39.9**
Total OPEC			**21.8**	**31.3**	**55.2**

* Also member of OPEC.
** Were not members of OPEC in 1970.
*** Established in 1922 to allow for free movement of the nomadic tribes.

[2] Figures on world production and reserves in this and the following charts are taken from *The Oil and Gas Journal* (Tulsa, Oklahoma: The Petroleum Publishing Company).

Oil Consumption[3]

(Thousand Barrels Daily)

Country/Area	*1960*	*% Annual Average Increase 1955-1960*	*1965*	*% Annual Average Increase 1960-1965*	*1970*	*1973*	*% Annual Average Increase 1968-1973*
United States	9,677	+ 3	11,300	+ 3	14,370	16,815	+ 5.1
Canada	856	+ 6½	1,150	+ 6	1,500	1,755	+ 4.9
Mexico	276	+ 9	360	+ 4	490	625	+ 8.7
Caribbean	532	+ 6	720	+ 4½	1,020	1,335	+ 7.2
South America	817		920		1,250	1,530	+ 7.1
Total Western Hemisphere	**12,158**	**+ 3½**	**14,450**	**+ 3½**	**18,630**	**22,060**	**+ 5.4**
Belgium & Luxembourg			840	+15	550	650	+ 8.2
Netherlands					730	835	+ 6.5
France			1,100	+14	1,940	2,555	+11.9
West Germany (FRG)			1,590	+18	2,700	3,070	+ 7.6
Italy			1,070	+17	1,720	2,100	+ 8.3
United Kingdom			1,500	+ 8½	2,080	2,285	+ 4.6
Scandinavia			680	+ 9	1,130	1,120	+ 4.8
Spain					480	730	+14.9
Other West Europe				+14	1,380	1,810	+10.3
Total West Europe	**4,051**	**+12**	**7,730**	**+13½**	**12,710**	**15,155**	**+ 8.2**
Mideast	528	+12½	660	+ 5	990	1,230	+ 8.9
Africa	463	+ 6	680	+ 7	870	985	+ 5.7
South Asia			360	+ 8	590	670	+ 7.6
Southeast Asia			490	+10	1,160	1,455	+ 8.9
Japan			1,770	+24½	4,030	5,425	+13.4
Australia	266	+ 8	410	+ 9½	600	670	+ 4.7
USSR, East Europe & China (PRC)	2,890	+15	4,500	+ 9	6,980	8,775	+ 8.9
Total Eastern Hemisphere	**6,529**	**+11½**	**16,600**	**+12**	**27,930**	**34,365**	**+ 9.0**
Total World	**21,577**	**+ 7**	**31,050**	**+ 7½**	**46,560**	**56,425**	**+ 7.5**

[3] *BP Statistical Review of the World Oil Industry, 1975* (London: The British Petroleum Company Limited).

Proved Oil Reserves

(In Billion Barrels)

	1960	1965	1970	1974	% of World Total 1974
OAPEC					
Saudi Arabia*	50.0	60.0	128.5	164.5	
Kuwait*	62.0	62.0	67.1	72.8	
Iraq*	27.0	25.0	32.0	35.0	
United Arab Emirates* (Abu Dhabi, Dubai & others)	n.a.	10.0	11.8	32.4	
Libya*	2.0	10.0	29.2	26.6	
Algeria*	5.2	7.4	n.a.	7.7	
Qatar*	2.5	3.0	4.3	6.0	
Egypt	n.a.	n.a.	4.5	3.7	
Bahrain	.25	.23	.634	.336	
Syria	n.a.	n.a.	1.2	1.5	
Neutral Zone (Kuwait & Saudi Arabia)	6.0	12.4	25.7	17.3	
Other Mideast					
Iran*	35.0	40.0	70.0	66.0	
Oman	n.a.	n.a.	1.7	6.0	
Israel (Includes captured Sinai fields)	n.a.	n.a.	.013	.002	
Other OPEC					
Venezuela	18.5	17.25	14.0	15.0	
Indonesia	9.5	9.5	10.0	15.0	
Nigeria	.15	3.0	9.3**	20.9	
Ecuador	.03	.02	.7**	2.5	
Gabon (Associate Member)	n.a.	n.a.	.7**	1.7	
Other					
United States	33.5	35.4	37.1	35.3	4.9
USSR	31.5	32.0	77.0	83.4	11.6
Canada	5.0	7.7	10.7	9.4	1.3
China (PRC)	.75	.32	20.0	25.0	3.5
West Europe	1.7	2.6	3.7	25.8	3.6
Mexico	2.2	2.5	n.a.	n.a.	n.a.
World Total	**305.0**	**357.3**	**611.4**	**715.9**	**100.0**
Total OAPEC			**312.6**	**367.9**	**51.4**
Total Mideast			**384.3**	**439.9**	**61.4**
Total OPEC			**399.6**	**489.0**	**68.3**

*Also a member of OPEC.
**Were not members of OPEC in 1970.

Index

A

Abu Dhabi, GNP per capita, 151
Afghanistan, area of, **19**
  critical mass of, **21**
  politectonic zone of, **93**
  population of, **17**
Albania, Chinese affiliation of, 25, 94
  GNP, **151**
  military expenditures of, 79
  perceived military capability of, **85**
  politectonic zone of, **93**
  population of, **17**
Algeria, area of, **19**
  critical mass of, **21**
  energy, **42**
  oil statistics for, 164, 166
  OAPEC and OPEC membership of, 155
  politectonic zone of, **23**
  population of, **17**
Alliances, power factor of, 9
"American Age," 104, 132, 134
Andorra, population of, **17**
Anti-Ballistic Missile Treaty (ABM), 62
Antisubmarine-warfare forces (ASW), 62, 82
Arab-Israeli War of 1967 ("Six Days' War"), 112, 157
Arab-Israeli War of 1973 ("October War"), 113, 114, 155
Argentina, area of, 18, **19**
  critical mass of, **21**
  energy, **43**
  grain exports of, **46**
  GNP of, **40**
  perceived strategy and will, **130**
  politectonic zone of, **23**
  population of, **17**
  strategy, 123
Athenian League, 133, 134, 135, 138
Atlantic Alliance, 91
Atlantic Community, 25, 129, 134
Australia, area of, 18, **19**
  critical mass of, **21**
  energy, **42**
  foreign trade of, **48**
  grain exports of, **46**
  GNP of, **39, 149**
  GNP per capita, **148, 149**
  military expenditures of, 79
  non-fuel mineral production of, **44**
  "Oceans Alliance" status of, 135, **136**
  oil consumption of, **165**
  perceived strategy and will, **130**
  politectonic zone of, **23**
  population of, **17**
  steel production of, **45**
Austria, energy, **43**
  foreign trade of, **48**
  German occupation of, 108
  GNP of, **40, 149**
  GNP per capita, **149**
  membership in IEA of, 160
  politectonic zone of, **93**
  population of, **17**

B

B-1 bomber, 71, **72**
B-52 bomber, 70, 72, **72**
B-58 bomber, 71
Backfire bomber, 71, 72
Bahamas, population of, **17**
Bahrain, GNP, **150**
  oil statistics for, **164, 166**
  OAPEC membership of, 155
  population of, **17**
Bangladesh, critical mass of, **21**
  politectonic zone of, **93**
  population of, 16, **17**
Barbados, population of, **17**
Belgium, energy, **43**
  foreign trade of, **48**
  GNP of, **39, 149**
  GNP per capita, **149**
  membership in IEA of, 160
  oil consumption of, **165**
  perceived military capability of, **86**
  politectonic zone of, **93**
  population of, **17**
  steel production of, **45**
Berlin, 25, 106
Bhutan, population of, **17**
Bipolarity, 9, 75, 89
Bolivia, area of, **19**
  population of, **17**
Botswana, area of, **20**
  population of, **17**
Brazil, area of, 18, **19**
  armed forces of, **80**
  critical mass of, **21**
  energy, **43**
  foreign trade of, **48**
  GNP of, **39, 149**
  GNP per capita, **148, 150**
  military expenditures of, **79**
  non-fuel mineral production of, **44**
  perceived military capability of, **85**
  perceived strategy and will, **130**
  politectonic zone of, **23**
  population of, 16, **17**
  steel production of, **45**
  strategy, 123
Brezhnev, Leonid, 99, 100, 101, 103, 107, 112, 113, 116
Bulgaria, armed forces of, **80**
  energy, **43**
  GNP of, **40, 150**
  perceived military capability of, **86**
  politectonic zone of, **92**
  population of, **17**
Burma, area of, **19**
  critical mass of, **21**
  grain exports of, **46**
  military expenditures of, 79
  perceived military capability of, **85**
  politectonic zone of, **23**
  population of, **17**
Burundi, population of, **17**

C

Cambodia, North Vietnamese defeat of, 54
  population of, **17**
Cameroon, area of, **20**
  population of, **17**
Canada, area of, 18, **19**
  critical mass of, **21**
  energy, **42**
  foreign trade of, **48**
  grain exports of, 46, **46**
  GNP of, **39, 149**
  GNP per capita, **148, 149**
  membership in IEA of, 160
  military expenditures of, 79
  non-fuel mineral production of, **44**
  "Oceans Alliance" status of, 135, **136**
  oil statistics for, 158, **164-166**
  perceived military capability of, **86**
  perceived strategy and will, **130**
  politectonic zone of, **23**
  population of, **17**
  steel production of, **45**
  strategy, 132
  relations with U.S., 10, 122
Cape Verde Islands, population of, **17**
Central African Republic, area of, **20**
  population of, **17**
Central Intelligence Agency, 108
Chad, area of, **19**
  politectonic zone of, **93**
  population of, **17**
Chile, area of, **19**
  energy, **43**
  GNP of, **40**
  non-fuel mineral production of, **44**
  politectonic zone of, **93**
  population of, **17**
China, mainland: See People's Republic of China
China/Taiwan, armed forces of, **80**
  Communist claims to, 26
  critical mass of, **21**
  foreign trade of, **48**
  GNP of, **40**
  military dependence on U. S. of, 137
  military expenditures of, 79
  "Oceans Alliance" status of, 135, **136**
  perceived military capability of, **85**
  perceived strategy and will, **130**
  politectonic zone of, 5
  population of, **17**
  strategy, 125
Chou En-lai, 24, 120

von Clausewitz, Carl, 53
Colombia, area of, **19**
critical mass of, **21**
energy, **43**
GNP of, **40**
politectonic zone of, **23**
population of, **17**
COMECON countries, 160
Command economies, 37, 38
Congo (Brazzaville), area of, **20**
population of, **17**
Containment strategy, 105-109, 111, 113
Conventional weapons, 54, 58, 76, 85, 87
"Core alliances," 133-135, 137-139
"Correlation of forces," 99, 101, 102, 132
Costa Rica, population of, **17**
Counterforce, 56, 65
Critical mass, definition of, 11, 14, 20
Cuba, GNP, **151**
military expenditures of, 79
perceived military capability of, **85**
perceived strategy and will, 130
politectonic zone of, 22, **92, 94**
population of, **17**
Soviety client status of, 89, 132
special strategic significance of, 123, **125**
Cuban missile crisis, 54, 109-111
Cyprus, population of, **17**
Czechoslovakia, armed forces of, **80**
communist coup in, 106
critical mass of, **21**
energy, **42**
foreign trade of, **48**
German occupation of, 108
GNP of, **40, 150**
GNP per capita, **150**
perceived military capability of, **85**
perceived strategy and will, **130**
politectonic zone of, **91**
population of, **17**
Soviet suppression of, 25, 112, 132
special significance of, **125**
steel production of, **45**

D

D-I submarine, 68, **69**, 70
D-II submarine, 68, **69**, 70
Dahomey, population of, **17**
Democratic Republic of Germany, armed forces of, **80**
critical mass of, **21**
energy, **42**
foreign trade of, **48**
GNP of, **39, 150**
GNP per capita, **150**
military expenditures of, 79
perceived military capability of, **85**
perceived strategy and will, **130**
politectonic zone of, **51**
population of, **17**
steel production of, **45**
Denmark, foreign trade of, **48**
GNP of, **40, 149**
GNP per capita, **149**
membership in IEA of, 160
perceived military capability of, **86**
politectonic zone of, **93**
population of, **17**
strategy, 123
detente, 55, 82, 92, 99, 103, 113-115, 125, 131-132, 139
deterrence, 11, 54, 55, 58, 75, 81
Dominican Republic, non-fuel mineral production of, **44**
population of, **17**

E

East Germany: See Democratic Republic of Germany
economic growth, as power factor, 143, 144
Ecuador, area of, **20**
oil statistics for, **164, 166**
OPEC membership of, 155
population of, **17**
Egypt, area of, **19**
armed forces of, **80**
critical mass of, **21**
energy, **43**
grain exports of, **46**
GNP of, **40**
military expenditures of, 78
oil statistics for, **164, 166**
OAPEC membership of, 155
perceived military capability of, **85**
perceived strategy and will, **130**
politectonic zone of, **23**
population of, **17**
strategy, 123
Electronic counter-measures (ECM), 60, 73
El Salvador, population of, **17**
Equatorial Guinea, population of, **17**
Ethiopia, area of, **19**
critical mass of, **21**
Italian occupation of, 108
politectonic zone of, **23**
population of, **17**
Eurasia, heartland of, 3, 107-108
land area of, 10
rimlands of, 5, 135, 137, 139
European Economic Community (EEC), 24, 159

F

FB-111A, fighter-bomber, 71, 72
Federal Republic of Germany, area of, **20**
armed forces of, **80**
critical mass of, **21**
energy, **42,** 158-159
foreign trade of, 46, **48**
GNP of, 36, 39, **39, 149**
GNP per capita, **148, 149**
membership in IEA of, 160
military expenditures of, 79
"Oceans Alliance" status of, 135, **136**
oil statistics for, 158-159, **165**
perceived military capability of, **85**
perceived strategy and will, **130**
politectonic zone of, **23**
population of, 16, **17**
steel production of, **45**
strategy, 125
Fiji, population of, **17**
Finland, area of, **20**
foreign trade of, **48**
GNP of, **40, 149**
GNP per capita, 149
politectonic zone of, **93**
population of, **17**
"Finlandization," 56, 94
"force-loadings," definition of, 59
Ford, Gerald, 113, 116, 126
France,
area of, **20**
armed forces of, **80**
critical mass of, **21**
energy, **42,** 159
foreign trade of, **48**
grain exports of, **46**
GNP of, **39, 148**
GNP per capita, **148, 149**
military expenditures of, 79
non-fuel mineral production of, **44**
nuclear forces of, 60, 67
"Oceans Alliance" status of, 135, **136**
oil statistics for, 159, **165**
perceived military capability of, **85**
perceived strategy and will, **130**
politectonic zone of, **23**
population of, 16, **17**
steel production of, **45**
submarine forces of, 70
free world alliances, 108, 111, 132

G

Gabon,
area of, **20**
energy, **43**
GNP, **150**
non-fuel mineral production of, **44**
oil statistics for, **164, 166**
OPEC membership of, 155
population of, **17**
Gambia, population of, **17**
geopolitics, 4
Ghana, population of, **17**
Gorshkov, Admiral Sergey, 81
Great Russians, 7, 22
Greece,
GNP of, **40, 150**
GNP per capita, **150**

military expenditures of, 79
NATO status of, 132
non-fuel mineral production of, **44**
Persian expedition against, 133
perceived military capability of, **86**
politectonic zone of, **93**
population of, **17**
gross national product, per capita, 144, **148**
gross national product (GNP), as power factor, 36, 38, 143
growth rates, **146**
Guatemala, population of, **17**
Guinea,
area of, **20**
non-fuel mineral production of, **44**
population of, **17**
Guinea-Bissau, population of, **17**
Guyana,
non-fuel mineral production of, **44**
population of, **17**

H

Haiti, population of, **17**
Helsinki agreements, 113
Honduras, population of, **17**
Hungary,
armed forces of, **80**
energy, **43**
foreign trade of, **48**
GNP of, **40, 150**
GNP per capita, **150**
non-fuel mineral production of, **44**
perceived military capability of, **86**
perceived strategy and will, **130**
politectonic zone of, **92**
population of, **17**
Soviet suppression of, 25, 111, 112

I

Iceland,
GNP per capita, **149**
population of, **17**
India,
area of, 18, **19**
armed forces of, **80**
critical mass of, **21**
energy, **42**
GNP of, **39, 150**
GNP per capita, **148, 150**
military expenditures of, 79
non-fuel mineral production of, **44**
nuclear forces of, 61
perceived military capability of, **85**
politectonic zone of, **23**
population of, 16, **17**
steel production of, **45**
Indochina, North Vietnamese takeover of, 24, 26, 54, 79, 91
Indonesia,
area of, 19, **19**
armed forces of, **80**
critical mass of, **21**
energy, **42**
GNP of, **40**
military expenditures of, 79
non-fuel mineral production of, **44**
oil statistics for, **164, 166**
OPEC membership of, 155
perceived military capability of, **85**
perceived strategy and will, **130**
politectonic zone of, **23**
population of, 16, **17**
International Energy Agency (IEA), 160
Iran,
area of, 19, **19**
critical mass of, **21**
armed forces of, **80**
cultural distinctiveness of, 25, 26
energy use of, **42**
foreign trade of, **48**
GNP of, **39**
military expenditures of, 78
oil statistics for, **164, 166**
OPEC membership of, 155
perceived military capability of, **85**
perceived strategy and will, **130**
politectonic zone of, **23**
population of, **17**
strategy, 125
Iraq,
area of, **20**
energy, **42**
military expenditures of, 79
oil statistics for, **164, 166**
OAPEC and OPEC membership of, 155
perceived military capability of, **85**
politectonic zone of, **93**
population of, **17**
Ireland,
GNP, **150**
membership in IEA of, 160
population of, **17**
"Iron Curtain," 25
Islam, 25
Israel,
armed forces of, **80**
cultural distinctiveness of, 25, 26, 93
energy, **43**
GNP of, **40**
military expenditures of, 78
"Oceans Alliance" status of, 135, **136**
oil statistics for, **164, 166**
perceived military capability of, **85**
perceived strategy and will, **130**
politectonic zone of, **93**
population of, 15, **17**
special strategic significance of, 123, 124, **125**
strategy, 125
Italy,
area of, **20**
armed forces of, **80**
critical mass of, **21**
energy use of, **43**
foreign trade of, **48**
grain exports of, **46**
GNP of, **39, 150**
GNP per capita, **148, 150**
membership in IEA of, 160
military expenditures of, 79
"Ocean Alliance" status of, 135, **136**
oil statistics for, 159, **164**
perceived military capability of, **85**
perceived strategy and will, **130**
politectonic zone of, **23**
population of, 16, **17**
steel production of, **45**
Ivory Coast,
area of, **20**
population of, **17**

J

Jamaica,
non-fuel mineral production of, **44**
population of, **17**
Japan,
area of, **20**
armed forces of, **80**
critical mass of, **21**
energy, 41, **43,** 159
foreign trade of, **48**
grain exports of, **46**
GNP of, 36, 39, **39, 149**
GNP per capita, **148, 149**
membership in IEA of, 160
military dependence on U.S. of, 27, 137
military expenditures of, 79
non-fuel mineral production of, **44**
"Ocean Alliance" status of, 135, **136**
oil statistics for, 159, **164**
perceived military capability of, **86**
politectonic zone of, **23**
population of, 16, **17**
post-war recovery of, 150
steel production of, **45**
strategy, 123
Johnson, Lyndon B., 112
Jordan,
military expenditures of, 79, 89
perceived military capability of, **85**
politectonic zone of, **93**
population of, **17**

K

Kellogg-Briand Pact, 103
Kennan, George F., 105, 106-107
Kennedy, John F., 104, 109
Kenya,
area of, **20**
critical mass of, **21**
politectonic zone of, **93**

population of, **17**
Khrushchev, Nikita, 43, 45, 99, 101, 107, 109, 120
Kilotons, definition of, 58
Kissinger, Henry, 113, 116, 120
Korean War, 76-77, 111, 118
Kosygin, Aleksei, 107, 112
Kuwait,
energy, 42
GNP, **149**
oil as unique asset of, 89
oil statistics for, **164, 166**
OAPEC and OPEC membership of, 155
politectonic zone of, **93**
population of, **17**

L

Land-based missiles, 56-57, 60-63
Laos, population of, **17**
Lebanon, population of, **17**
Lenin, Vladimir, 99, 100, 117
Lesotho, population of, **17**
Li-Hsien-ning, 121
Liberia,
non-fuel mineral production of, **44**
population of, **17**
Libya,
area of, 19, **19**
critical mass of, **21**
energy, **42**
GNP, **150**
oil statistics for, **164, 166**
OAPEC and OPEC membership of, 155
politectonic zone of, **93**
population of, **17**
Liechtenstein, population of, **17**
"linkage," 114, 115
Lin Piao, 118
Lippmann, Walter, 9, 133
"little red book," 117
Luxembourg,
GNP, **149**
membership in IEA of, 160
population of, **17**
oil consumption of, **165**
steel production of, **45**

M

Mackinder, Sir Halford, 3, 4
macrometrics, measuring technique of, 12, 35, 58, 86, 97
Malacca Straits, 91, 124
Malagasy, Republic,
area of, **20**
population of, **17**
Malawi, population of, **17**
Malaysia,
area of, **20**
non-fuel mineral production of, **44**
population of, **17**
Maldives, population of, **17**, 26
Mali,
area of, **19**
population of, **17**
Malta, population of, **17**
Manchuria, Japanese occupation of, 108
manned bombers, 57, 61, 63, 70, 72
Mao Tse-tung, 104, 116-117, 119-120, 125
Marshall Plan, 105, 108
Marxist-Leninist thought, 100, 102, 105, 131
Mauritania,
area of, **19**
population of, **17**
Mauritius, population of, **17**
megatons, definition of, 58
Mexico,
area of, 19, **19**
critical mass of, **21**
energy, **42**
GNP of, **39**
oil statistics for, **165-166**
perceived strategy and will, **130**
politectonic zone of, 23
population of, 16, **17**
strategic alignment of, 10
strategy, 122
Minuteman-2, **65**
Minuteman-3, 60, 62, **64-65,** 66, 70, 72
Mirage-IV, 72
MIRV, 61, 62, 64, **65,** 66, 68, 69, **69**
missile defenses, 61
mobile ICBMs, 64, 67
Monaco, population of, **17**
Mongolia,
area of, **19**
critical mass of, **21**
friction along frontier of, 22, 94
GNP, **151**
perceived military capability of, 86
politectonic zone of, 22, **94**
population of, **17**
Morrocco,
area of, **20**
critical mass of, **21**
politectonic zone of, **93**
population of, **17**
Mozambique,
area of, **19**
population of, **17**
MRV, 61, **65, 69**
multipolarity, 9
Mya-4 bomber, 71, **72**

N

nation state, 8
National Security Council, 125-126
national strategy, 97, 125-126, 129, 131, 134, 135
national will, 75, 97, 123, 125-126, 129
Nauru, population of, **17**
Nehru, Jawaharlal, 24
Nepal,
critical mass of, **21**
politectonic zone of, **93**
population of, **17,** 89
Netherlands,
critical mass of, **21**
energy, **42,** 159
foreign trade of, **48**
GNP of, **39, 149**
GNP per capita, **149**
membership in IEA of, 160
"Oceans Alliance" status of, 135, **136**
oil statistics for, 159, **165**
perceived military capability of, **86**
perceived strategy and will, **130**
politectonic zone of, **51**
population of, **17**
steel production of, **45**
New Zealand,
area of, **20**
GNP of, **40, 149**
GNP per capita, **148, 149**
"Oceans Alliance" status of, 135, 136
perceived strategy and will, **130**
politectonic zone of, **93**
population of, **17**
special strategic significance of, 123-125
Nicaragua, population of, **17**
Niger,
area of, **19**
non-fuel mineral production of, **44**
population of, **17**
Nigeria,
area of, **19**
armed forces of, **80**
critical mass of, **21**
energy, **42**
GNP of, **40**
military expenditures of, 78
oil statistics for, **164, 166**
OPEC membership of, 155
perceived military capability of, **85**
perceived strategy and will, **130**
politectonic zone of, **23**
population of, 16, **17**
Nixon, Richard, 99, 101-102, 113-115, 117-118, 120, 125
North America, land area of, 10
North Atlantic Treaty Organization (NATO), 24-25, 79, 83, 94, 108, 135, **148, 151,** 157, 159
North Korea,
armed forces of, **80**
critical mass of, **21**
energy, **43**
GNP, **151**
military expenditures of, 79
perceived military capability of, **85**

perceived strategy and will, **130**
politectonic zone of, **94**
population of, **17**
relations with China of, 94
special significance of, **125**
threat to South Korea of, 26, 27
North Vietnam (Indochina),
armed forces of, **80**
critical mass of, **21**
GNP, **151**
military expenditures of, 79
perceived military capability of, **85**
perceived strategy and will, **130**
politectonic zone of, 90
population of, **17**
special significance of, **125**
Norway,
area of, **20**
energy, **43**
foreign trade of, **48**
GNP of, **40, 149**
GNP per capita, **149**
oil statistics for, 158-159
perceived military capability of, **86**
politectonic zone of, **93**
population of, **17**
"nuclear club," 53
nuclear parity, 38, 56, 73, 110
nuclear weapons, 9, 53, 55-59, 76, 87

O

"Oceans Alliance," 134-135, 137-139
oil-producing countries, political role, of, 41, 42, 129, 132, 152, 155-157, 160, 162, 166
Oman,
energy, **43**
oil statistics for, **164, 166**
population of, **17**
"one-megaton equivalent," 58
Organization of Arab Petroleum Exporting Countries (OAPEC), **151,** 155-157, 160, **164, 166**
Organization for Economic Cooperation and Development (OECD), **151,** 160
Organization of Petroleum Exporting Countries (OPEC), 144, 149, 151, 152, 155-156, 160, **164, 166**

P

Pakistan,
area of, **19**
armed forces of, **80**
critical mass of, **21**
energy, **43**
grain exports of, **46**
GNP of, **40**
military expenditures of, 79
perceived military capability of, **85**
perceived strategy and will, **130**
politectonic zone of, **23**
population of, 16, **17**
Panama, population of, **17**
Panama Canal, 22
Paraguay,
area of, **20**
population of, **17**
"peaceful coexistence," 24, 99, 100-102, 113, 116
People's Republic of China
area of, 18, **19**
critical mass of, **21**
energy, **42**
entry into the U.N. of, 119, 122
foreign trade of, 37, 38, **48**
grain exports of, **46**
GNP of, 39, **151**
GNP per capita, **148, 151**
identification with third world of, 38, 119, 121, 122, **153**
military expenditures of, 79
non-fuel mineral production of, **44**
nuclear forces of, 60-61, 67
oil statistics for, 162, 164-166
perceived military capability of, **85**
perceived strategy and will, **130**
politectonic zone of, 5, **23,** 24
population of, 16, **17**
steel production of, **45**
strategy of, 95, 98, 116, 118-120, 122, 125
submarine forces of, 70
perceived power, 8, 11, 15, 54, **87,** 89, 124, 129, **130**
Peru,
area of, **19**
critical mass of, **21**
GNP of, **40**
non-fuel mineral production of, **44**
politectonic zone of, **93**
population of, **17**
Philippines,
area of, **20**
critical mass of, **21**
GNP of, **40**
non-fuel mineral production of, **44**
politectonic zone of, **93**
population of, **17**
pluralism, 104
Poland,
area of, **20**
armed forces of, **80**
critical mass of, **21**
energy, **42**
foreign trade of, **48**
GNP of, **39, 150**
GNP per capita, **150**
perceived military capability of, **85**
perceived strategy and will, **130**
politectonic zone of, **51**
population of, **17**
steel production of, **45**
strategy, 123
Polaris missile, 67-69, **69**
politectonics, definition of, 3, 4
Portugal,
armed forces of, **80**
Communist threat to 129, 132
GNP of, **40**
military expenditures of, 79
perceived military capability of, **85**
perceived strategy and will, **130**
politectonic zone of, **94**
population of, **17**
Soviet influence on, 94
special significance of, **125**
Poseidon missile, 60, 68-69
Pravda, 102
private-enterprise economics, 37, 38
Puerto Rico, GNP per capita, **148, 150**

Q

Qatar,
energy, **43**
GNP per capita, **149**
military expenditures of, 79, 89
oil statistics for, **164, 166**
OAPEC and OPEC membership of, 155
perceived military capability of, **85**
politectonic zone of, **93**
population of, **17**
Quemoy and Matsu Islands, 120

R

redistributive world economy, 38, 152
Rumania,
armed forces of, **80**
critical mass of, **21**
energy, **42**
GNP of, **40, 150**
GNP per capita, **150**
perceived military capability of, **86**
perceived strategy and will, **130**
politectonic zone of, **51**
population of, **17**
special strategic significance of, 123-125
steel production of, **45**
Rwanda, population of, **17**

S

SALT I, 57-59, 61-62, 64, 66, 68-70, 82, 113
SALT II, 59, 64, 113
San Marino, population of, **17**
Saudi Arabia,
area of, **19**
critical mass of, **21**
energy, **42**
GNP of, **40**
GNP per capita, **150**
military expenditures of, 79

oil statistics for **164, 166**
OAPEC and OPEC membership of, 155
perceived military capability of, **85**
perceived strategy and will, **130**
politectonic zone of, **25**
population of, 16, **17**
Senegal, population of, **17**
Sierra Leone, population of, **17**
Singapore,
perceived military capability of, **85**
perceived strategy and will, **130**
politectonic zone of, **93**
population of, **17**
special strategic significance of, 123-125,
Sino-Soviet split, 119-120
Somalia,
area of, **20**
military expenditures of, 79
perceived military capability of, **85**
politectonic zone of, **93**
population of, **17**
South Africa,
area of, **19**
critical mass of, **21**
energy, **42**
foreign trade of, **48**
grain exports of, **46**
GNP of, **40**
military expenditures of, 79
non-fuel mineral production of, **44**
perceived strategy and will, **130**
politectonic zone of, **23**
population of, **17**
steel production of, **45**
strategy, 123
South Korea,
armed forces of, **80**
critical mass of, **21**
dependence on U. S. of, 27
energy, **43**
GNP of, **40**
military expenditures of, 79
perceived military capability of, **85**
perceived strategy and will, **130**
politectonic zone of, 90
population of, **17**
South Vietnam,
critical mass of, **21**
North Vietnamese defeat of, 54, 75, 108, 115, 132
politectonic zone of, **92**
population of, **17**
U. S. military involvement in, 3, 113, 118, 120, 132
Southern Rhodesia,
area of, **20**
population of, **17**
U.N. status of, 7
Spain,
area of, **20**
armed forces of, **80**
critical mass of, **21**
energy, **43**
foreign trade of, **48**
GNP of, **39**
GNP per capita, **150**
membership in IEA of, 160
military expenditures of, 79
oil consumption of, **165**
perceived military capability of, **85**
perceived strategy and will, **130**
politectonic zone of, **51**
population of, **17**
steel production of, **45**
strategy, 123
Sri Lanka,
critical mass of, **21**
politectonic zone of, **93**
population of, **17**
SS-17, 60, **65**
SS-18, 60, **65,** 66
SS-19, 60, **65**
Stalin, Joseph, 99, 101, 104-107, 116-117
submarine-launched missiles, 60, 61, 63, 68
Sudan,
area of, **19**
critical mass of, **21**
military expenditures of, 79
perceived military capability of, **85**
politectonic zone of, **23**
population of, **17**
Surinam, non-fuel mineral production of, **44**
Suslov, Mikhail A., 102, 107
Swaziland, population of, **17**
Sweden,
area of, **20**
foreign trade of, **48**
GNP of, **39, 149**
membership in IEA of, 160
non-fuel mineral production of, **44**
politectonic zone of, **93**
population of, **17**
steel production of, **45**
Switzerland,
foreign trade of, **48**
GNP of, **40, 149**
GNP per capita, **149**
membership in IEA of, 160
politectonic zone of, **93**
population of, **17**
Syria,
energy, **43**
military expenditures of, 79, 89
oil statistics for, **164, 166**
OAPEC membership of, 155
perceived military capability of, **85**
politectonic zone of, **93**
population of, **17**

T

Tanzania,
area of, **19**
critical mass of, **21**
politectonic zone of, **93**
population of, **17**
tectonic plates, 4
Teng Hsiao-ping, 121
Thailand,
area of, **20**
critical mass of, **21**
grain exports of, **46**
GNP of, **40**
politectonic zone of, **93**
population of, **17**
Third World nations, 38, 119, 134, 152-153, 162
throw-weight, 59-60, 64, 66
Tibet, Chinese control of, 24
Titan-2, **65,** 68
Togo, population of, **17**
Tonga, population of, **17**
totalitarianism, 104, 107, 125, 135, 138-139, 153
Trident submarine, 69, 72
Trinidad & Tobago,
energy, **43**
population of, **17**
Truman, Harry S, 105
Tu-16 bomber, 71-73
Tu-95 bomber, 71-72
Tunisia, population of, **17**
Turkey,
area of, **19**
armed forces of, **80**
critical mass of, **21**
cultural distinctiveness of, 26
energy, **43**
GNP of, **40**
membership in IEA of, 160
NATO status of, 132
perceived military capability of, **85**
perceived strategy and will, **130**
politectonic zone of, **23**
population of, **17**
strategy, 123

U

Uganda, population of, **17**
USSR,
area of, 18, **19**
critical mass of, **21**
deployed manpower of, 79
energy, 41-42, 160, 161
foreign trade of, 37, **48**
GNP of, 36, 39, 75, 106, **151**
GNP per capita, **148, 151**
military expenditures of, **77**
(Soviet) Navy, 81, 82

non-fuel mineral production of, **44**
oil statistics for, 160-161, **163-165**
perceived military capability of, **85**
perceived strategy and will, **130**
politectonic zone of, 5, **23**
population of, 7, 16, **17**
sphere of influence of, 9, 10
steel production of, **45**
strategy of, 95, 98, 100-101, 125
visible economic might of, 38-39
United Arab Emirates,
energy, **42**
GNP per capita, **149**
military expenditures of, 79
oil statistics for, **164, 166**
OAPEC and OPEC membership of, 155
perceived military capability of, **85**
politectonic zone of, **93**
population of, **17**
United Kindom,
area of, 19, **20**
armed forces of, **80**
critical mass of, **21**
energy, **42**
foreign trade of, 47, **48**
GNP of, **39**
GNP per capita, **148-149**
membership in IEA of, 160
military expenditures of, 78
nuclear forces of, 60, 67
"Oceans Alliance" status of, 135, **136**
oil statistics for, 158, **165**
perceived military capability of, **85**
perceived strategy and will, **130**
politectonic zone of, **23**
population of, 16, **17**
steel production of, **45**
submarine forces of, 70
United Nations, 6, 9, 135
United Nations Conference for Trade and Development (UNCTAD), 38
United States,
area of, **18-19**
critical mass of, **21**
deployed manpower of, 79, 84-85
energy, 41, **42**
foreign trade of, 46-**48,** 166
global reach of, 76, 81, 84-85
grain exports of, 45, **46**
GNP of, 36, **39,** 76, 106, **148**
GNP per capita, **149**
managerial expertise of, 38-39
membership in IEA of, 160
military expenditures of, 76-78
Navy, 81-82
non-fuel mineral production of, **44**
"Oceans Alliance" status of, 135, **136**
oil statistics for, 157, **164-166**
perceived military capability of, **85**
perceived strategy and will, **130**
politectonic zone of, 5, **23**
population of, 16, **17**
power alignment of, 5, 9-10
steel production of, **45**
strategy of, 3-5, 8-9, 95, 98, 103-104, 106-107, 109, 114, 126, 138-139
Upper Volta,
area of, **20**
population of, **17**
Uruguay, population of, **17**

V

V-Bombers, 60, 72
Vatican City,
area of, 24
population of, **17,** 24
Venezuela,
area of, **19**
critical mass of, **21**
energy, **42**
foreign trade of, **48**
GNP of, **40**
GNP per capita, **150**
non-fuel mineral production of, **44**
oil statistics for, **164, 166**
OPEC membership of, 155
perceived strategy and will, **130**
politectonic zone of, **51**
population of, **17**
special significance of, **125**
Vladivostok agreement, 61, 66, 68, 71, 113

W

Warsaw Pact countries, 83-84, 91, **148, 151,** 160
West Europe, potential power of, 50, 91
West Germany: See Federal Republic of Germany
Western Samoa, population of, **17**
"world cities," 118, 119, 131
world population, statistical table for, **147**
world product, statistical table for, **145**
World War I, 103
World War II, 3, 54, 98, 103, 105, 108, 111, 126, 132-133, 137, 150

Y

Y-class submarine, 68-70
Yemen (Aden),
area of, **20**
military expenditures of, 79
perceived military capability of, **85**
politectonic zone of, **93**
population of, **17**
Yemen (Sana), population of, **17**
Yugoslavia,
area of, **20**
armed forces of, **80**
critical mass of, **21**
energy, **43**
GNP per capita, **151**
military expenditures of, 79
nonalignment with USSR of, 25, 50, 91, 94
non-fuel mineral production of, **44**
perceived military capability of, **85**
perceived strategy and will, **130**
politectonic zone of, **51**
population of, **17**
strategy, 123

Z

Zaire,
area of, **19**
critical mass of, **21**
military expenditures of, 79
non-fuel mineral production of, **44**
perceived strategy and will, **130**
politectonic zone of, **23**
population of, **17**
special significance of, 125
Zambia,
area of, **19**
non-fuel mineral production of, **44**
population of, **17**